# ISTAI

## *Also in the series*

Clark, Peter, 1939–
Istanbul : a cultural
history /
2011.
33305223800610
mi            02/07/12

# ISTANBUL

*A Cultural History*

Peter Clark

Interlink Books

An imprint of Interlink Publishing Group, Inc.
Northampton, Massachusetts

First published in 2012 by

INTERLINK BOOKS
An imprint of Interlink Publishing Group, Inc.
46 Crosby Street, Northampton, MA 01060
www.interlinkbooks.com

Text copyright © Peter Clark, 2012

Published simultaneously in the United Kingdom by Signal Books

All rights reserved. The whole of this work, including all text and illustrations, is protected by copyright. No parts of this work may be loaded, stored, manipulated, reproduced or transmitted in any form or by any means, electronic or mechanical, including photocopying and recording, or by any information, storage and retrieval system without prior written permission from the publisher, on behalf of the copyright owner.

Library of Congress Cataloging-in-Publication Data

Clark, Peter, 1939-
Istanbul : a cultural history / by Peter Clark. -- 1st American ed.
    p. cm.
British ed.: Oxford : Signal Books, 2010, with subtitle A cultural and literary history.
Includes bibliographical references and indexes.
ISBN 978-1-56656-845-6 (pbk.)
1. Istanbul (Turkey)--Civilization. 2. Istanbul (Turkey)--History. 3. Istanbul (Turkey)--Intellectual life. 4. Istanbul (Turkey)--Social life and customs. 5. Cultural pluralism--Turkey--Istanbul--History. I. Title.
DR726.C55 2011
949.61'8--dc23                                        2011035697

Cover images: Burdem/istockphoto.com; Ayhan Altun/istockphoto.com; Alex Nikada/istockphoto.com
Images: istockphoto.com: i, viii, xviii, 2, 13, 20, 38, 53, 46, 79, 83, 186, 226, 228, 231, 236, 239, 248; Wikipedia Commons: 41, 48, 62, 68, 72, 89, 98, 104, 111, 117, 129, 133, 134, 140, 145, 150, 160, 166, 168, 182, 191, 196, 201, 215, 244; courtesy Ian Strathcarron: 206

Printed and bound in the United States of America

To request our 48-page full-color catalog, please visit our website at: www.interlinkbooks.com, call us toll-free at:1-800-238-LINK, or write to us at: Interlink Publishing, 46 Crosby Street, Northampton, MA 01060 e-mail: info@interlinkbooks.com

# Contents

# Preface and Acknowledgements

I first went to Istanbul in 1962. I returned occasionally during the following three decades but my love affair with the place started only in 1993 when I took my son, Gabriel, then aged twelve, to the city. We stayed at the Pera Palas Hotel. Gabriel was a fan of James Bond films and we toured Istanbul locating sites that appeared in the film, *From Russia with Love*. We found five, and enjoyed discovering one huge deception in the film: the Russian consulate general is not, and never has been, immediately above any of the Byzantine cisterns. That visit also deeply affected Gabriel. Eleven years later, in 2004, with a qualification in teaching English as a foreign language, he moved to Istanbul. He has lived there ever since, and is married to a Turkish girl to whom he says, most gallantly, "Coming to Istanbul was the second best thing I have done in my life." His parents are equally delighted for it gives us an excuse to spend time in the most wonderful city in the world.

Indeed, Gabriel has been following in a family tradition, for each of his parents, at the age of twenty-three, went to Turkey to teach. In 1962 I went to Ankara and taught mathematics for a year, and visited Istanbul two or three times from there. Gabriel's mother, Theresa, had a profounder exposure to the city.

In 1964 Theresa went to Istanbul for two years. She and her then husband had a contract, guaranteed by the British Council, with the English High Schools to teach mathematics. They had just graduated from the University of Keele and this was their first job. The Boys' School was in Nişantaşı and the Girls' School, originally founded by the wife of the legendary nineteenth-century British Ambassador, Stratford Canning, was on İstiklâl Caddesi.

They arrived on a Qantas plane en route for Australia and were met in the middle of the night by two other British teachers, one of whom had arrived a few weeks earlier. They were taken to Kodoman Caddesi in Nişantaşı, and moved straight into the basement apartment which nonetheless overlooked a valley, covered with hastily erected unofficial housing. Kodoman Caddesi then was full of local bakeries, grocery stores and greengrocers. Today it seems to specialize in designer clothes' shops for fashion-conscious and often pregnant wealthy women. The following morning they were taken into the school a few blocks away.

The two schools had about twenty British staff. The principal of the Boys' School was Walter Birks, who was one of the great scholars of Catharism. Indeed, thirty years earlier he had been the amanuensis to the leader of the sect at Ussat-les-Bains, in southern France. Antonin Gadal, known as the Cathar pope, actually anointed Birks, who was twenty-five at the time, as his spiritual successor in 1938. When war broke out the following year, Birks chose not to be the Cathar pope but to serve in British intelligence in Syria. Over the years he became disillusioned with Catharism and resumed the more humdrum task of being a teacher overseas, though in 1987 he did co-author *The Treasure of Montsegur*, the standard work on the subject.

At both schools English, mathematics and the sciences were taught through the medium of English, by native speakers of English. The syllabus was set by the Turkish Ministry of Education, but the text-books were British and teachers were able to set the exams. Other subjects—Turkish, history, geography and religion—were taught by Turkish staff. Teachers and pupils for both schools were drawn disproportionately from the middle-class Jewish, Greek and Armenian communities.

One of Theresa's colleagues at the Boys' School was Richard Deleon, who lived with his wife and son in an apartment opposite the school. Richard was from an old Istanbul Jewish family, whose surname suggests that they originally came from León in northern Spain, and were among those Jews invited by Sultan Beyazit to settle in Istanbul at the end of the fifteenth century after the Catholic re-conquest. Richard spoke perfect, if archaic—"My dear chap"—English, and never failed to be impeccably dressed. Each summer he would go, at the school's expense, to London where he always had a meal at the Café Royal. To his own family he was known as Izak. He had moved with his parents to Egypt in the 1930s and he was educated at Victoria College Alexandria, modeled on a British public school. As well as teaching at the school he had one other job as a translator at one of the Spanish-speaking embassies. His family language would have been Ladino, the fifteenth-century Spanish brought to Istanbul by the expelled Jews. Izak/Richard had a son, Jak, no longer alive, who was a historian of Istanbul and the author (in English) of books on some of the byways of the city.

Both schools were reminders of the cosmopolitan Istanbul of fifty or a hundred years earlier. In 1982 such schools were taken over by the government, but some features were retained. The former English High Schools continued to be an English medium for math and the sciences, but they became part of the Anatolian High Schools network. Other schools, such as Galatasaray, continue to teach subjects through the medium of French. All now work to a special Turkish government syllabus.

Theresa remembers nothing but warmth and kindness from staff and pupils. It was difficult to get to know the ethnically Turkish staff. Sometimes there was a language barrier, but most of the Turkish teachers had one (or more) other job/s. There were restrictions on the number of hours Turkish teachers could teach in "foreign" schools, so they were not on the school premises as much as the British teachers. One teacher who did leave an impression was Faranisa Hanım, who was very keen on opera. She used to organize trips of staff and pupils to the opera house at Tepebaşı, in the former Petits Champs, near the Pera Palas. Theresa remembers a trip to see *Eugen Onegin* when senior pupils dozed off.

Each of the schools had a housekeeper. The housekeeper of the Boys' School was Madame Sobiewski, who was—it was believed—a White Russian refugee. She had a roomy wooden house on Büyükada and invited some of the British teachers over for weekends on that island. Theresa and her husband would wake up to breathe in the fresh pine-scented air and find an empty beach for an early morning swim. When she had to teach at the Girls' School, Theresa traveled with Madame Christides, the housekeeper of that school, who also lived in Kodoman Caddesi. She was married to Suat Bey, a former national tennis champion.

An overwhelming memory is the food of Istanbul. It was possible then—more than now—to eat well and cheaply. Friends would explore the fish restaurants of the Bosphorus. There were two favorites in Tarabya, Feliz and Fidan, near to each other. The road ran between the restaurants and the Bosphorus, traffic was light and tables and chairs were set at the water's edge and waiters crossed the road to bring the food.

One British teacher had a car, and summer weekends were often spent at the Black Sea village resort of Kilyos, where there was a beach of white sand and a single one-story hotel. The drive there was through the Belgrade Forest, with its water buffaloes and ancient aqueducts. School holidays were generous and there was the opportunity to travel outside the city, both in Turkey and further afield to neighboring Middle Eastern countries. But Istanbul was also explored, mostly with visitors from

Britain: friends, parents and family needed little encouragement to come out.

The schools provided most of the social life. The British Council had a good library, but Theresa and her husband were no part of a British official circle. The regional representative of the British Council was a man who had "had a good war" and was treated with enormous deference. They were occasionally invited to functions, but would escape afterwards to the Rejans restaurant and eat a meal of borsch and piroshky, and filet mignon, washed down with lemon vodka. There was little contact with the older British community, though Theresa remembers one of the last Istanbul Whittalls taking a fatherly interest in the single women who had come to the city to teach at the Girls' School.

I have not had the good fortune to have lived in Istanbul. I have, however, for several years been leading tours of Belle Epoque Istanbul for ACE Cultural Tours. I have spent over twenty years living in six Arab countries that formed part of the Ottoman Empire. Istanbul has had an impact—architectural, administrative and cultural—on each of those countries, and I have been fascinated by the way the empire operated and the interconnections between capital and province. I therefore see Istanbul as a provincial.

&#8493;&#8365;

This book is neither a guide nor a history of the city. There are excellent volumes that instruct, enlighten and inspire. I have relied on many of these. What this book aims to do is to celebrate Istanbul as a global city, to draw attention to places and buildings that give insights into the richness of Istanbul's past and to note how it has seized the imagination of those who have visited it or who have made it their home.

Among the many guides to the city, the prodigious output of John Freely has been enormously valuable, though I do not always accept his aesthetic judgments. Jane Taylor has also written illuminatingly, and I have benefitted from reading the work of Godfrey Goodwin as well as the excellent *Architectural Guide to Istanbul*, produced by the Istanbul Metropolitan Branch of the Chamber of Architects of Turkey.

Many books on Byzantine Constantinople are instructive. The older classics by Vasiliev, Ostrogorsky, Baynes and Runciman are still essential reading. More recent surveys by Joan Hussey, Cyril Mango, Judith Herrin and John Haldon make use of the latest scholarship. The Byzantine writers themselves who are easily available—Procopius, Psellus and Anna Comnena—reveal much of Byzantine frames of reference. The best and most up-to-date work on Ottoman history is *Osman's Dream* by Caroline Finkel. Philip Mansel's book on Istanbul is brilliant. There are other very good general surveys of the last two centuries or so by Şükrü Hanioğlu, Suraiya Faroqhi and Donald Quataert. In the last ten years Istanbul has hosted exhibitions on aspects of what one may call the Belle Epoque. The catalogues have been full of insights.

On the Republic Andrew Mango's biography of Atatürk cannot be beaten. Erik Jan Zürcher has written on the evolution of the Ottoman Empire into twenty-first century Turkey in a way that has replaced the pioneering book by Bernard Lewis, *The Emergence of Modern Turkey*.

This book follows a rough chronological sequence, but should be supplemented by some of the works cited. As we walk around the city we see the past mixed up with the present. Byzantine, Ottoman, Republican: all are woven into the physical and cultural environment of those who live in and visit Istanbul. I have perhaps been easily distracted by people, buildings and stories that—I think—add to an appreciation of the bigger picture. One chapter looks at aspects of the Bosphorus and the Islands, separate but essential parts of the city. Another chapter touches on the impressions of some of those from abroad whose imagination has been stirred by time spent here.

cro

I have received help, guidance and insights from many people.

I am grateful to Professor Robin Thelwall for permission to quote from the unpublished memoirs of Sir Hamilton Lang, and to Osman Streater for references to an unpublished article about his Menemçioğlu family history. Gamon McLellan read the whole book with meticulous attention, made many most helpful suggestions and steered me away from infelicities and howlers. Those that have survived are my own responsibility.

I owe debts to Omer Namouk, the late Osman Osmanoğlu, Can Dyson, Cemil Bezmen, Canan Alioğlu, Gülbikem Ronay, Pars Tuğlaci,

Penny Young, Philip Mansel and participants in successive tours I have led of Belle Epoque Istanbul for ACE Cultural Tours.

My greatest debt is to my family who have shared my love of the city—my wife Theresa, my son Gabriel, my daughter-in-law Funda and my step-grandson Ferhat.

# Foreword

In my young days in Istanbul, when films and television were still the preserve of the affluent, we had a plethora of storytellers—extraordinarily adept—for entertainment.

My favourite raconteur was an ancient man who, according to various rumours, had been a hero of the War of Independence; a university professor commissioned by Atatürk to teach the nation the Roman alphabet; and an advocate of socialism who had been jailed in Bursa Prison along with his mentor, the sublime poet, Nâzım Hikmet.

This patriarch would set up his stage in the grounds of Rumeli Fortress by the Bosporus, every sundown—that being the time, he asserted, when our godly beverages, coffee and rakı, pervaded the mind with intuition.

No one knew his name. He was simply known as Bulutsultan, meaning "sultan of the clouds." He had acquired this sobriquet, over many years, by always contemplating the sky before beginning his narratives, then, by bestowing on to the clouds specific identities and attributes. Clouds, he maintained, endowed humankind with continuity, insight, civilization and culture. Thus, we in Turkey, especially in Istanbul, constantly imbibed not only Hittite and Greek, Persian and Jewish, Muslim and Christian, Ottoman and Sufi cloudbanks, but also the countless noble ones from Africa, Europe, India, China, Australia, Oceania, North and South America. He further maintained that we were luckier than most of the world's inhabitants because our diverse peoples always remembered the tutelage imparted by these peregrinators of the firmament.

When some of us pointed out that, at least half of the year, Istanbul had blue skies—a phenomenon that conferred on her both during the day and at night her unique lambency—he smiled like a cherub and pointed at the landscape around us. "Look," he said, "when the heavens are clear, it's because the clouds have imprinted themselves on the sea and on the land, even on rooftops and the tips of the minarets. Observe the way they limn life by coupling with light, earth and water. See the myriad hues they compose as they refract. It's their way of showing to us everything that has happened in the past and all that we can expect to happen in the future. Behold, right here, Fatih Sultan Mehmet transports his fleet over the hills onto the Golden Horn to conquer Byzantium. Across, on the Asian shore, Alexander the Great drives his chariot towards Darius. Beyond, in Ankara,

Tamerlane wrestles with his soldiers after defeating Sultan Beyazıt. On the northern horizon, in Kagul, Catherine the Great rewards Marshall Pyotr Rumyantsev's victory over the Ottomans by taking him to her bed. To the south, in Jerusalem, Saladin cures Richard the Lionheart's fever. Further west, Roxana seduces Attila the Hun and stops him from marching to Rome. Way east, in Mongolia, Chengiz Khan rescues his wife, Börte, from the Merkits…"

And then he unfolded a new romance…

I listened to his fables for many years, always in awe of the fact that, but for certain tales which had become his listeners' favorites, he never retold the same story. Thus I learned many things about many peoples. But most importantly, I learned that, in the fragile world we live in, divisions created by religions, races, flags, cultures and wealth offend Creation's miracle of multiplicity, that instead of extolling conflict and bloodshed, we must worship the sanctity of life—all life.

I have reclaimed this memory, in joyous nostalgia, indeed, in gratitude, while reading Peter Clark's *Istanbul*. I have always claimed that Istanbul, a metropolis straddling two continents and a mother of cosmopolitanism, is the most bewitching city in the world—the author rightly delineates her as "The Queen of Cities"—and every page of this painstaking and erudite work not only strengthened my conviction, but also kept reminding me the price I have paid by exiling myself from her. Equally, by exploring her bounteous nurturing of all the diverse peoples who made her their home, it has reinforced the ethos of coexistence that has forged my beliefs. And, not least, it has apprised me of so much that I did not know and, but for this oeuvre, would never have come to know. There have been many exceptional books on Istanbul—and, no doubt, there will be many more; some chronicled her history from her birth in Antiquity to her ensuing development as Constantinople and to her coronation as an imperial capital of the Roman, Byzantine and Ottoman Empires; others expounded on her cosmopolitanism and belle-époque; yet others on her status as a haven for the arts and enlightenment. But I have yet to encounter an opus that aims to produce a biography of this unique city and succeeds in doing so with such palmary authority. Here, the reader will not only become acquainted with Istanbul's history, but also and, most importantly, with her spirit.

I am very tempted to continue acclaiming Peter Clark's Herculean labor. But I will desist. That pleasure should be the exclusive privilege of those who will peruse it.

Dear Reader, I urge you to surrender to Peter Clark's inspired study of Istanbul's anima and be motivated by her maturation as a crucible for the legion of peoples of Europe and Asia. The sensibility of this book would have, most certainly, induced the old storyteller, Bulutsultan, to compose new stories which, abhorring wars and ideologies, would celebrate life and coexistence. And when you alight in Istanbul, take a good look at her skies, seas and land. Observe the clouds even if you don't see them. They will tell you that no matter who we are or where we come from, we are all citizens of Istanbul, citizens of the world, born under the same clouds.

Moris Farhi

*Introduction*

# CENTER OF EMPIRE

The best point from which to see the city of Istanbul is the top of the Galata Tower, 220 feet high. From the viewing gallery, to the east, is the ship-studded Bosphorus, the windy strait connecting the Black Sea and the Mediterranean, and separating Europe from Asia. You can easily see the first bridge built (in 1973) over that waterway from above Ortaköy to the hills of the expanding suburbs on the Asian side. A couple of miles to the right is the major Asian suburb of Üsküdar, then Haydarpaşa railway station on the waterfront. Behind and above are the Selimiye barracks, where Florence Nightingale had her base. The gash of the Golden Horn is a European inlet of the Bosphorus and lies half a mile to the south of the tower, dividing older Muslim Istanbul—until half a century ago often referred to as Stamboul—from Pera/Beyoğlu, which was built more as a cosmopolitan city. Such distinctions have become blurred in recent decades, although all the major mosques are in old Stamboul.

The land of Stamboul tapers to the left, to Sarayburnu jutting into the Bosphorus. Much of that peninsula, in contrast to the rest of the city, is uncluttered. Above the green of Gülhane Park are the buildings, dating from the fifteenth to the nineteenth century, of Topkapı, the sprawling palace-city of the Ottoman sultans. You have a clear view of Ayasofya, built as Justinian's Christian cathedral in the sixth century, transformed to a mosque after the Turkish conquest in 1453, and into a museum by the secular Atatürk in 1935. To the right is the seventeenth-century Sultan Ahmet Mosque, Camii, with its six minarets. Then further to the right can be seen the Süleymaniye Mosque, the masterpiece of the sixteenth-century architect, Sinan, built for his Ottoman emperor, Süleyman Kanuni, otherwise Süleyman the Magnificent.

Galata Tower was built in 1348, a fortification in the walls of a Genoese city, divided by the Golden Horn from the Greek Byzantine city. If you look down you can still see some of the Genoese walls. But on this side of the Golden Horn the whole area is crammed with buildings. Between the tower and the port buildings on the northeastern shores mosques, churches, schools, blocks of flats and synagogues are huddled together. Nearer the first bridge, Galata Bridge, you can make out the solid confident constructions of the nineteenth-century banks. If we turn to the north we see the crowded streets of Beyoğlu, earlier known as Pera and formerly cosmopolitan, full of bars, cinemas, cafés, nightclubs and more recently shops, often the outlets of international chains. On the horizon to the north you can make out some of the skyscrapers of the modern financial quarter of Levent.

## Byzantium/Constantinople/Istanbul

The city that spreads out around the Galata Tower was for 1600 years an imperial capital. Few metropolises have had such a prolonged career as a major political, economic, cultural and social player. Over a millennium and a half it has been influenced by or had an impact—direct or indirect—on most of the rest of the world. Only the Americas and Australasia have been outside its direct reach. As Napoleon said, "If the Earth was a single state, Istanbul would be its capital."

This name Istanbul, the city's official title since 1930, is seen as the Turkish designation of the city in contrast to Constantinople, the city of Constantine, which is how Anglophone Greeks will call it. The word Istanbul can actually be traced back to the tenth century and meant in Greek "to the city." There was no other city like it and so it was simply called by its inhabitants "The City." Byzantium was the name of the city before it became the capital of the Roman Empire in the fourth century. The term Byzantine then became common only in the nineteenth century and referred to the empire, originally Roman but culturally Greek, which lasted from Constantine in the fourth century until the Turkish conquest in 1453.

Constantinople was the capital of the Roman Empire. The western half of the empire fell to "barbarians" from the north of the Alps. This was the fall of the Roman Empire *in the West*. One limb, a major limb, dropped off but the rest of the body lived on until 1453, and has been known by modern historians as the Byzantine Empire. The last emperor, Constantine, saw himself as the legitimate successor of the first Constantine, who had founded the city on the site of the earlier Greek city of Byzantium. Outsiders after the Turkish conquest referred to the successor state of the surviving fragment of the Roman Empire as the Ottoman Empire. The capital was officially Kostantiniyye.

The Ottoman Empire stretched over much of the territory of the Byzantine Empire—Greater Syria, Egypt and North Africa, Asia Minor and the Balkans. Both empires had intimate cultural and commercial relations with the people of the Italian peninsula. Both empires, over the course of time, had the same enemies, especially the countries to the north and east.

Byzantine Constantinople and Turkish Istanbul had much in common. They were the capitals of universal states driven by a God-given mission. They received Divine support and it was their mission to spread the true word beyond the frontiers of the state. Both states devised policies of hegemony, limited in their physical capacity to exercise control, but willing to accept tribute or deference. This hegemony and assumption of authority was extensive. Medieval Serbia or nineteenth-century Egypt may have been formally subject to a Byzantine or an Ottoman sovereignty, but there was not a lot the ruler could do if and when the outlying province went its own way. The Byzantine Empire at its zenith had influence and interests as far south as Abyssinia. Support for the nineteenth-century Ottoman Empire came from India. Each of the two states was a global commercial center, with trade extending from China to the Atlantic.

For both empires the capital was all-important, attracting people from every corner of the empires. Men and women who fashioned Byzantine and Ottoman civilization came from all places over which Constantinople/ Istanbul cast its shadow. In each empire the patronage of the city and the politics of the court were paramount. Byzantine history—political, military, social, economic, cultural—radiated from the court of the Byzantine emperors. It was the same with the Ottoman sultans.

Both empires were multicultural and multi-ethnic. The capital was open to all people of talent. The racial mix of the people of Constantinople/Istanbul may be compared with London, Marseille, New York or San Francisco but no other city has had such a sustained history of multiculturalism. Outsiders have made the city their home. People in some of its many communities have been able to live enclosed, self-sufficient lives, but generally there has been regular interaction between individuals of the different communities.

The maker of modern Turkey, Mustafa Kemal Atatürk, in creating a new country, moved the capital to Ankara and initially turned his back on the city that represented to his generation all that was wrong with the empire he replaced. The multiculturalism of the city veiled abuses and injustices of which the Muslim Turks saw themselves as the victims. The country was in debt to outsiders who were interested in returns on their investments with no thought of the moral and economic damage it might have on the people of the country. Foreigners had controlled the economy with the assistance of local clients who were, very often, neither ethnically Turkish nor Muslim. During Ottoman times, these clients were often exempt from paying taxes, serving in the army or appearing before Ottoman courts. Mustafa Kemal's constituency, the Muslim Turks, had to serve the interests of the foreigners physically and financially. Istanbul was the city where the abuses were most blatant. From the 1920s, Istanbul remained the cultural and intellectual center of the country, and was the major commercial port for the Republic. But the center for major decision making was now Ankara, and modern Turkey was not going to be an imperial country. Istanbul's multiculturalism was irrelevant, and occasionally offensive. Ankara represented the future.

Mustafa Kemal avoided Istanbul for eight years, but its lure brought him back regularly. He built a typically modest home at Florya in the western suburbs and spent his last months in and around the city, dying in that citadel of sultanic financial extravagance and aesthetic excess, the Dolmabahçe Palace.

## COSMOPOLITAN CITY

Since the 1970s Istanbul has seen a renaissance. The population has increased tenfold. Most migrants have come from provincial Anatolia, but in the last ten years there has also been migration from the countries of the former Soviet Union (in particular Moldova, Georgia, Armenia and Azerbaijan). Istanbul has also experienced an artistic revival. The architecture of its newest parts to the north of Taksim is as stunning as anything in Milan, Paris, London or New York. Istanbul is a major city on the global map of the arts, sport and fashion. Today's Istanbul is unmistakeably Turkish and Islamic but there is also a sense in which the positive aspects of its multicultural openness can still be found, fashioned to the norms of the twenty-first century.

There are cycles and continuities throughout Istanbul's history. In some ways these have been determined by its geographical location. It has always been an extraordinary commercial and cultural meeting point, looking east, west, north and south. It is possible to identify a Russian Istanbul, an Arab—and especially an Egyptian—Istanbul and a west European Istanbul. From early Byzantine times the population came from all over the then "known world." In the fourth, as in the twenty-first century, you heard the languages of Asia and Europe. In the twelfth century the Spanish Jewish visitor, Benjamin of Tudela, wrote of Syrians, Palestinians, Persians, Egyptians, Patzinaks, Bulgarians, Lombards, Spaniards, Georgians, Armenians, Turks, Christian and Muslim, Latin and Greek, all jostling together in the narrow streets. People from eleventh-century England and from Scandinavia—where the city was known as Miklagård—settled to become a Byzantine mercenary army. A Scot—or was he a Welshman?—served as an engineer in the dying days of the Christian empire. There were mosques in Christian Byzantine Constantinople. Jews fled from those parts of Europe that were re-conquered by Christians—Spain and the Balkans—to settle here. In the tenth century, as also in the nineteenth century, Bulgarians derived cultural support from what they—as well as the Slavs—called Tsarigrad, the city of the Caesars. Nineteenth-century Poles shared with Turks hostility towards Russia and were made welcome.

Today Istanbul's population is still mixed. The Greek population has been reduced to a few hundred elderly people, but there are still sizable Jewish and Armenian communities. Because of massive immigration, fewer than 10 percent of inhabitants have parents who were born in Istanbul, while in the wider suburbs there are encapsulations of rural Anatolia. Another distinctive ingredient of the last decade of the twentieth century was that of the Turks who have returned from many years in western Europe, largely Germany, but also Belgium, the Netherlands, France and Britain. Many have come back with a bicultural approach to the world. Turkish identity overlaps with Muslim identity. But a Turk today may also have roots that are Arab, Circassian, Albanian or Laz. His or her forebears may have come from North Africa or from the Balkans. As the European empire shrank in the nineteenth century, each withdrawal saw an increase in Muslim migrants to the city—and to Anatolia. Their descendants are all *Istanbullus* today and share the identity forged by the Republic. Many Kurds, however, have maintained a distinctive culture and identity, to the puzzlement of some Turks who have seen the successful absorption of other Muslims.

Most historians have seen Ottoman Istanbul as being divided vertically, with distinct communities, particularly different varieties of Christians and Jews. There is a concept of an egalitarian Muslim community: all equal in the sight of God, men worshipping collectively without distinction in serried rows at the mosque, or dressed identically in the *ihram* on the pilgrimage to Mecca. This has also been true in a formal sense in the case of non-Muslim communities—with the head of each community negotiating on its behalf with the Ottoman authorities—but more recent scholarship has drawn attention to horizontal social and economic divisions. Poor Greeks, Jews and Armenians have shared the same space as poor Muslim Turks. The same has been true of wealthier classes. Moreover, poorer women of any community have often had more in common with other poor women, regardless of confession, than they did with men of their own confession. The most important markers of confessional identity were location of worship (if they worshipped) and marriage partners. The quarters that have been mainly Christian or Jewish were never exclusive ghettos. For the literate, minority languages and scripts were also markers of identity, but none of the languages of the city kept its purity, except for ritual religious functions. Communities were never all-embracing, though the more articulate community leaders may have wished them so, for that would have emphasized their authority.

An Istanbul Armenian once chided me for referring to "minorities." The use of that word, it was argued, delegitimizes the community. Democracy implies the rule of the majority. If there is a conflict of interest, then democracy means that the interests of the majority should prevail exclusively. But for millennia the eastern Mediterranean world was made up of different communities, with loosely varying functions. Communities were interdependent, and the size of separate communities was meaningless. The general pattern over the centuries has been one of mutual acceptance and often mutual support. People celebrated each others' festivals. Jews and Christians made allowances for the Muslim Ramadan. Christians and Jews respected the Jewish Shabbat. In Ottoman times, shops were closed on Friday or Saturday or Sunday, depending on the confession of the proprietor. Nineteenth-century nationalism imposed exclusive choices of identity on people. This led to alienation, dislocation and ultimately the cantonization—by nationality and confession—of the eastern Mediterranean world that we have today.

Sometimes it has been necessary to argue the case for Istanbul in a way that is not required for Paris, Vienna or Rome. Negative baggage accompanies the approach to the history of both the Byzantine and the Ottoman Empires. The Late Roman—Byzantine—Empire lasted until 1453. But the western European narrative has been reluctant to acknowledge the extraordinary success of the Byzantine Empire. Was it the negative influence of the Crusaders, whose approach to the Islamic Middle East lacked the nuances and subtleties of the policy makers of Constantinople? The Crusaders saw the Byzantines as unmanly and effete. Or has it been the influence of Edward Gibbon's work of genius, *The Decline and Fall of the Roman Empire*? ("Decline and fall" over the course of a millennium?) For Gibbon, the history of medieval Europe saw the triumph of barbarism and religion. His work had a great influence on the attitudes and writings of the following century and more. To this day "Byzantine" has a negative sense (like Kafkaesque) of unreasonable administrative complexity. "Of that Byzantine Empire," W. E. H. Lecky, a widely read historian, wrote in 1869, "the verdict of history is that it constitutes, without a single exception, the most thoroughly base and despicable form that civilisation has yet assumed."

Part of the problem of perceptions of the Byzantine Empire is that there was no heir. Or rather there were many heirs. Russia took over the mantle, when the Khan of Muscovy assumed the title of tsar, a corruption of Caesar, and one tsar married a niece of the last Byzantine emperor. Catherine the Great coveted Constantinople. But nineteenth- and twentieth-century Greece also gazed longingly at the city. The Church and the language might suggest that that country has inherited the Byzantine mantle, but the heritage of Byzantium is scattered. The Ottoman Empire inherited the territory. The Orthodox churches inherited the ecclesiastical legacy. But the whole Mediterranean world has derived aspects of Byzantine civilization: spirituality, a sense of the sacred, ceremonial, military architecture, respect for scholarship, humanism, a political culture that accepts diversity.

There has been a similarly negative approach to the Ottoman Empire, especially in the nineteenth century. It was "the sick man of Europe," a polity in decline. The implosion of the Ottoman Empire in the First World War retrospectively vindicated the negative views. The same simplistic approach is not applied to the Russian or the Hapsburg—or even the British—empires. In the 1850s Ottoman Turkey was the political and military partner of France and Britain during the Crimean War. Some British felt uncomfortable with their ally. Byron had inspired a generation with a historically dubious concept of Hellenism that was in a kind of existential conflict with the Ottoman Empire. The decision-makers and opinion-formers of Western Europe were educated on the Greek classics and on the New Testament; this predisposed them to a political bias towards Greeks and Christians. Some—perhaps most—British writings on Turkey in the late nineteenth and early twentieth centuries were hostile, uncomprehending and racist. In 1876, at a packed public meeting in the presence of the former and future prime minister W. E. Gladstone, another popular historian campaigned against a possible military alliance with the Ottoman Empire. "Were then the English people," Edward Freeman thundered, "prepared to wage war for one hour, or to shed one drop of English blood, in order to prop up as foul and bloody a fabric of wrong as ever a shuddering world had gazed upon? Would they fight to uphold the integrity and independence of the Empire of Sodom?"

There were exceptions to this knee-jerk antagonism towards Turkey. Observers such as Adolphus Slade and Marmaduke Pickthall were prepared to come to terms with the dynamics of the Ottoman Empire, but they were themselves often marginal individuals. After the First World War, the Ottoman Empire was replaced by a dozen or more successor states. All of them, including the new Republic of Turkey, owed their identity to a political rejection of that empire. It has only been in the last twenty years that there has been a new appreciation of the Ottoman Empire. In Turkey the Islamists have reclaimed Ottomanism: some want to restore Ayasofya, the Byzantine Church of the Holy Wisdom, to the function it had from 1453 to 1935 as a mosque. But a western liberal can also note that the Ottoman Empire has been the most successful Islamic political institution ever. Nineteenth-century Constantinople may not have been as liberal as Paris or London, but it was certainly freer than Berlin, St. Petersburg and Vienna.

The Republic that emerged from the disasters of the First World War has evolved into the democracy of modern Turkey, a candidate for entry into the European Union. Istanbul in recent decades has suffered from terrorism—acts committed in the name of Islam, or of Armenians, or of

Kurds, or of the far left. There are orthodoxies—liberal, Kemalist, Islamist—that protest when they feel threatened, but, broadly speaking, Istanbul is going through one of the best periods of its history. In the last generation there has been an increase in openness of debate. Creativity has been as vibrant as ever. There is an appreciation of what the rest of the world can offer and what Turkey and Istanbul can offer the rest of the world. Istanbul has produced a novelist of the standing of Orhan Pamuk, whose works are translated into forty or more languages and are sold globally in their millions. His later works have been expertly translated by Maureen Freely who was brought up in the city and has written her own Istanbul novels. Orhan Pamuk was awarded the Nobel Prize for Literature in 2006. At great personal risk, he has been pushing the boundaries of open debate on the darker areas of Turkey's history.

Today we are able to see the evidence of the artistic heritage of both empires, and also of the Republican decades. The history of the city can be read in its streets and buildings. Cycles and continuities can be seen and appreciated. Fashions come and go, but the architectural creativity is as full of life today as it ever has been. And what is cheering is that there is today an enthusiasm for the variety—sometimes eclecticism—of the legacy of the past.

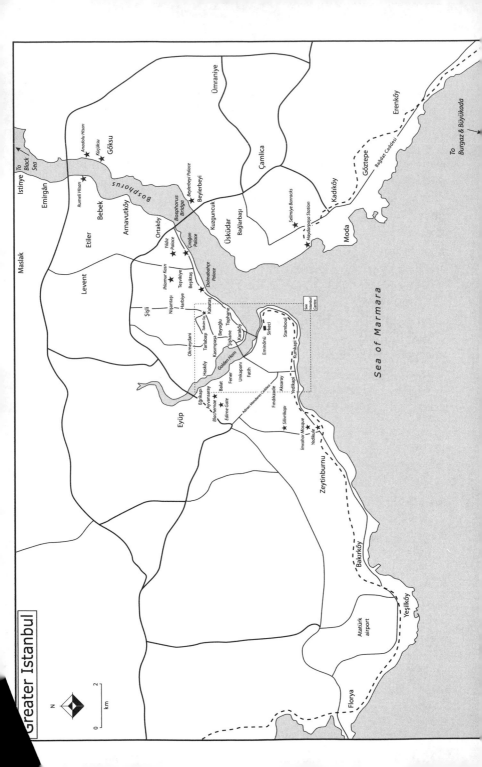

# Chapter One

# THE QUEEN OF CITIES

## THE BIRTH OF AN EMPIRE

The city of the Roman Emperor Constantine the Great was inaugurated on 11 May 330, the culmination of a decade of planning and six years of building. Constantine was the son of a Roman army officer and was born in Niš in modern Serbia—one man in a series of people of Balkan origin who have had a profound impact on the city. Constantinople, wrote Edward Gibbon,

> appears to have been formed by nature for the center and capital of a great monarchy. Situated in the forty-first degree of latitude, the Imperial city commanded, from her seven hills, the opposite shores of Europe and Asia; the climate was healthy and temperate, the soil fertile, the harbour secure and capacious, and the approach on the side of the continent was of small extent and easy defence. The Bosphorus and the Hellespont may be considered as the two gates of Constantinople... When the gates of the Hellespont and Bosphorus were shut, the capital still enjoyed within their spacious enclosure every production which could supply the wants or gratify the luxury of its numerous inhabitants. The sea-coasts... still exhibit a rich prospect of vineyards, of gardens, and of plentiful harvests; and the Propontis has ever been renowned for an inexhaustible store of the most exquisite fish, that are taken in their stated seasons, without skill, and almost without labour.

The hill overlooking the Golden Horn and the Marmara Sea (known to the Greeks as the Propontis) was an obvious place for settlement, and an acropolis was already there when, in the middle of the seventh century BC, one Byzas founded a city that immortalized his name. Other settlements had been founded by migrating Greeks on the Asian shores of the Bosphorus and the Marmara, such as Chalcedon (today's Kadıköy), Cyzicus (at the isthmus of the Kapıdağı Peninsula on the southern shore

Emperor Constantine, Ayasofya Mosque

of the Sea of Marmara) and Lampsacus (Lapseki, opposite the town of Gallipoli, Gelibolu).

For centuries Byzantium remained a small, significant and prosperous port. In the fifth and fourth centuries BC Byzantium was an outlying partner in the shifting alliances of Greek states. In the year 400 BC Xenophon brought his ten thousand Greek troops back from a Persian campaign and received a cool reception in the city. He had to restrain his troops from looting the place. It was not deemed important enough for Alexander to add it to his conquests. In 150 BC the city agreed a treaty with Rome and two centuries later the Emperor Vespasian incorporated it into the Roman Empire. In the civil war at the end of the second century, Byzantium backed the wrong rival for emperor. The winner, Septimius Severus, besieged the city, took it and sacked it. However, he appreciated its setting and enlarged and rebuilt it and its walls. He gave it the name, Augusta Antonina, in honour of his son Antoninus, but the name did not stick.

Nothing above ground is left of the pre-Constantine city.

The eastern half of the Roman Empire in the early fourth century was richer and more populated than the west. It provided the main intellectual and artistic input to the empire. The leading professionals were from the east, a region that was the source of new and old faiths: Judaism, Mithraism, Christianity. The Roman Empire owed its inspiration to the city of Rome, but imperial commitments had reduced the strategic status of that city. Emperors were frequently on the move, on campaign or on morale-boosting inspection tours, and the central government, the "capital," as it were, moved with them. Some emperors had their favorite cities, and Constantine had spent years in Treves (Trier), on the Moselle, at Serdica (Sofia in Bulgaria) and at Nicomedia (İzmit) before he felt the need to found his own eponymous city.

Contemporary writers did not make much of the foundation of the new city, which initially did not have the preeminence it later acquired. Nor was the city on the Bosphorus Constantine's first choice. Other possible bases for the empire were considered, including Nicomedia and Troy. The latter might have been an appropriate choice, for one of the "foundation myths" of the city of Rome was that Romans came from Troy with Aeneas.

There were disadvantages to the site. The area suffered from earthquakes—there were thirteen between 395 and 565—and the tribes of the

Thracian hinterland had a reputation for fractious independence.

The full name of the freshly launched city was "The New Rome Which is Constantinople." It was not unusual for emperors to give their names to cities but the full name indicates that the Emperor Constantine saw it as a complement to the city of Rome. Like Rome, the new city had seven hills and was divided into fourteen regions. Constantine encouraged many of the Roman upper class to migrate, but the status of the senatorial class who migrated as *clari* (noblemen) was lower than the senators of Rome who were *clarissimi* (most noblemen). But over the centuries the power base shifted to the east and people who pursued power also moved, leaving the old city, as a later courtier said, to "vile slaves, fishermen, confectioners, poulterers, bastards, plebeians, underlings." At first the new city received special privileges, such as free rations of corn shipped from Egypt. The indigenous population was Greek but for the first three centuries Latin was the official language.

Like Washington DC, Canberra or Ottawa, Constantinople's *raison d'être* was government. Trade came later. There was initially something flashy and brash, perhaps *nouveau riche*, about the place. Antioch (modern Antakya) and Alexandria had for centuries been the great opulent cities of the eastern Roman Empire. The emperor adorned the squares and open places of his city with plunder from Athens, Rome and Antioch. His mother, Helena, later canonized, had, in 326 in her old age, gone to Jerusalem and discovered relics relating to the life and death of Jesus Christ three hundred years earlier. The most important find was the True Cross, but other finds included the Lance that pierced Jesus's side, the Sponge used to comfort His wounds as well as the Crown of Thorns. The adze which Noah had used to fashion the ark also turned up. She brought the True Cross back to Constantinople where it was joined by other relics— the crosses of the thieves crucified at the side of Jesus and the baskets that held the miraculously reproducing loaves and fishes. The empire was slowly identifying itself with Christianity and the amassing of holy relics gave the city a religious standing, making it a magnet for pilgrims from all over the Christian world.

On the slopes between today's Hippodrome and the Marmara Sea the Emperor Constantine built a palace. It was actually a small self-contained city consisting of several separate buildings, with wide terraces overlooking the sea. It was the first of such self-contained cities within the city, the

Topkapı and Yıldız palaces following a similar pattern in Ottoman times. It remained a focal point of Byzantine Constantinople until the Turkish conquest of 1453. Here was located the Porphyry Palace ("Purple Palace"), reserved for imperial confinements; hence the phrase "born in the purple." All that remains of Constantine's palace are cisterns and cellars, scattered among later buildings.

Thus "the Byzantine Empire" was founded, to last for over a thousand years, a pretty remarkable record for any institution. In 1453 the last in a line of nearly one hundred emperors was also named Constantine. There was a very real continuity from the fourth to the fifteenth century. Although the empire was often seen as rigid, conservative and unchanging, it was actually in a constant state of flux. The political institution based in Constantinople responded to pressures from states and civilizations that rose and subsided around the eastern Mediterranean. Some emperors made important administrative changes that affected the pattern of social and economic relationships. The roles of the military, the landed aristocracy, the imperial bureaucracy, the Church and the people of the city—craftsmen, smallholders, traders—were constantly changing.

Three features characterized Byzantine Constantinople. It was the capital of the Roman Empire. It was the center of the Christian world. And it was the heir to Hellenic civilization.

## A ROMAN AND CHRISTIAN CITY

To the end—1453—the people of Constantinople regarded themselves as Romans. Their name for the state was Romania. The word Byzantine was a much later term, devised by western Europeans. (Incidentally the word Byzantine is the only trisyllabic word where the stress can be on any of the three syllables.) For western Europeans the Roman Empire was associated with Rome. Rome fell to "the barbarians" in the fifth century, and so what there was further east could not be the Roman Empire. Moreover, Constantinopolitan was a bit of a mouthful and for long it was known as the Greek Empire. But the citizens of Constantinople did not like being called Greeks. In the last centuries of the empire, some westerners deliberately insulted the emperor by calling him "the Greek king." ("Greek" or "Hellene," in the early and central Middle Ages, had overtones of paganism.)

In the early centuries the titles of all offices in the city were Latin, a replication of the procedures and institutions of Rome. The emperor was proclaimed by Senate, army and populace. Until 457 he was given his crown by an official. Only after that was he crowned by the head of the Church. The currency was initially based on the *solidus* (the s of the British pre-decimal money £.s.d., known in English as shilling), a Latin name, and for centuries (notwithstanding name changes to *nomismata* and later *hyperon*) it was the stable currency for Mediterranean trade, known to outsiders as the bezant.

The renovated city suggested rebirth, a notion that happily overlapped with Christian ideas of renewal and regeneration. From the start Constantinople was the Christian city, while Rome was seen, by contrast, as the home of paganism. In Rome the senatorial class, the higher grades of the civil service and the senior army officers had, for the most part, not caught up with the new religion. It is interesting to note that, in the first centuries of Constantinople the language of administration was Latin, whereas the major new churches were known by their Greek names: Hagia Sophia or the Church of the Holy Wisdom, Hagia Irene or the Church of the Holy Peace.

Constantine was not himself baptized until he was on his deathbed but he had made Christianity the official religion of the Roman Empire. He was flattered by Christians who designated him the Equal of the Apostles, Isapostolos. "You others are Bishops within the Church," he said, "whereas I am divinely-appointed Bishop-General outside the Church." In the first centuries of Christianity the Church organized itself on a territorial pattern that paralleled the state—with supervisors of provinces (*episcopi*, bishops, literally overseers). Before Constantine, the Bishop of Byzantium had been rather a minor figure, subordinate to the see of Heraclea in Thrace (Marmara Ereğlisi).

Very little of Constantine's construction work remains. He built at speed and perhaps too hastily. Building materials were at hand. Wood came from the forests that surrounded the city. Stone came from the island of Proconnesos (Marmara Adası) in the Sea of Marmara. "If Rome wasn't built in a day," observed George Young in 1926, "New Rome very nearly was." Constantine is believed to have built the first Church of the Holy Apostles (replaced since the fifteenth century by the Fatih Mosque), the Hagia Irene and the Hagia Sophia. None of these buildings survives today in its Constantinian form: Justinian rebuilt the Church of the Holy Wisdom and the Church of the Holy Peace in the sixth century, after they were burned by rioters. The latter was also restored after an earthquake in the eighth century.

The mother of the emperor, Helena, brought her holy finds from Palestine. The Church of the Holy Apostles became the repository of relics, with the bodies of St. Andrew, St. Luke, St. Timothy as well as the Prophet Samuel. Six red porphyry columns have survived from this church and were reused and incorporated into the mosque, built by Sultan Mehmet after his conquest of the city in 1453.

## Paganism Persists

The triumph of Christianity was not absolute. Sometimes Constantine seemed to be keeping his options open: one of the statues he looted from Rome for public display was of Athena, allegedly brought to Rome from Troy by Aeneas. Old fashioned sun worship merged with the new official Christian cult. In 321 the emperor inaugurated a habit that has persisted by enacting that law courts and workshops should close, and the urban—but not the rural—population should rest on "the venerable day of the Sun." There was even a hint of sun worship on his coinage, with the inclusion of a reference to Sol Invictus. Moreover, Christians in their worship faced the rising sun and their God was, according to the Christian holy writings, the Sun of Righteousness.

For most of the fourth century other religions were tolerated but only from 380 was there an imperial edict that all subjects of the empire were to follow "the faith of the Bishops of Rome and Alexandria." In the 360s Constantine's nephew, the Emperor Julian, subsequently called the Apostate, tried to reverse the religious policies of his predecessors and reinstate paganism. That reaction did not last long but pagan or pagan-derived rites competed with the officially backed Christianity. Constantine and his immediate successors retained the pre-Christian Roman religious title, Pontifex Maximus. Many people managed to combine commitment to the new religion with respect for the ancient rites. Men and women dressed up, danced in the streets and sang songs in honour of Dionysius. At the new moon young men leapt over funeral pyres lit in front of houses. Such rites were forbidden from the sixth century and a militant popular Christianity kept an eye on backsliding on the part of the authorities. In 576 one man was openly practicing pagan rites. The authorities caught him and sentenced him, but people thought the punishment too lenient. They seized the offender, who was mangled by wild beasts, then impaled and his body thrown to be devoured by wolves.

Pagan Greek culture could not be easily eradicated. Among the elite—the landed aristocracy, the senior clergy and the upper bureaucracy—there was a high level of education that was both Christian and pre-Christian. The Greek classics were part of their mental furniture. Hellenism was grafted on to Christianity. This can be seen in some of the art from the early Byzantine centuries. Hermes was recast as the Good Shepherd. Orpheus was transmuted into David. Jesus, sometimes unshaven, was Apollo.

In some ways the pre-Christian culture never disappeared and asserted itself periodically over the course of time. Herodotus was always the model for historians. The eleventh-century scholar and official, Michael Psellus, was steeped in ancient Greek literature. One of his students threw himself off a rock into the sea with the words, "Take me Poseidon!" In the following century, the historian, Anna Comnena, wrote in an archaic Greek, very different from the prose writing of the Byzantine Greek of her contemporaries.

THE EMPEROR AT THE CENTER

The central institution of the Byzantine Empire was the emperor. There were eighty-eight over the 1233 years, mostly men. The first emperors were from the family of Constantine. Then other dynasties took over. Emperors were chosen from and by the army, but there was sometimes continuity with a son, son-in-law or nephew following a father, father-in-law or uncle. The great Justinian I, who reigned for thirty-eight years from 527, was the nephew of a soldier from the Balkans who became the Emperor Justin I. Justinian's own nephew, Justin II who followed, was mentally unstable. One dynasty was founded by Heraclius (610-41), a soldier who had campaigned in North Africa. A century later came the Isaurian dynasty and then the Phrygian dynasty. But the empire was at its most glorious under the Macedonian dynasty, starting with Basil I in 867 and ending with Michael VI in 1057. The last four hundred years of the empire saw rule by the Comnenian and finally the Palaeologan dynasty, the longest lasting of them all. The Palaeologi ruled for almost two hundred years until the last emperor, Constantine XI, fell with the empire in 1453.

Among the emperors were saints, murderers, madmen, soldiers, bureaucrats, pedants and poets. Some stand out as outstanding historical personalities.

The emperor was, in theory, all powerful. By the fifth century he was seen as being chosen by God and under divine protection. The person of the emperor was special. He withdrew from the people, wore special costumes and employed eunuchs as ministers. People as they approached him had to prostrate themselves. The empire was identified with the emperor and his household. The emperor, as the historian George Ostrogorsky wrote,

> is entire master of the government of the Empire, commander-in-chief of the army, supreme judge and sole law-giver, protector of the Church and guardian of the true faith. With him rest decisions of war and peace, his judicial sentence is final and irrevocable, his laws are considered to be inspired by God.

He (or occasionally she) was at the apex of a state whose activities extended far beyond those of its contemporaries. The Byzantine state organized industrial production: a mint, foundries for weaponry, textile workshops and brick-kilns. Constantine, with the foundation of the new city, created an absolutist state. He headed an elaborate bureaucracy that was structured on militaristic lines—officials even wore a military belt. Many elite families of Rome, with traditional memories of the more democratic republic, had declined to migrate to the new city. Constantine's elite was based on senior civil servants who owed everything to the emperor: this increased the autocratic tendencies in him and his successors. A vast bureaucracy was sustained by a system of taxation that was elaborate and inescapable. In time taxes were complemented by customs duties imposed on foreign merchants, who were mainly Syrian, Egyptian, Jewish or Armenian. But there were tacit limits to the authority of emperor and state, and some emperors were deposed for incompetence or as a result of palace revolutions.

Deposed emperors often changed their names and retired to a monastery, sometimes on one of the Princes' Islands. Occasionally they might be mutilated and murdered, by soldiers, by family or by the mob. None suffered a more awful fate than Andronicus in 1185 who was deposed, had an eye gouged out, his teeth torn out, his beard pulled out and his right arm cut off. He was then paraded through the streets of the city on a mangy camel. The mob poured human and animal excrement on him and pelted him with stones. A prostitute emptied a pot of her own piss over his face. As if that was not enough, in the Hippodrome, near the Blue Mosque in today's Istanbul, he was hanged upside down and castrated. Some of the crowd stuck swords into his mouth, others up his backside. Only then did he die. But such a death was unusual.

## THE EMPEROR AND THE CHURCH

Most emperors were content with seeing themselves as the regent of God on earth, a demotion from the pre-Christian emperors who claimed to be gods themselves. Constantine was both the protector and the master of the Church. It was his duty to adjudicate when there were disputes among Christians. "What higher duty have I in virtue of my Imperial office and policy," declared Constantine, "than to dissipate errors and repress rash indiscretions, and so to cause all to offer to Almighty God true religion, honest concord and due worship?" Imperial control over the Church meant the management of dissent and diversity, especially in the fourth and fifth centuries which were characterized by intricate dogmatic and liturgical issues that baffle minds in the twenty-first century. In those centuries everyone had a strong opinion on theological issues. "All places," wrote the fourth-century St. Gregory of Nyssa,

> lanes, markets, squares, streets, the clothes' merchants, moneychangers, and grocers are filled with people discussing unintelligible questions. If you ask someone how many obols you have to pay, he philosophises about the begotten and the unbegotten; if I wish to know the price of bread, the salesman answers that the Father is greater than the Son; and when you enquire whether the bath is ready, you are told that the Son was made out of nothing.

The first major dispute arose in the third century and revolved around the doctrine of the Trinity. Was Jesus Christ lesser than God the Father? Was Jesus of the same substance as God, or only similar? An Alexandria-based theologian, Arius, maintained that he was only similar. Arius suffered from intellectual arrogance but was allegedly attractive to women: he is said to have had 700 holy virgins among his supporters. The doctrine called after him, Arianism, led to the most ferocious controversies that were only resolved at the first Ecumenical Church Council in 325. The council was convened by the Emperor Constantine, who was not yet a baptized Christian, at the town of Nicaea (today's İznik), fifty miles from the capital. It was attended by 250 bishops from east and west. The council decided that the Father and the Son were of the same substance and co-eternal. Jesus was "begotten not created." The council also resolved other issues, such as determining the date of Easter and the condemnation of self-castration. The Council of Nicaea set a pattern for eastern Christianity: discussion, debate, bitter disputes over words and subtle meanings.

In the following century the Church was racked by a further controversy over how precisely Jesus Christ combined human and divine qualities in His single person. Were there two natures merged as one, or was there just one nature? Theologians from Egypt in particular, led by Cyril of Alexandria, stressed the unity of Christ's person. Other theologians from Syria, together with Nestorius, Archbishop of Constantinople from 428 until 431, stressed the separation of the two natures, and argued that Mary could not thus be designated the Mother of God: she was the mother only of Christ's humanity. By this time many in Constantinople considered the Blessed Virgin Mary as having a special protecting role over the city, and Nestorius's views were not popular. Another Church Council, convened at Ephesus in 431, condemned the teachings of Nestorius, and proclaimed Mary as *Theotokos*, Mother of God.

But the dispute was never settled. In 451 a further council was convened at Chalcedon, Kadıköy today, across the Bosphorus from Constantinople. The Council of Chalcedon confirmed the decisions of the Council of Ephesus, but condemned what it called the confusion of the human and divine natures of Jesus, anathematizing those who maintained that there were two natures before the incarnation, but one after. The Egyptian Church in particular could not accept the wording of the decisions of Chalcedon, and together many in Syria and Palestine persisted with their understanding of the nature of Christ and were therefore treated as heretics by the established Church in Constantinople. But the imperial arm was unable to discipline heresy far from the capital, and the Coptic Church in Egypt, the Syrian Orthodox (Jacobite) Church and the Armenian Church rejected Chalcedonian orthodoxy and quietly persisted in different beliefs and practices. The Arab Muslims, when they overran these countries in the seventh century, extended a disinterested tolerance to all. Dissenting Christians found this more acceptable than the censoriousness of Constantinople. Together with the Church of Ethiopia, the non-Chalcedonian or Ancient Oriental Churches remain a distinct group of Christians today.

The imperial role of guide to the Church initiated by Constantine was thus followed by his successors, leading to what has been called Caesaropapism. "The emperor is undoubtedly God on earth," said a Visigoth chieftain, "and whoso raises a hand against him is guilty of his own blood."

The 451 Council of Chalcedon reaffirmed the status of the Archbishop of Constantinople as equal to that of the Bishop of Rome. He came to be designated patriarch, but he was never appointed without the approval of the emperor. Herein lay another feature of Byzantium that led to a cultural difference between the eastern and western churches. Because of the collapse of the civil political structures in Western Europe the pope as Bishop of Rome ceased to have a secular authority overseeing him. There was no emperor with the backing of the machinery of a state. When in the eleventh century, a reformed papacy did claim to be an infallible medium of God's wishes on earth, popes claimed to appoint and to dismiss western emperors.

## THE CITY FROM CONSTANTINE TO JUSTINIAN

Only the design of the eastern part of the city survives from the time of Constantine. A rough column, still standing outside the entrance to the Yerebatan Cistern, the Milion, was the point from where distances to and from the city were measured, fulfilling the same function as the London Stone. The Column of Constantine—Çemberlitaş—used to be on the Forum of Constantine: now on Yeniçeriler (Janissaries') Caddesi. Originally it was topped with a statue of the Emperor Constantine as Apollo. It has suffered from earthquakes, fires and has been struck by lightning. It was restored in the twelfth century and again in 1955. Today it is undergoing further restoration.

The basic plan of the central part of the city bears the stamp of Constantine—the central roads, one leading to the Edirne Gate, and another nearer the Marmara leading to the Golden Gate. The planning of the Hippodrome (Atmeydanı), 1,440 feet (440 meters) long with a rounded southern end, had been started by the Emperor Septimius Severus and

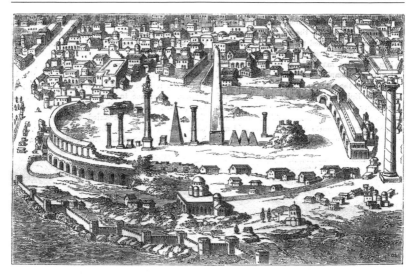

The Hippodrome, a nineteenth-century impression

was completed by Constantine. As it was next to the palace, it was here that the emperor met the people, who would shout their demands to him when he appeared.

Later in the fourth century the Emperor Valens (who died at Edirne fighting invading Goths) built the still surviving aqueduct (known today as Bozdoğan Kemeri), in about 373. It brought water to the central part of the city along a channel that has a gradient of one in 1,000. It functioned for 1500 years, during which time it has undergone much restoration. The lower story is mostly fourth-century work, with large cut stones. The upper story is made up of smaller stones, indicating later Byzantine and Ottoman work.

Five cisterns providing clean water for the city date from these early Byzantine times. Yerebatan near the Sultan Ahmet Mosque is well known. About 250 meters to the west is the Binbirdirek (One Thousand and One Columns) Cistern, to the south of Yeniçeriler Caddesi. It is believed to date from the fourth century. Like other surviving Byzantine buildings, it has suffered vicissitudes of fortune and in the nineteenth century it housed a spinning mill. There are three other cisterns that can be identified, "large rectangular holes in the urban landscape," in the words of the architectural historian, Zeynep Çelik. One is the Aetios Open Cistern, on the main road heading towards the Edirne Gate. It brought in water from Thrace. In Ottoman times it was a vegetable garden and is now the Vefa football stadium. Another open air cistern, dating from the fifth century but abandoned as a reservoir before the end of the Byzantine Empire, is the Mocius Open Cistern in the area of Fındıkzade, west of Aksaray. It too became a vegetable garden in later Byzantine and Ottoman times. Today it is an "education park," with gardens, tennis courts, a baseball pitch and a giant chess set. A third vast cistern is the Aspar Cistern near the Sultan Selim mosque.

In the early fifth century the walls were rebuilt, a mile or so further out to contain suburban developments. They may also have been extended to secure water supplies, for three of the five great Byzantine cisterns were brought into the walled city by the extension. But the massiveness of the walls also protected the city from the increasing raids from "barbarians." Although they are called the Theodosian walls and attributed to the Emperor Theodosius II, that emperor was only twelve years old when the work was undertaken. The man responsible was his minister, Anthemius. The walls that we can see today are substantially those built then. With ninety-six towers, the construction alternated bands of brick with stone: the brick acted as shock absorbers during earthquakes. They were of military value for over a thousand years, and lost that value only when the development of artillery made walled cities obsolescent. They were of symbolic value even longer. For a thousand years citizens were ready and happy to maintain the masonry. The people of the city felt safe behind those walls which complemented the protection provided, as it was believed, by the Blessed Virgin Mary.

This extension indicates how, between the reigns of Constantine and Justinian I, the city was expanding. As Themistius, a pagan philosopher of the time, who specialized in writing panegyrics of successive emperors, wrote,

> No longer is the vacant ground of the city more extensive than that occupied by buildings; nor are we cultivating more territory within our walls than we inhabit; the beauty of the city is not as heretofore scattered over it in patches, but covers the whole area like a robe woven to the very fringe. The city gleams with gold and porphyry... were Constan-

tine to see the capital he founded, he would behold a glorious and splendid scene, not a bare and empty void; he would find it fair, not with apparent but with real beauty.

Constantinople's "vacant ground" was filled up in the fourth and fifth centuries by people who came to the city from all directions. Constantinople was becoming a city of immigrants, a role it has maintained to the present day. Older citizens were worried. "I am astonished at our folly," petitioned Synesius, himself a migrant from Cyrene in present day Libya, in 399. "In every more or less prosperous home," he went on,

> we find a Scythian [Goth] slave; they serve as cooks and cupbearers; also those who walk along the street with little chairs on their backs and offer them to people who wish to rest in the open, are Scythians. But is it not exceedingly surprising that the very same light-haired barbarians with Euboic headdress, who in private perform the function of servants, are our rulers in political life? The Emperor should purify the troops just as we purify a measure of wheat by separating the chaff and all other matter, which, if allowed to germinate, harms the good seed.

The city was also establishing itself as a center of education and learning. When it was founded scholars migrated from Athens, then the main center for pagan teaching and philosophy in the Roman Empire. Higher education was reorganized during the long reign of the Emperor Theodosius II (408-50). Thirty-one professors were appointed to what has been called a university. Subjects included Latin, Greek, jurisprudence, philosophy and rhetoric. The professors and their staff received a salary from imperial funds.

## THE EMPEROR JUSTINIAN

Justinian was the bright nephew of an allegedly illiterate soldier who had worked his way up in the army to become at the age of sixty-six the Emperor Justin. Justin was the first Greek emperor, although the family had been Romanized and probably had Latin as their native language.

Justinian was well educated and had more impact on the Byzantine Empire than any other emperor. Ambitious, ruthless, a spendthrift and multitalented, he was versed in the Christian scriptures and relished joining in religious discussions. He even wrote a few hymns. He saw himself as Emperor of the Roman Empire and had no concept of a separate eastern empire. He set himself the task of recovering the lost territories of the west—including North Africa—and reuniting the empire. By the end of his life the empire stretched from the Pillars of Hercules—Gibraltar today—to the River Euphrates. For his ambitious policies he imposed a ruthless taxation system, increasing revenue further by selling offices.

In the first decade of his reign he faced a rebellion—the Nika riots (see below)—which led to the destruction of much of central Constantinople. He turned this calamity into a triumph by the rebuilding of much of central Constantinople, and above all the Church of the Holy Wisdom, today's Ayasofya.

In his work Justinian was supported by an able team. Constantinople was, then as now, a melting pot, a place for the exercise of talent. There was a Constantinopolitan elite, but for real achievements emperors drew on the resources of talent from an empire. Thus his leading military commander was Belisarius, also a man from the Balkans. When Belisarius fell into disfavour, Justinian called on the services of another outstanding general, Narses, an Armenian eunuch. Justinian's tax collector was John of Cappadocia. The architects of the Church of the Holy Wisdom were Anthemius of Tralles and Isidore of Miletus. Tralles (present-day Aydın) and Miletus (Milet) were two cities in south-western Asia Minor. The head of the commission that carried out the legal reforms was Tribonian who came from Pamphylia, the area around present-day Antalya. The men who realized Justinian's visions were all provincials.

In his domestic life Justinian relied on his wife, the remarkable Empress Theodora. Her father was allegedly a bear tamer in the circus, originally from Crete (according to some) or northern Syria (according to others). Our perception of her as a cruel and heartless nymphomaniac has been colored by *The Secret History* by her contemporary, Procopius. This is an extraordinary work. Procopius was a lawyer, another provincial—a Palestinian from Caesarea—who came to the capital and accompanied Belisarius in his military campaigns. Before *The Secret History* he wrote two other major works of history—on the military campaigns and on the buildings of Justinian. In both he writes with respect and restraint of the emperor and Belisarius, but in *The Secret History* he is so unsparingly bitter and scurrilous that it is hard to realize that the works come from the same pen.

## THE NIKA RIOTS

Wars and buildings require funding and Justinian's extortions created enemies among the professional and well-to-do classes, from which Procopius sprang. His *Secret History* reflected popular discontent at the burden of taxation imposed to pay for wars. Discontent took the more direct form of the Nika riots.

For the previous century factions had represented political, social and economic interests, and were called the Greens and the Blues. (There were also Reds and Whites but these had relatively little influence.) The Blues, of which the Emperor Justinian was seen as leader, represented the interests of the senior bureaucracy and landed magnates who backed the regime. The Greens represented traders and artisans. The factions were almost like political parties in eighteenth-century England and competed for power and influence, and the distribution of taxation. They made themselves most visible (and audible) during chariot races held in the Hippodrome, today's Atmeydanı. The Hippodrome had always been the scene of festivals and political assemblies, as well as of popular sporting contests. The main races occurred in the first week of January and on 11 May, commemorating the city's foundation. Twenty-four races were held, when the chariots charged seven times round the course. The charioteers wore the colors of the factions and were cheered by their factional supporters. In the intervals between the races the crowds would be entertained by displays of boxing and wrestling. The emperor had a box half way down the length of the Hippodrome, backing on to the palace. A frieze, dating from half a century before Justinian's reign, has survived on the base of the obelisk in the Hippodrome. It shows the emperor in his box presiding at the games, flanked by spectators in two tiers.

Soon after his succession Justinian found the factions united in opposition to him. During the races chants of "Long live the humane Greens and Blues" were heard. Then things turned ugly and the demonstration became a riot. With the slogan *Nika*—Conquer!—rioters broke into the jail, released prisoners and started to torch buildings. In the next few days the unrest spread. The Church of the Holy Wisdom was burned, as well as parts of the palace. The emperor responded to demands to sack some of his senior civil servants, but the rebellion went on. Shops and workshops were destroyed. Justinian offered an amnesty if the riots were to stop. The emperor contemplated flight by slipping across the Bosphorus to Chalcedon, Kadıköy. But the Empress Theodora, who seemed on this occasion to have shown the qualities of a mixture of Lady Macbeth and Margaret Thatcher, told him to fight it out. The factions were still in the Hippodrome and Belisarius was ordered to bring his soldiers out of the palace. They charged the packed mass of people. Tens of thousands were killed.

## JUSTINIAN'S LEGACIES: CHURCH, LAW AND TRADE

Far from reducing taxation, the riot had the opposite effect. The sacking of the city meant the need for funds for rebuilding it, and taxation was increased to rebuild the center. Justinian did not patch up or restore older damaged buildings; he built afresh. There are consequently today very few buildings from before Justinian's reign.

The most celebrated new building was the Church of the Holy Wisdom. The senior architect, Anthemius of Tralles, was a very Byzantine personality. Inventor of a steam engine and a searchlight, he was one of several brothers. One brother taught literature in the city; two others were doctors, one staying in Tralles, the other migrating to Rome. Anthemius himself was a mathematician, fascinated with the connection between mathematics and architecture; in particular, how to create a dome on a basilica base. The answer was to create colossal pendentives, a device that had not before been tried. His theories were tested by speedy construction of the new church over the next five years.

Anthemius died before the work was completed, but when the building was twenty years old, the eastern part of the dome collapsed. A nephew of Isidore of Miletus, the junior partner—also called Isidore—undertook the restoration. Four hundred years later, the western arch collapsed and restoration was entrusted to an Armenian, Trdat, who had built Ani Cathedral in the far east of Asia Minor.

Since the time of Justinian the great church has been the symbol of Byzantium. In spite of earthquakes it has stood for 1500 years. Perhaps it had been given strength by the first masons mixing the spittle of very holy men into the binding cement. In 1204 it was the scene of abuse by the Latin occupiers of the city. In 1453 the Turkish conqueror Sultan Mehmet II turned the church into a mosque. He had a hair of the Prophet Muhammad inserted into building materials used for repairs. Many new mosques of the Ottoman Empire were inspired by the Church of the Holy Wisdom which has also indirectly inspired St. Peter's in Rome and St. Paul's Cathedral in London. Few buildings in the world have meant so much to so many.

In 1847 the Sultan Abdülmecid I invited two Swiss Italians, the Fossati brothers, to survey and repair it. The structure was reinforced with girders and the mosaics were uncovered, cleaned and covered again. In the following century Atatürk secularized it and turned it into a museum.

For centuries Greek nationalists and their supporters dreamed of restoring it to a church. Today Islamists want to insist on the city's Islamic character and restore it to Muslim worship. Although one philistine has likened Ayasofya Mosque, with its minarets, to a blancmange surrounded by candlesticks and Byron thought it "not a patch on St. Paul's," it remains one of the most instantly recognizable and iconic buildings in the world.

What we see today is substantially the work of Anthemius and Isidore. Western European occupiers looted the interior in 1204, but the exterior was left largely unchanged. The occupiers may have strengthened the structure by adding the flying buttresses at the west end, as well as the slender gothic-influenced buttresses on the other three sides and a belfry to the west. Sultan Mehmet the Conqueror converted the belfry into a minaret, and in later years four minarets were added. The first, at the southeast, was built in the time of Sultan Mehmet II towards the end of the fifteenth century. His son and successor Sultan Beyazit II added another at the northeast corner. Then the great Sinan completed the quartet, a work of expiation of the sins of the empire that had led to the naval defeat at the Battle of Lepanto in 1571. The Fossatis in the nineteenth century added the imperial loggia inside.

Justinian's building program was paid for both by draconian taxation and by the plunder of other buildings. One chronicler reported that schools had to close down because unpaid teachers were starving, and that lead pipes, guaranteeing a water supply had been taken and melted down to be made into gutters for the new church.

Another legacy of Justinian was a code of civil law. Under his direction all previous legislation was codified and legal training was reformed and concentrated in Constantinople after he closed legal schools in Beirut and Athens. The Christian religion was given a monopoly and non-Chris-

Ayasofya Mosque, formerly Church of the Holy Wisdom

tians suffered civil disadvantages. On the other hand, there was less savagery in the punishments. One Christian principle that influenced Justinian and successive emperors was *philanthropia*, the need to temper justice with mercy.

Constantinople became, under Justinian, a global city and during his reign trade extended from China to the Atlantic. The Persians were the intermediaries for the Far East trade. There were two trade routes. An overland route from China went to Bokhara and the Persian frontiers. From there Persians transferred goods to Byzantine customs houses. The sea route went by Ceylon (Sri Lanka) which provided ports for the transshipment of goods which were then brought up the Euphrates to the eastern customs houses of the empire. The principal import from China was silk, whose technology of production the Chinese long kept secret. Other goods from the east included spices, cotton and precious stones.

Justinian tried to break the dependence on Persian middlemen by building up a Byzantine merchant fleet in the Red Sea. He established diplomatic relations with the Christian kingdom of Abyssinia, but failed in his wish that these Christian allies might replace Sassanid Persia as intermediaries. But by a stroke of luck the secret of silk production was discovered and a home silk industry rapidly developed as a state monopoly, with a factory in the capital. Constantinople then became an exporter of silk wares to Western Europe for the palaces and residences of royalty and the wealthy.

Much information on the Red Sea and Indian Ocean routes appears in the writings of Cosmas Indicopleustes, a sixth-century merchant who later became a monk, wrote about his travels and mused on geographical issues. In Lyn Rodley's words, he wrote about "rain, earthquakes, the Flood, the migration of Noah, the silk routes, sources of the Nile, unicorns (although he admits to not having seen one), measurement of the earth, the destruction of old empires and the primacy of the Roman one, the life of Christ and, to his great credit, the equality of men and women."

Justinian was succeeded by a feeble-minded nephew who liked to be drawn through the palace in a child's cart. He was succeeded by a son. Then a soldier, Maurice, who married into the family, took over. Wars with Persia preoccupied the empire. The capital was eclipsed by the provinces, and it was a provincial soldier, perhaps of Armenian origin, Heraclius, who became emperor in 610, declaring himself emperor while in Carthage. A man with light golden hair, he was an effective administrator and able soldier with a strategic vision. The empire was harassed by enemies on all sides and at one point he considered moving the capital from Constantinople to Carthage. In the first part of his reign he was reversing Persian invasions of Syria. Exhausted by that, he then had to face emerging Muslim invasions from the Arabian Peninsula, during which Syria and Palestine were lost.

For a thousand years Syria and Palestine had been under a Hellenic cultural hegemony. Aramaic and other Semitic languages may have been the language of the people but Greek was generally the language of education, culture and administration. There had been strong links between Syria and Constantinople. Antioch was an older Christian center than the capital, to which it had provided philosophers, poets and preachers. Then Egypt fell to the Arab Muslims later in the seventh century. After that, the areas under Byzantine control were more homogenously Greek. It was also more homogenously Orthodox.

## THE ICONOCLAST CONTROVERSY

The eighth century was marked by the iconoclast controversy. The Emperor Leo III was a soldier from Germaniceia (Kahramanmaraş) who became emperor in 717. He spent his first years resisting the last major attack from Muslim Arabs. A tough man, he was an able soldier, an administrator and something of a thinker. Just as the successes of the first Constantine were attributable to Divine favor, so the reverses of the seventh century were to be attributed to Divine displeasure, in particular wrath against the use of images. Arguments about the acceptability of images went back to interpretations of the Ten Commandments, and Leo's arguments were not new. But he had the power to implement a policy of the destruction of graven images.

The iconoclastic period, from 726 to 843, with a break when images were favoured from 780 to 813, saw concerted campaigns against holy images in churches, a vandalism comparable to that of the Commonwealth period in English history. And, like that period, one needs to go beyond the destruction to understand what was behind it. In both periods, each side produced a literature of polemic. Some historians have argued that Byzantine iconoclasm was influenced by the Islamic prohibition of images. But it seems more probable that both sprang from the same regional and ideological roots. The Muslim prohibition of images took time to develop, and the legal proscription was decreed a century after the emergence of Islam by an Umayyad Caliph in Damascus, roughly at the same time as the Byzantine ban. In both cases, the iconoclasts were in search of a purer sense of worship, believing that the devotion to images derived from a pagan past.

In the Byzantine case, iconoclasm was accompanied by an attack on monasticism, on the grounds that it took young men away from the army and from productive activity in agriculture and industry. The Emperor Leo wanted to wrest education from the control of the Church. Support for iconoclasm was widespread from the higher officials and higher clergy—the selection of both groups would have been strongly influenced by imperial patronage—and from the army. It seems there was a regional bias in the conflict. The emperors who were the most vigorous iconoclasts were from eastern provinces. Soldiers tended—as they were to the end of the Ottoman Empire—to be drawn from Asia Minor. Opposition came from Thrace and the west. The popes deplored iconoclasm and excommunicated iconoclasts. It was the emperors of Greek origin, including the first empresses, who reversed iconoclastic policies. Sacred images were popular among the ordinary people of the capital and, of course, among monks and those involved in the manufacture and distribution of icons.

Iconoclasm was implemented capriciously. Pro-image patriarchs were replaced, and image worshippers were liable to be exiled, imprisoned, tortured or executed. But bans were not uniform, and met with resistance. Most surviving evidence is about iconoclasm in the capital. Representations of church councils in the center of the city were replaced by sporting scenes. In the patriarchate room over the southwest ramp of the Church of the Holy Wisdom, mosaic decorations that included medallions of the face of Christ and of saints were replaced by crosses. The mess resulting from the changes can still be seen. Some painters, such as one Lazarus, continued to practice until, on the orders of the Emperor Theophilus, his hands were burned. Many artistic works, especially illuminated religious books, were concealed in monasteries.

The campaign against monasticism became personal. Some monks were compelled to marry. On one occasion monks were forced to walk in file through the Hippodrome, each holding a woman by the hand, to jeers and taunts from the crowd. This treatment was gentler than that meted out by a governor in Asia Minor who gathered together the monks and nuns of Ephesus and said to them, "Let each who wishes to obey the emperor put on a white dress and take a wife immediately; those that do not do so shall be blinded and exiled to Cyprus." He was congratulated by the emperor who wrote, "I have found in you a man after my own heart who carries out all my wishes." Monasteries were turned into barracks. Thousands of monks migrated to Italy. Others fled to the caves of Cappadocia where they were able to continue their lives free from harassment.

One positive artistic consequence of iconoclasm was a growth in secular art. Scenes of nature—trees and animals—and illustrations of hunting and racing became popular, and other art forms such as the painting of enamels were developed.

The craze against icons was relaxed between 780 and 813, but was restored after a military humiliation. In 811 the Emperor Nicephorus I, on a campaign against the aggressive Bulgarian Khan Krum, was captured and killed. His skull was fashioned into a bowl from which the Bulgar nobles were obliged to drink. The Bulgars advanced towards Constantinople but the khan died suddenly and the threat petered out. Iconoclasm was restored two years later, again in response to what was seen as Divine wrath, but with less conviction. Measures against images were largely restricted to the capital, which also saw the most articulate opposition. The monastery of St. John of Studios (Imrahor Mosque today), the ruins of whose church are still standing to the west of the city towards the point where the walls meet the Marmara Sea, was the base for resistance, led by Theodore of Studios (later canonized). This monastery was one of the richest among the hundred or so in the city and owned income-generating properties such as mills, vineyards, workshops and dockyards. In later centuries the monastery became a center for the production of illuminated manuscripts, icons and also hymns. Iconoclasm was finally ended in 843.

## PHOTIUS AND EDUCATION

In 858 a man of great secular and religious learning became patriarch: Photius. He taught at the university in Constantinople where students could study at state expense on a campus that occupied part of the palace area. The syllabus consisted of a *trivium* of three subjects—grammar, rhetoric and dialectics—and a *quadrivium* of four subjects: arithmetic, geometry, astronomy and music. Medieval Western European universities adopted this program of studies. In addition students were able to study philosophy and the old classical writers. Photius was a charismatic teacher who used to run a reading group, and made the books of his library available for students. He wrote critical summaries of books and so can be regarded as the father of book reviewing.

He counted the Muslim Emir of Crete among his friends. One of Photius's students wrote to the emir's son that Photius "knew well that, although difference in religion is a barrier, wisdom, kindness, and the other qualities which adorn and dignify human nature attract the affection of those who love fair things; and, therefore, notwithstanding the difference of creeds, he loved your father, who was endowed with those qualities."

Ninth-century Constantinople was a center of learning with a reputation that traveled far. The Muslim Caliph Ma'mun in Baghdad, begged the emperor to allow one scholar, known as Leo the Mathematician, to come to his court. With the university reorganized, Leo became its head, before moving on to become Archbishop of Thessalonica.

It was two brothers from Thessalonica who were to bring Christianity to the Slavs, whose language still had no written form. In 862 the ruler of Greater Moravia wrote to the emperor and asked for a teacher who could teach them the Christian faith in their own language. The emperor sent two of his most distinguished scholars: Constantine, an accomplished linguist and a theologian, and his brother Methodius, abbot of a monastery and former administrator. They set off the following year. Constantine is better known by his monastic name, Cyril. He invented an alphabet based on the Macedonian Slav dialect, believed to have been the alphabet now known as Glagolitic. A century later another alphabet using more Greek letters was devised, and is called Cyrillic. Cyril translated the New Testament, the Orthodox liturgy and other service books into the language now known as Old Church Slavonic, which is used today for worship by the Russian, Serbian and Bulgarian Orthodox Churches.

Higher education was generally, though not exclusively, a male pursuit. Ninth-century Constantinople did produce a female poet and hymnographer, Kassia, who came from a family of senior officials and studied privately. She was shortlisted as a bride for the Emperor Theophilus. An archaic classical ritual was arranged whereby the emperor walked between two lines of potential brides, with a golden apple in his hand. Gibbon records how Kassia (whom he calls Icasia) caught the emperor's eye, who said, guardedly, alluding to Eve, "Women have been the cause of much evil," whereupon Kassia answered back, referring to the Blessed Virgin Mary, "And, surely, Sir, in this world, they have likewise been the occasion of much good." What Gibbon calls her unseasonable wit displeased the emperor who chose a more silent bride, perhaps bearing in mind the Byzantine precept applied to women, "Silence is an ornament." (Things were slow to change. In the nineteenth century a young Black Sea Greek woman who moved into the household of her husband was expected to keep totally silent until she had produced a son.) Kassia's compositions have become part of the Orthodox canon and are used in services to this day. Indeed, there has been a revival of interest in her life and work.

The Emperor Theophilus was the last of the iconoclasts. He did not object to luxury, and used to sit on a golden throne and preside over entertainments where lions cast in bronze spouted wine into fountains. The Emperor Theophilus also developed the palace at Blachernae, on the heights where the walls sweep down to the Golden Horn. He inaugurated the custom of riding to the Church of the Blessed Virgin Mary at Blachernae, giving his subjects the opportunity of presenting petitions. Blachernae was actually more secluded as a palace than the palace city near the Church of the Holy Wisdom. It was near the forests beyond the walls, convenient for hunting, for which boars were carefully protected. Life at Blachernae became increasingly luxurious. It was here that in later centuries that emperors would meet western Crusaders.

## THE MACEDONIANS: IMPERIAL ZENITH

The first post-iconoclast emperor was Michael III. He made one of his favourite courtiers, Basil, co-emperor, but in 867 Basil, known as the Macedonian, turned on his patron, murdered him and seized absolute power. He inaugurated what has been seen as a golden age for the empire. He and his descendants ruled for nearly two hundred years, interrupted only by two usurping, though successful, soldiers. During these centuries the empire recovered territory in the Balkans and in southern Asia Minor. A grandson and namesake of Basil met the challenge of a rejuvenated Bulgarian empire and crushed it at a battle in the Struma valley in 1014.

To the north these centuries were times of cultural expansion. The Balkans became Christianized. Russia, after a failed assault on Constantinople, was won over by flattery, concessions and a sumptuous ceremony when the Russian princess Olga visited the city. In the Balkans there was competition between Latin and Greek missionaries for people's souls. The Latins were more prescriptive, the Greeks content with acknowledgement of the supremacy of the Constantinopolitan church. For the Greeks, there was no problem in the liturgy being celebrated in another language. The empire had colossal self-confidence, and operated on the assumption of superiority. Although, as we have seen, there were armies and aggressive warfare, there was no cult of heroism in the practice of warfare. War was never holy. Security was pursued by other means—by duplicity, by diplomacy or by encouraging a third party to attack a potential enemy.

The Macedonians, as the emperors following Basil I were called, presided over a cultural flowering in Constantinople. Basil I (867-86) was illiterate, an excellent breaker in of wild horses, but he nonetheless respected learning. His son became known as Leo VI the Wise (886-912). He was pious, a writer of sermons and liturgical poems. His first three wives all died without leaving him an heir. The Orthodox Church teachings expressly forbid fourth marriages under any circumstances, and any children are regarded as illegitimate. Leo took a mistress who did produce a son, but then needed to legitimize him by marrying his mother, thereby reluctantly but dutifully taking a fourth wife. He was duly excommunicated by the patriarch. The child eventually succeeded to the throne as the Emperor Constantine VII, with the epithet Porphyrogenitus, "born in the purple," to underline his legitimacy and perhaps to offset the dubious accession to power of his grandfather. The mosaic over the central door of the narthex of the Church of the Holy Wisdom dates from shortly after his death. It shows the Emperor Leo, in penitence for his fourth marriage, groveling before Christ as stern judge. Above are medallions of the Blessed Virgin Mary and of an Archangel. The latter is presumably the "avenging angel" displayed in penitence scenes. The presence of the Blessed Virgin Mary denotes her role as intercessor.

The product of this fourth marriage, Constantine, was the most intellectual of emperors. He tended to leave the actual running of the empire to his tutor and father-in-law Romanus Lecapenus, while he devoted himself to scholarship. When he did have to transact public business, he would do so with his youngest daughter, Agatha, who sat at his side. He was a musician and left several works of interest. His *Ceremonies of the Byzantine Court* is replete with the details of offices, titles and court ceremonies. He wrote a biography of his grandfather and an account of the geography and administration of the empire. Constantine was a polymath, anticipating the "Renaissance man" of half a millennium later. His interests and enthusiasms extended to shipbuilding, architecture, painting and sculpture. Under his influence, the university in Constantinople was reorganized by decree. Professors received a good state salary, full board, silk garments and gifts at Easter. The practical objective of the university education was to train civil servants.

The state was extensive in its control over the social and economic life of the capital, with an elaborate system of taxation, which extended to all private economic activity, including beggars and prostitutes, male and female.

## TRADE AND ARCHITECTURE

The state derived an income from customs dues, with a fixed amount, varying between 10 and 12.5 percent on all goods in transit. If merchants thought they could evade the great customs house in the capital, there was another one at the Dardanelles, policing any boats heading for the Bosphorus. And Constantinople was a center for exchange and sale of an enormous variety of goods: cotton from the Aegean island of Cos, purple cloth from Syria, glass from Sidon, paper, glass and textiles from Alexandria, parchment from Pergamon, furniture from Thessaly, wines from Lesbos and from Palestine, raisins and figs from Rhodes, cheese from Damietta at the junction of the Nile and the Mediterranean. From further afield came spices and gems from India, and slaves, furs and amber from Russia. The city's customs house, called the Kommerkion, was the major source of state revenue. The Ottomans took over the word from which the modern Turkish word, *gümrük*, is derived. The English word, commerce, derived through the Latin *commercium* is thus an etymological cousin of the Turkish word.

The state, where it could, controlled other aspects of society. The sale of arms to private people was forbidden. Economic activity was controlled through craft guilds.

At the end of the nineteenth century a document was discovered in Geneva that sheds dazzling light on the social history of the city in the tenth century. The state official in charge of its affairs was known as the eparch and *The Book of the Eparch*, dating from the reign of Leo VI ("the

Wise"), outlines his duties. He was responsible for law and order, and was supported by a large staff. The document lists the craft guilds which included everyone from notaries to tavern-keepers. Each guild had a monopoly and there were penalties for those who pursued more than one trade. Shops had to close at 8 p.m. each evening, on Sundays and on holidays. Exceptions were made for candle-sellers who might practice their trade outside churches. Artisans were instructed to complete work undertaken, and not to charge more than the amount for which they had estimated, and to make good faulty domes that might collapse within ten years. Apart from the penalties for defaulting—which included flogging, head-shaving or banishment—there is a curiously modern ring to it all.

Two surviving churches from the tenth century show important developments in church architecture. The prototype of much church building had been the Church of the Holy Wisdom, a vast construction, a statement of the triumph of Christianity, a show place to overawe the infidel. By the tenth century such a church was no longer necessary. Instead, the religious sensitivities of the worshippers were of greater importance: intimacy, a close relationship between priest and congregation, popular worship.

The tutor of the Emperor Constantine VII Porphyrogenitus, Romanus Lecapenos, had a palace in the area now known as Aksaray. The palace church, which survives today as the Bodrum Mosque, was built in about 920 in what has been called an "inscribed-cross" form, in which a cruciform plan is set within a square enclosing outer wall. This form, which may have developed first in Armenia, became the prototype for Byzantine churches for the next half-millennium and beyond. Today the Bodrum Mosque is hidden behind shops. Bodrum is the Turkish for crypt, basement or cellar. Below the mosque is a cistern, which, drained of its water, is now a small shopping mall, targeted at the immigrants and visitors from the former Soviet Union who have made Aksaray their quarter in today's city. There is even a small Russian restaurant in this basement.

The other example is now the Isa Mosque on Adnan Menderes (formerly Vatan) Caddesi, built as the church of a monastery by a general, Constantine Lips. Both churches have suffered damage and have undergone conversion to mosques and heavy restoration over the last thousand years.

In the later centuries of Byzantium the city became more visibly international in its population and culture. The Italians were the first to set up colonies with quays and warehouses allotted to them on the southern shores of the Golden Horn, around today's Eminönü. Amalfiots were settled in 944, followed by Venetians in 992. Pisans and Genoese followed in the twelfth century. In later years there were communities of Germans and people from the south of France—Marseille and Narbonne. Jews and Muslims were also welcomed in the city. Jews were assigned a district in Galata, but persisted in remaining in Eminönü. Eyüp, the area along the Golden Horn outside the Theodosian walls, was a place for Muslim pilgrimage even in Byzantine times.

## THE IMPACT OF THE CRUSADES

The eleventh and twelfth centuries were to bring a series of challenges to the proud, self-admiring world of Byzantium.

The city and the empire owed their supremacy and their utter assurance to a number of factors. Their confidence relied on an identity that was unquestioned. In the first place Constantinople, or Byzantium, was the capital of the Roman Empire, the center of the civilized world, the culmination of known history. And so, monuments and relics of past civilizations had from the earliest years been brought to the city. Moreover, its unquestioned primacy as the capital of the Roman Empire was given divine sanction because it was the Christian empire. There may have been variations in liturgy and localized practices from place to place, but the hierarchy of the Church as well as the rituals linked the emperor and the Church. The emperor was the man to whom St. Peter had referred when he urged Christians to "fear God, honor the Emperor." The city's moral integrity had been secured by the presence of the vast collection of holy relics, associated with the life of Jesus Christ and the Apostles. The mother of the Emperor Constantine I had been the first collector of relics, but the gatherings continued over the centuries. As well as pieces of the Holy Cross, another priceless relic was the Mandylion, a face cloth on which Jesus had wiped His face, leaving an everlasting impression. Some relics were housed in a chapel of the principal palace that was between the Hippodrome and the Sea of Marmara. This chapel now contained the Crown of Thorns, the lance that pierced Jesus's side and even a phial of His blood. "The relics," Geoffroy de Villehardouin, who accompanied the Crusaders of 1204 observed, "were beyond all description; for there were at that time as many in Constantinople as in all the rest of the world."

Constantinople had a special relationship with the Blessed Virgin Mary, who watched over her city. At times of crisis a wonder-working icon, the Hodegetria (she who shows the way)—allegedly painted by St. Luke—was paraded around the city walls.

Visitors to the city were staggered by its wealth and size. The population was probably larger than the whole of the then population of England. The fine buildings were intended to impress.

The political system was sustained by a political elite who were educated in a range of classical subjects. The supreme and most articulate exemplar of this culture was Michael Psellus, who was a counselor to several eleventh-century emperors and has left us highly readable memoirs, translated as *Fourteen Byzantine Rulers*. In this book Psellus reveals himself as a bumptious and self-confident gossip, full of good stories and vivid sketches of life at the top of the city. He is contemptuous of others who lack his scholarship, and his intellectual arrogance has few boundaries. He assumes an expertise in medicine and military strategy and suggests that the Battle of Manzikert (Malazgirt) in 1071 was lost because the emperor did not take his advice. His references and allusions range from the Bible to classical authors, to Greek and Roman history. Indeed, he would not be out of place in the senior civil service or the cabinet in nineteenth-century Britain. But he sheds much light on the city in his time. The sea and the Golden Horn were highways, and boats were used not just to go from one bank to the other. Emperors traveling from their palace next to the Church of the Holy Wisdom and the Hippodrome to the Palace of Blachernae up the Golden Horn would go by trireme rather than overland. This would also be their mode of transport to the monastery of St. John of Studios near the walls on the Sea of Marmara.

The people, "the reasonable folk who preferred to live a simple honest life and took no part in public affairs," were kept loyal by spectacles. When the military rebel, George Maniaces, was defeated in battle in 1043, the Emperor Constantine IX decided to celebrate with a Triumph.

> He had a genius for organizing shows on a grand scale. The procession, worthy of its author, was arranged as follows: the light-armed troops were ordered to lead, armed with shields, bows, and spears, but with ranks broken, in one conglomerate multitude; behind him were to come the picked knights in full defensive armour, men who inspired fear, not

only for their forbidding appearance, but by their fine military bearing; next came the rebel army, not marching in ranks, nor in fine uniforms, but seated on asses, faces to the rear, their heads shaven and their necks covered with heaps of shameful refuse. Then followed the pretender's head, borne in triumph a second time, and immediately after it some of his personal belongings; next came certain men armed with swords, men carrying rods, men brandishing in their right hand the rhomphaia—a heavy one-edged iron sword—a great host of warriors preceding the army commander—and, in the rear of them all, the general himself on a magnificent charger, dressed in magnificent robes and accompanied by the whole of the Imperial Guard.

Psellus is revealing of the values of his class. The qualities in a ruler or a senior advisor are listed. He should come from a good family. He should be eloquent, with an eloquence based on scholarship such as his own. And he should be handsome. Psellus is very conscious of physical beauty and is meticulous in describing the personal appearance of the gallery of emperors in his memoirs.

Into this world burst the Crusaders. In the second half of the eleventh century, the empire was fighting on two fronts. Wave after wave of Turks from central Asia were settling in Asia Minor. Many became organized into political states and were edging into territory that had owed allegiance to Constantinople. In 1071 the Emperor Romanos IV went to face them and suffered defeat and humiliating capture in eastern Anatolia at Manzikert. Meanwhile to the west, another upstart race of gifted adventurers from Normandy was chipping away at Byzantine possessions on both shores of the Adriatic Sea. The Emperor Alexius I Comnenos appealed to the west for support against the Muslim Turks. He got more than he bargained for. The First Crusade was launched.

In 1096 the first Crusaders arrived on the outskirts of the city, with the aim of relieving Jerusalem from the Muslims and "helping" the Byzantines to recover lost territory. The emperor's daughter, Anna, later wrote her memoirs and describes with aristocratic disdain the vulgar habits of the French and Italians who arrived. As soon as possible they were shipped across the Bosphorus to minimize damage to the city. Close political, military and diplomatic relations led to an acute strain in relations between the Christians of east and west. This exacerbated the growing gulf in the religious field. The Greek east thought final religious authority rested with Church councils. In the west a reformed papacy in the tenth century aspired to complete authority, to papal supremacy. There were differences of doctrine and ritual. The presence of the Crusaders forced the issue. When Crusaders set up statelets in previous Byzantine lands, a religious hierarchy owing allegiance to Rome was established.

Where possible western pilgrims and Crusading soldiers were persuaded to stay out of the city—or allowed only for short supervised visits to stare in wonder at the sights. The monastery of St. Cosmas and Damian near the present Eyüp became the base for the Normans of southern Italy, and for a couple of centuries became known as Bohemond's Tower. Others stayed at the monastery of St. Stephen, later San Stefano, today Yesilköy, on the Sea of Marmara four miles west of the walls. Most camped on the heaths and hills outside the walls.

Throughout the twelfth century all the Byzantine diplomatic skills were exercised to reduce the damage the Crusaders were doing. Deep distrust was mutual. Constantinople became dependent on the commercial expertise of the Italian city states whose loyalty to the papacy was tempered by the pursuit of commercial advantage.

The Crusaders were not the only visitors from the west to record their impressions of the city.

## A Jewish Visitor

Benjamin of Tudela was a twelfth-century rabbi from Navarre in northern Spain, then still under Muslim rule. He set out in 1165 on a long journey to the lands of the east and later wrote up his travels in a vivid account. It is not clear why he traveled—commerce? curiosity? pilgrimage?—but wherever he went he made contact with Jewish communities. He may have intended his writings to be a guide for future Jewish pilgrims to the Holy Land.

He reached the city after having traveled overland from Thessalonica, Salonica. Constantinople's circumference was eighteen miles, he noted. The city was full of traders from all over the known world. He visited the Church of the Holy Wisdom and observed that the Pope of the Greeks is "at variance with the pope of Rome." He marveled at the riches of the church, "ornamented with pillars of gold and silver, and with innumerable lamps of the same precious metals." In the Hippodrome Benjamin saw a motley crowd of international entertainers performing

> surprising feats of jugglery. Lions, bears, leopards, and wild asses, as well
> as birds, which have been trained to fight each other, are also exhibited.
> All this sport, the equal of which is nowhere to be met with, is carried
> on in the presence of the king and the queen.

The rabbi visited the Blachernae Palace with its pillars of gold, and with pictures of all the wars of ancient times, as well as those fought by the Byzantines, a practice that was resumed seven centuries later in Dolmabahçe Palace.

Towers in the city stored the tribute brought in from all parts of the empire: silks, purple cloths and gold. The state had a huge money income, from rents of hostelries and bazaars and the duties paid by merchants. Benjamin was impressed by the wealth of the city, where the inhabitants rode on horseback, dressed in garments of silk, ornamented with gold. There was ample bread, meat and wine.

> The Greeks hire soldiers of all nations, whom they call barbarians, for
> the purpose of carrying on their wars with the sultan of the Thogarmim,
> who are called the Turks. They have no martial spirit themselves, and,
> like women, are unfit for warlike enterprise.

Benjamin estimated that there were 2,500 Jews in Constantinople of whom 500 were Karaites, who lived on the Galata side of the Golden Horn. They included some extremely rich merchants, mainly dealing in silk. No Jew was allowed to ride on a horse except Rabbi Solomon Hamitsri, who was the emperor's physician. He interceded with the authorities to enable the Jews to enjoy some privileges, but their general lot was grim:

> … the hatred against them is increased by the practice of the tanners,
> who pour out their filthy water in the streets and even before the very
> doors of the Jews, who, being thus defiled, become objects of contempt
> by the Greeks. Their yoke is severely felt by the Jews, both good and
> bad; for they are exposed to be beaten in the streets, and must submit
> to all sorts of bad treatment.

## 1204: HUMILIATION

The Fourth Crusade has been seen as the death blow to the Byzantine civilization that radiated from the city of Constantinople. Crusaders were diverted from advancing to the Holy Land to wrest Jerusalem from the hands of the infidel by materialist Venetians, who inaugurated the sacking and the plundering of the wealthiest city in Christendom. That is certainly one point of view, but the reality was a little more nuanced. The events of 1203–04 did not come out of the blue. There were longstanding grievances between Venice and Constantinople. Western Crusaders believed eastern Christendom was heretical. In some ways the Crusade was an extension of Byzantine internal politics. And although the plunder was unprecedented in its scale and insensitivity, it has to be remembered that Constantinople was itself full of plunder taken from sites in the ancient world and holy relics acquired from the countries around the eastern Mediterranean.

Venice had come with its new naval power to the support of the Byzantine Empire during the eleventh century, before the First Crusade, helping it recover some territory that had been taken by the Turks. Venice was also the ally of Byzantium in the struggle with the Normans on the Adriatic. The city, in acknowledgement, gave concessions to the Venetians and to other Italian city states—Amalfi, Pisa and Genoa. Venetians were exempt from the *kommerkion* customs duties. They were awarded quays, warehouses and a quarter along the Golden Horn. There was mutual advantage in the arrangements. But these privileges were resented by indigenous Constantinople merchants. Reflecting this resentment, in 1171 the Emperor Manuel I suddenly ordered the arrest of Venetians and the seizure of their goods. Venice sent an envoy, Enrico Dandolo, to try to resolve the dispute. Negotiations were prolonged and reached no agreement. After Manuel's death in 1180, the politics of the city were in confusion. An old soldier from the Comnenus family seized power in 1182. His troops went on the rampage against the west Europeans; this time the victims were mostly Pisans and Genoese. A hospital managed by the Hospitallers was raided and the sick murdered in their beds. One story—and of course it may have been malicious propaganda—was that a visiting Roman cardinal was killed and his decapitated head tied to the tail of a dog. Some survivors reached Crusader Palestine. The historian William of Tyre met them, reflecting on the Byzantines as "the perfidious Greek nation, a brood of vipers." Venetians and western Europeans no longer felt any loyalty to the city.

The old soldier was the Emperor Andronicus who terrorized the people of Constantinople, until he was pushed aside in 1185 by a cousin. The particularly grisly end of the deposed Andronicus has already been mentioned. The cousin, the Emperor Isaac II, was himself deposed ten years later, blinded and replaced by his brother, who became the Emperor Alexius III. The story now becomes confusing, for Isaac had a son, also called Alexius, who fled to the courts of his German relations. He claimed to be a pretender to the imperial throne. He got to know potential Crusaders from Germany and France, and offered them rewards from the imperial treasury if they helped him to become emperor.

The Crusaders needed money and ships to reach the Holy Land. These could be provided by Venice and a deal was made. The old envoy, Enrico Dandolo, now aged about ninety, was the Doge of Venice. Unfortunately, the expected number of Crusaders was a third of the number anticipated in the deal. The doge persuaded the Crusaders to take Zara, a former Venetian city on the eastern shores of the Adriatic Sea, and then to go on to Constantinople. The Byzantine state had been in touch with the Muslims, and was therefore an obstacle and a legitimate target. It would be a righteous diversion, for not only would they be collecting outstanding debts, but they would also be putting on the throne the legitimate heir to the empire.

And so in 1203 the Crusaders headed for Constantinople, landed at Galata and settled there. A boom joined the two shores of the Golden Horn. On the Galata side it started at the old fort that is now the Yeraltı Camii ("Underground Mosque") and stretched to Sarayburnu, Seraglio Point, now dominated by the statue of Atatürk. The Crusaders raised the boom, allowing their ships to enter the Golden Horn. The city was besieged and stormed on 17 July 1203. The Emperor Alexius III fled. The old blind emperor, Isaac, was taken out of his detention at the Blachernae Palace and reinstated as emperor, jointly with his son, the pretender, who became the co-Emperor Alexius IV. At this stage the Crusaders remained outside the city, settling at Galata or beyond the walls or on the Asian shore.

But the new Emperor Alexius IV did not deliver the required goods to the Crusaders to whom he owed his position. Nor did he find much support among the people of the city. He lasted on the throne for barely six months. Another old soldier, called Alexius Ducas, from one of the aristocratic families and nicknamed Murtzuphlus, "Bushy Eyebrows," was a court official and in January 1204 arrested, deposed and imprisoned the Emperor Alexius IV. "Bushy Eyebrows" had himself crowned Emperor Alexius V. By now there had been in the previous twelve months four emperors, three of them called Alexius: all were still alive. The new emperor did not offer even the pretence of an alliance with the Crusaders. Open war seemed inevitable.

In early April the city was besieged. The Crusaders were effectively led by the nonagenarian doge, whose earlier visits to the city as Venetian envoy had given him an insight into its vulnerability. The besiegers had a force of 20,000 men and concentrated on the sea walls overlooking the Golden Horn. The Emperor Alexius V had his headquarters at a church on a hill overlooking the Golden Horn. On 9 April the city was stormed and captured three days later. The emperor of three months was captured.

The Crusaders had already worked out how the spoils were to be divided, but for three days the soldiers went berserk. Churches were plundered for relics. The Church of the Saviour Pantocrator (Zeyrek Camii) had been closely associated with the imperial Comnenus family and was a repository for relics from monasteries both within and without the walls. The Church of the Holy Apostles—on the site of the present Fatih Mosque—had been the burial place of emperors, including the great Justinian. Ornaments and chalices were seized, and the royal tombs were opened up, and jewels taken. Even the Church of the Holy Wisdom, defiant symbol for seven hundred years of a triumphant Christianity, was not spared. The high altar, richly ornamented doorways and the silver pillars of screens were hacked into pieces. Silver was torn off the pulpit gates. Twelve large crosses above the altar were dragged down. The silver lamps suspended from the ceiling were tossed into a pile for removal. Plunder was loaded on to the backs of donkeys brought into the church. Once the church was ransacked, the soldiers perched one of the camp followers, described by a Greek chronicler as "a priestess of devils," on the patriarch's throne. She entertained the soldiers with bawdy songs.

"Entry of the Crusaders into Constantinople" by Gustave Doré

A Greek contemporary wrote sadly of

war-maddened swordsmen, breathing murder, iron-clad and spear bearing, sword-bearers and lance-bearers, bowmen, horsemen, boasting dreadfully, baying like Cerberus and breathing like Charon, pillaging the holy places, trampling on divine things, running riot over holy things, casting down to the floor the holy images (on walls or on panels) of Christ and His holy Mother and of the holy men who from eternity have been pleasing to the Lord God.

After the three days of bedlam the invaders restored some sort of peace. The deposed Emperor Alexius V was imprisoned, blinded, underwent a show-trial and was later executed. The mode of execution was one that had been practiced in Bruges. The prisoner was taken to the top of the column of Theodosius and pushed out to die, smashed to pieces on the ground.

The Crusaders elected a new Latin emperor, who became known as the Emperor Baldwin. He did not last long, for he was captured the following year at Edirne, Adrianople, in a battle against Bulgarians. His fate is unknown for certain, but one report says that his captors chopped off his feet and arms and left him to be picked to pieces by vultures. Six hundred years later, however, he became a cult hero in the new Kingdom of Belgium, where he has been celebrated in stories and songs.

The Byzantine Empire, like the high altar of the Church of the Holy Wisdom, was irreparably shattered. Outlying parts of the empire, such as Trebizond (Trabzon) and Epirus to the west, maintained a Greek character. Large parts of the Aegean islands and what is today modern Greece became Frankish principalities, adorned to this day with an intriguing diversity of medieval military architecture. Nicaea (İznik), only a few days ride from Constantinople, became the focus for hopes of a restoration of the empire, a kind of mini-Byzantine Empire in exile.

The Latin empire lasted in the city until 1261. One historian, John Godfrey, has called it "one of the most useless political creations in history." The Latins lacked any legitimacy, though the papacy tried to encourage westerners to give it support. Its memory was an embarrassment, but in 2001 Pope John Paul II issued an apology: "It is tragic that the assailants, who set out to secure free access for Christians to the Holy Land, turned against their brothers in the faith. That they were Latin Christians fills Catholics with deep regret."

## AFTERMATH: RESTORATION, CREATIVITY AND DECLINE

The relationship with Venetians was destroyed by the Fourth Crusade of 1204. The beneficiaries were the Genoese, who were allocated Galata. By the fourteenth century Galata became a distinctively separate town, with walls, gateways and its own government. Walls were built in 1304 and enclosed the Genoese city. Other walls divided quarters within Galata. Some of the walls still stand, and can be identified either from the top of the Galata Tower, or near the Arap Camii, where a gateway still has the cross of St. George, symbol of the city of Genoa, and the heraldic arms of two major Genoese families, Doria and De Merude. Most of these walls were destroyed in 1864–65.

Meanwhile the city had been crippled. Even before the Latin occupation parts of the empire that acknowledged the suzerainty of Constantinople were becoming semi-independent. This tendency increased in the following centuries. Some of the Frankish possessions in the Aegean area developed a distinctive culture. Mystras—by classical Sparta—in the Peloponnese, where imperial authority was restored, became a flourishing center of art and architecture, and was usually headed by a member of the imperial family.

Between the Byzantine recovery of the city in 1261 and the fall in 1453, the emperors all came from one family, the Palaeologi. The empire had lost its *élan* and the successive emperors had to resort to makeshift strategies in order to survive. They tried to continue the policy of dividing enemies, and relying on their prestige, but it was not the same. They became a tributary to the Ottomans who were quietly and relatively peacefully annexing and colonizing Asia Minor. Turks and other Muslims were able to come and go in the city. Indeed, there was even a slave market for the sale of Christian slaves.

Constantinople had become, as George Young expressed it, "a sucked orange." One interesting building survives from his time, the Church of St. Mary of the Mongols. This has the distinction of being the only Orthodox building from before the Fall/Conquest of 1453 to have remained a continuously functioning church. (The Roman Catholic Church of SS. Peter and Paul in Galata, though rebuilt in 1475 and again in 1843, can

Mosaic in the Kariye Camii

also claim to have a continuity going back to before the Conquest.) In 1265 the first of the restored emperors, Michael VIII, had an illegitimate daughter, Maria, who was sent to the Mongol Khan Hulagu (who seven years earlier had devastated Baghdad, killing tens of thousands—at least). Some Christian powers saw the possibility of a Christian-Mongol alliance that would encircle and ultimately crush the Muslim states and remove what was seen as the Turkish threat. Maria was given the role of being an agent for Mongol conversion. Unfortunately Hulagu died before she arrived at the Mongol court, so the bride-to-be was married off to his successor Abagu. After sixteen years of marriage, Abagu was killed and Maria returned to Constantinople. Her father wanted to marry her off to another Mongol khan but she declined, and retired to the nunnery attached to this church probably built just before Maria's eastern travels. Hence the commonly accepted name of the church, though officially it is dedicated to Mary, the All Holy Mother of God.

The city in this last phase has left one extraordinary monument. The Kariye Camii (now a museum), originally the monastic Church of the Saviour in Chora, lies within the Theodosian walls of the city. But the name, *chora*, indicates it was originally in the country. Between 1315 and 1321 a public servant and scholar, Theodore Metochites, restored the building as a place for his retirement, donated his library and was responsible for the mosaics and frescoes on the walls and ceilings. He entered the monastery as a monk with the name Theodoulos and spent his last two years here. The mosaics and frescoes represent a break from the more formalistic art of earlier Byzantine times. One mosaic has Theodore himself presenting his church to Jesus Christ. A favorite is a mosaic illustrating the Mother of Christ as an infant taking her first steps, her arms held out with the expectation of parental support. It is intensely moving, an exquisite anticipation of the humanism of the Renaissance. The work in Kariye Cami is outstanding but similar contemporary work was being executed in outlying parts of the crumbling empire such as Mystras and Trebizond (now Trabzon on the Black Sea shores of Turkey).

## A MUSLIM VISITOR

Ibn Battuta, as he is generally known, was born in Tangiers, in today's Morocco, in 1304. He was educated for a legal career but from 1325 he set off on travels that lasted nearly thirty years. On his return he was encouraged to write an account of his wanderings that took him all over the Arab and Islamic worlds, to India, China and islands in the Indian Ocean and to West Africa. He practiced law and married and settled for short periods of time, but he had a restless curiosity about people and places. One of the few places outside the world of Islam that he visited was the Byzantine capital. He came to Constantinople in 1332 after travels in the Crimea where he had attached himself to the camp court of the Khan of the Golden Horde. One of the khan's wives was probably the illegitimate daughter of the Emperor Andronicus III. She had assumed the name of Bayalun after her mother-in-law. She was pregnant and the khan gave her permission to give birth in her native city. Ibn Battuta persuaded the khan to let him join the royal progress through southern Russia, Ukraine, Romania and Bulgaria.

The party camped ten miles from the city and the following morning a huge crowd came out to greet them with bands playing on drums and trumpets. The emperor himself appeared. Ibn Battuta entered "Constantinople the Great" at about noon. The citizens struck their church-gongs until the skies shook with the din. They advanced to the first of the palace gates and met a group of men who called out, "Saracens! Saracens!" and refused any further advance. After negotiation they were allowed into the palace. The emperor allocated a house for Ibn Battuta and gave an order that he should be allowed to travel around the city without any trouble. He stayed at the house for three days and was provided with food—"flour, bread, lamb, chicken, butter, fruit and fish"—as well as money and carpets.

On the fourth day Ibn Battuta called on the emperor, whose father, according to Ibn Battuta, had opted for the religious life. But either looseness in the use of the word father or a faulty memory has made Ibn Battuta's text misleading. The emperor at the time of Ibn Battuta's visit was Andronicus III. His father had died over ten years before his visit.

The khan's wife arranged for an Indian eunuch called Sunbul to escort Ibn Battuta on his visit to the emperor. He passed through four gateways, by each of which was a group of armed men sitting on a bench. At the fifth gate he was searched—"We do to do this to everyone, high or low, stranger or local"—by four Greek eunuchs. Ibn Battuta understood; they did the same thing in India. These four guards then escorted him to a large reception room, two holding him by the shoulders. Unintimidated by this treatment, Ibn Battuta was able to note (and remember decades later) the details of the room which had on the wall a huge mosaic of a rural scene, with a stream flowing among trees. In silence he was taken up to three more men, who checked him again for weapons. Another man came up to him, a Jew from Syria who was to be his interpreter. "Don't worry," he said reassuringly in Arabic. "This happens to everyone."

He was then taken to a large dais. The emperor was sitting on a throne, his wife in front of him. Six armed men stood to his right; four to his left and another four behind him. Ibn Battuta's nervousness must have made an impression on the emperor who gave a sign for him to take a seat and recover his composure. He then rose and declined a further invitation to sit down. The emperor asked Ibn Battuta about Jerusalem—the Mosque of Omar and the Church of the Resurrection—about Bethlehem, Hebron and other places he had traveled to. "My answers pleased him," recalled Ibn Battuta smugly. The emperor ordered that he be looked after and had him dressed in a robe of honor and given a horse in full harness and a parasol. Ibn Battuta asked for a guide to take him around the sites so he could later tell his own countrymen about them. This was agreed. It was the custom, Ibn Battuta noted, that a visitor who received a robe of honor from the emperor and was riding a horse from the imperial stables had to be accompanied on his tours of the city to the sound of trumpets, bugles and drums.

Constantinople, divided by what he saw as a large tidal river, reminded him of the Moroccan city of Salé. On one side was Istanbul (this is the word he uses), where "the Sultan" and top people lived. There were wide roads, paved with stone. People of each profession lived in the same neighbourhood and kept to their tasks. Each market area was closed at night. The whole city lay within the walls of thirteen villages. On the other side of the river was Galata, which reminded Ibn Battuta of Rabat opposite Salé. This quarter was exclusive to Frankish Christians—Genoese and Venetians and individuals from Rome and France. They were subject to the authority of the emperor who appointed one of their number to head them and organize the payment of a tribute. They were all devoted to commerce and Ibn Battuta saw a hundred large ships in their port as well as countless smaller craft. But the streets and also the churches were filthy.

He was unable to enter the Church of the Holy Wisdom, but described the exterior. The church was surrounded by a wall, with thirteen gates, as if it was a separate city. Anyone could enter the enclosure through which a stream flowed. There were shops, including one for perfumes, and platforms around which lawyers and scribes were seated. At the entrance were guards who had the job of sweeping the area, lighting the lamps and opening the gates. People were permitted to enter the church only after they knelt before a cross, allegedly part of the cross on which Jesus was crucified. As a good Muslim, Ibn Battuta could not do this. He was told that thousands were attached to the church, including descendants of the Apostles. In the enclosure was another church set aside for women, with more than a thousand serving virgins, as well as an even greater number of widows. The emperor and the citizens, great and small, came to the church every day, and the emperor paid daily homage to the patriarch.

Ibn Battuta compared the monasteries of Constantinople to the Muslims' *zawiya*. Two monasteries, with cells for men and for women, were within the enclosure of the Church of the Holy Wisdom. Others were outside the enclosure, one for the blind, another for old men over sixty. Most emperors, wrote Ibn Battuta, when they reached the age of sixty or seventy, built magnificent monasteries, resigned and devoted themselves to religious exercises until they died. Ibn Battuta together with a

Greek guide entered one monastery where in the church he saw five hundred virgins, "endowed with the most exquisite beauty." A young man with the sweetest voice was reading the Gospels to them. The virgins were "the daughters" of the emperor, given up to serve this church. Ibn Battuta was taken into other churches and monasteries and came to the conclusion that most of the population were monks or nuns or priests.

One day was spent calling on a monk whom he recorded was the emperor's father, George, who had retired to a monastery. The fatherhood may be as loosely used as the "daughters," the virgins serving the church. The monk was wearing a hair shirt and a felt bonnet and had a long white beard. He took Ibn Battuta by the hand and told the Greek, who knew Arabic, "Tell this Saracen, that is, this Muslim, that I salute the hand that has entered Jerusalem, the foot that has walked in the Mosque of Omar and in the great church of the Resurrection, and in Bethlehem." He placed his hand over Ibn Battuta's feet and then wiped it over his face. Ibn Battuta was surprised at the reaction of Christians towards those of another religion who had been to their holy places. The old man also quizzed him about Jerusalem and the Christians there. Ibn Battuta wanted to accompany the man he thought was the former emperor into the church. "Tell him," the man said to the Greek interpreter, "that anyone who enters must prostrate himself in front of the cross. This is the rule of the ancients and cannot be transgressed." Ibn Battuta therefore left him to enter the church alone and never saw him again.

Another day Ibn Battuta went to the scribes' market. A judge saw him and when it was explained that the visitor was a Muslim seeker after truth Ibn Battuta was invited to meet him. The judge rose. "You are the guest of the emperor," he said, "and we are pleased to treat you with honor." More questions about Jerusalem, Egypt and Syria followed.

The khan's wife then chose to stay in her birthplace, and her retainers set off with Ibn Battuta back to Astrakhan.

Bozdoğan Kemeri: Valens Aqueduct

## Chapter Two

# THE SIEGE OF 1453:
# REGIME CHANGE

The year 1453 is one of the turning points in European, indeed world, history. It formally marked the end of one empire that could trace its history back for two thousand years, and the coming of age of another empire that was to become the most successful Islamic political institution.

By the middle of the fifteenth century the Byzantine Empire was reduced to the city of Constantinople and a few coastal possessions. It traded on its memories and traditions. The Roman Empire has cast a shadow over the whole of Europe. Byzantium was the legitimate and acknowledged successor of the Roman story. For over a thousand years it had been a Christian empire. Meanwhile the Ottomans, descendants and clients of a Turkish family that had settled in northwest Anatolia, had been building up a state for the century and a half before 1453. They spread over much of Anatolia and into Europe. They were already a Mediterranean and a European power.

Constantinople in 1453 was not what it had been. And Istanbul was not in 1453 what it was to become in centuries to come. But the drama of 1453 took place around the city, and continuities can be traced from before and after the siege. For the Turks the taking of the city was the ultimate prize. The siege has been seen as a major advance of Islam and a setback for Christianity.

A closer look at the events of that year suggests that things were not so clear-cut. Christians fought in the army of the conquering Ottoman sultan, Mehmet II. One member of the Ottoman family fought among the defenders of the city. It is erroneous to project a "clash of civilizations" back to the fifteenth century. Since the time of the Crusades an ideology of conflict between the forces of Islam and the forces of Christianity had coexisted with other characteristic features of Levantine politics: compromise, adjustment, curiosity about the other. Sovereignty was never absolute. One

Ottoman troops, 1569

political entity might pay tribute to another more powerful entity, acknowledging the suzerainty of a more powerful state. This guaranteed immunity for the weaker, and was not unlike protection money. At the same time the resources of the eastern Mediterranean and the products of the Far East and the Far West stimulated trade. The Italian city states of Pisa, Venice and Genoa dealt with everyone, spreading prosperity, and in some ways sealed and underwrote Levantine policies of pragmatic coexistence.

In quite another way the siege did mark a turning point. The walls of Constantinople had stood fast against any invader for a millennium. But in the previous century gunpowder had developed. The use of artillery was in its adolescence, but the use of a big gun was perhaps the most significant factor in reducing the city. The walls of Constantinople had been admired and copied by military strategists for centuries. Provided there were adequate supplies of water and food, stone fortifications could outlast a siege. Campaigning in the Middle Ages was often seasonal, lasting from early spring to late summer—by early autumn soldiers were restless, eager to get home for harvests and the winter. The ground outside a city was not necessarily well supplied with the needs of a large army. Turkish winters—and the height of Turkish summers—can be grim, debilitating and potentially unhealthy for soldiers camped in close quarters in the open. The siege of Constantinople lasted under two months, and was over at the end of spring.

The use of artillery in 1453 led to a rapid development in arms technology during the next century. Gunpowder is seen as a marker of modern times and the end of the Middle Ages. Although castles had been losing their strategic importance in the previous century—and even though they continued to be constructed in the Mediterranean world in the next two centuries—the failure of the walls of Constantinople was symbolically the end of the primacy of the castle and the walled town in European defense thinking.

The story of the siege is dramatic and exciting. There are two excellent accounts available in English. The late Sir Steven Runciman's narrative, beautifully written, has to be supplemented by Roger Crowley's twenty-first century account. An older history was written by Sir Edwin Pears who spent forty years in the city before 1914. Many of the contemporary accounts are available in English translation. In contrast to the usual practice, the siege of 1453 was mostly recorded by the losing side.

## A Western Visitor Twenty Years Before 1453

Twenty years before the fall of Constantinople, a knight of Burgundy, Bertrandon de la Broquière came to the city. He set out in 1432 to make the pilgrimage to Jerusalem, then in the hands of the Cairo-based Mamluks. He was a man of great curiosity and recorded whatever he saw. He traveled to the Holy Land by boat from Venice to Jaffa, and decided to appraise the dominions under Turkish rule, and see how far the Ottomans were a threat to Constantinople. He traveled overland from Palestine, observing all sorts of everyday matters from horses to food. From Ottoman Bursa he traveled with a Spaniard, a runaway slave, to Scutari, Üsküdar, also in Turkish hands. The Turks imposed a toll on all who crossed the Bosphorus.

Bertrandon de la Broquière crossed in a Greek boat to the autonomous Genoese city of Galata, and, convincingly disguised as a Turk, was treated with deference. But when he started to make enquiries about a Genoese merchant called Christopher Parvesin, the disguise slipped. The boatman suspected that he was a western Christian and demanded more money. The knight was threatened but was rescued by a Genoese shoemaker.

Pera, de la Broquière wrote, was full of Greeks, Jews and Genoese. He noted the large Genoese vessels in the quays and commented on the strategic vulnerability of the walls on the Golden Horn near the gate that still stands not far from the present Atatürk Bridge.

After two days in Galata, or Pera as he called it, he crossed over to the main city. The open spaces of Constantinople within the walls were more extensive than the built-up areas. He admired the Church of the Holy Wisdom with its religious relics which included "a large stone in the shape of a wash-stand, on which they say Abraham gave the angels to eat, when they were going to destroy Sodom and Gomorrah." He attended a service in the church, attended by the Emperor John Palaeologus, his wife and mother, and his brother, Demetrius, Despot of the Morea. During the service a religious drama was performed, the subject of which was the story of the three youths cast by Nebuchadnezzar into the fiery furnace. Afterwards he hung around to see the empress come out and mount her horse. He was impressed.

> I was so near that I was ordered to fall back, and, consequently, had a full view of her. She wore in her ears broad and flat rings, set with several

precious stones, especially rubies. She looked young and fair, and handsomer than when in church. In a word, I should not have had a fault to find with her, had she not been painted, and assuredly she had not any need of it.

In the Hippodrome he observed the ancient columns and saw the emperor's brother and friends galloping along, tossing their hats into the air, and then shooting arrows at them: a custom, he says, adopted from the Turks.

The Burgundian knight visited other churches, including "one opposite to the passage to Pera, where mass is daily said after the Roman manner." He paused at more holy relics which, in his view, had saved the city from conquest by the Turks. Constantinople was full of merchants "from all nations," but the most powerful were the Venetians who were "independent of the emperor and his officers."

The emperor had heard of the story of Joan of Arc who had been captured by de la Broquière's feudal lord, the Duke of Burgundy—two years earlier—and his courtiers quizzed the knight about the matter. After attending some jousting to celebrate the wedding of a relation of the emperor, he left the city on 23 January 1433, traveling overland to the Ottoman capital Edirne (Adrianople). He wrote about the Ottoman army and methods of warfare. He then left the Ottoman world, passing on through the Balkans, Vienna, Munich and back home to France.

## CONSTANTINOPLE AND THE WEST

The Byzantines, penniless and weak, saw their only chance of survival in the practice of diplomacy, and sought support from Western Europe. But the appetite for Crusades against the Turks had been sated. The papacy demanded a union of the churches and the submission of the Eastern Church to Rome. The Byzantine emperor John VIII traveled extensively in Europe seeking help and at the Council of Florence in 1439 accepted union. This Byzantine concession had the support only of the emperor, his immediate court and the senior clergy. Most of the lower clergy, the monks and the people were opposed to the union. Popular memories of the humiliations of the Latin occupation after 1204 made them fiercely opposed to Western Europe. Could matters be any worse under a Turkish occupation? A western military expedition in 1444 ended in disaster at the hands of the Ottomans at Varna in Bulgaria, and confirmed the Ottomans in their possession of the Balkans. There was little spirit for further military ventures in support of Byzantium. What was the point?

Western outposts in the Eastern Mediterranean and Black Sea areas were motivated by commercial gain rather than religious zeal. The Genoese had trading colonies off the Aegean coast and in the Black Sea, of which Galata was simply one. Although only across the Golden Horn and although there was an obvious overlap of interest, Galata's political administration was quite independent of the empire. It was also much more prosperous than the empire, with an annual revenue seven times greater than that of Constantinople.

By 1453 the city's population had shrunk from its zenith in the twelfth century when it was home to over half a million people to about 100,000 or less. As a Russian survivor of the siege said, Constantinople was "as a vegetable storehouse in a garden." Most of the city was spread across a series of hills overlooking the Golden Horn from Seraglio Point to the Theodosian land walls. Almost all the major churches were in this area. The Golden Horn itself was lined with warehouses, behind which were the quarters of the various Italian commercial communities. There were also quarters for Jews, Ragusans (people from the city now called Dubrovnik) and Catalans. The city now consisted of a number of separate villages—a Moroccan visitor said there were thirteen villages when he visited in the 1340s—linked up with gardens and orchards. Sometimes the villages were themselves walled. The main road from the hub of the city around the palace to the Chariseus Gate (Edirnekapı) road was lined with shops and houses. The university quarter was around the monastery of St. John of Studios, in the southwest.

Warfare was costly and painful and Byzantium had survived because it practiced a policy of coexistence. Other powers were to be flattered, manipulated or appeased. Because of its size and enormous wealth, the city could not fail to impress people from humbler and more modest realms—whether Crusaders or Turks. A cultural authority dazzled Orthodox pilgrims from more recently Christianized lands such as the Balkans or Russia. It was an open city, and unlike cities in Western Europe had provision for Muslims to worship. Arab and Turkish travelers felt at home. It had also exploited its role as a commercial center. People were seduced by the opulence of the place, and exploited by the flattering charm of its rulers. War was avoided by bribery or tactful concessions. The policy of Levantine coexistence had sometimes been shattered—by the explosion of Arabs in the seventh century, by newly aggressive people from the Steppes or the Balkans from the fifth to the tenth centuries, by the Crusaders in the eleventh and twelfth centuries, by the Mongols in the thirteenth century and by the Turks in the fifteenth—but the city itself was rarely directly affected.

There was, to the end, no feeling of racial, religious, ethnic or cultural exclusiveness among the Byzantine elite. The last emperor, Constantine, had a Serbian mother. His father was half-Italian. Turks had long fought in the Byzantine army, just as Greeks fought with Ottomans and with Turkish regimes before them. There was a serene assurance in being a Byzantine, an aristocratic confidence, in spite of having fallen on hard times. But this openness could also mean that loyalties might be temporary. Lack of fanaticism might suggest lack of commitment.

The land walls had inspired military architecture for centuries. Massive walls extended for most of the seven kilometres (four miles) from the Marmara to the Golden Horn. Beyond the solid walls was a wide ditch—now often used as market gardens—and a lower wall. Beyond the lower wall was a fosse or trench, filled with water at times of danger, and a final wall facing the world. This pattern of multiple walls was replicated from the Levant to Wales. Midway along the walls the River Lycus, now

Remains of the old land walls

underground, flowed into the city down to the Marmara. It obliged the walls to drop a hundred meters into the stream's valley, aesthetically pleasing but tactically vulnerable. An invading force was in a position to place slings or catapults on the slope and to overlook, albeit diagonally, the defensive wall. Although the walls were conscientiously maintained, they were not always appropriate for defensive artillery and were unsuitable for gun platforms. Moreover, the towers were added on to the walls rather than built into them: this inhibited the mobility of troops.

Access to the city was by four principal gates—the most northerly being called then Chariseus, today Edirnekapı. This gate stands at the highest point of the whole city, and in 1453 a church dedicated to St. George stood inside the walls on land now occupied by the Mihrimah Sultan Mosque. To the south was the Gate of St. Romanus, now Topkapı. Further south was the third main gate, Pege, now the Silivrikapı. Finally there was the Great Golden Gate, built around a fort and used by the emperors for triumphal entries into the city. After the conquest this was adapted by the Ottomans and is now incorporated within the Yedikule or Seven Towers fortress. Between these principal gates were a number of military gates, giving access to the enclosure between the two higher walls.

The sea walls were less impressive, but, in spite of 1204, the defenders did not anticipate assault from the sea. The currents were too fast to stabilize ships and allow troops to land. A boom connected Seraglio Point to a fort on the Galata side, effectively sealing off the Golden Horn.

A further arm of defense was religious faith. A thousand years of experience—notwithstanding 1204—had taught its people that the city was under divine protection. There was a touching and persistent belief that, even at the last moment, divine intervention would chase off the invader. For diplomatic reasons the emperor had given in to Western Europe, and the union with Rome was celebrated in the Church of the Holy Wisdom. The name of the pope was included in the list of the heads of the other Orthodox churches commemorated during the celebration of the liturgy, in the hope that there would be military support from the west.

But diplomacy, the walls and faith were insufficient when the chips were down and Constantinople had to face actual fighting. And in 1453 the Byzantine Empire was most vulnerable. In the month before the siege, the emperor asked for a census of the potential fighting forces. His secretary, Theodore Phrantzes, told him there were 4,983 available Greeks and just under 2,000 others. The city still had fifty monasteries, and monks and priests were non-combatants. These figures were so demoralizing that they were not made public. They also suggest that the population was very much lower than 100,000. It is likely that many had been seen the writing on the wall and had slipped away to relative safety.

OTTOMAN ADVANCE

In the century before 1453 a steady decline in the city coincided with the growing dynamism of the Ottoman power. Since 1338 the Asian shore opposite the city had been in the hands of the Turks. By the mid-fourteenth century they advanced into Europe, making the port of Gallipoli, Gelibolu, their naval base. In the 1360s Adrianople was occupied and became Edirne, the new Ottoman capital. In the 1390s they built the castle, known as Anadolu Hisarı, on the Asian shore of the Bosphorus, eight miles north of the city. Strategically Constantinople was encircled. These years also saw a constant migration of Turks from Anatolia to Europe to the point where it has been estimated that there may have been more Turks in Europe than in Anatolia. The northeast Aegean was effectively a Turkish lake. The grandfather of Mehmet II had besieged the city but was diverted to confront the Mongols who, under Timur (Tamerlane), invaded Turkish-held lands to the east and sparked off a flight of refugees. Sultan Beyazit abandoned his plans of advancing on the city and sped east, to encounter humiliation and capture by Timur at Ankara. This postponed the conquest by fifty years. The sons of Beyazit fought among themselves, but over the next half century, the Ottomans reinforced their control of western Anatolia and of their European possessions.

Sultan Murat II ruled from 1421, pursuing a policy of ambiguous Byzantine pragmatism. But his son, Mehmet II, who, on the death of his father in 1451, succeeded to the full powers of the sultanate while in his early twenties, was a different and remarkable man. He was multilingual—it was claimed he was fluent in Turkish, Arabic, Persian, Greek, Latin and Hebrew—and had an intellectual curiosity and a strong sense of history. As sultan he possessed a strategic sense, great tactical resourcefulness and unlimited ambition. At once he planned to conquer the city. Ottoman lands now extended for hundreds of miles on both sides of the Sea of Marmara, and, for Mehmet, the city stood out as an island of perceived opulence and infidelity, an insulting check on expanding Islamic hegemony.

The revenues of its commerce would help the young expanding empire. The only snag was a potential army from the west. He was aware that the emperor and some leading churchmen had at the Council of Florence in 1439 exchanged their ecclesiastical independence for the hope of western Christian support against the Turks.

In his first year he secured the neutrality of the Christian powers in south-eastern Europe: Serbia and Hungary. He confirmed a treaty with Venice. He secured his rearguard by menacing the semi-independent Turkish warlords in southwest Anatolia. He had his only brother murdered and thereby sealed his primacy in his family. The only potential challenger was the uncle who was in Constantinople. Mehmet paid him a pension, hoping thereby to neutralize him as a threat.

In early 1452 Mehmet crossed the Bosphorus from Asia to Europe at its narrowest point by Anadolu Hisarı. He destroyed villages and monasteries in the lands to the west and on the Bosphorus, including the Asomaton church at today's Arnavutköy. At great speed he built the elaborate fortress now known as Rumeli Hisarı with plundered masonry. That was completed by August 1452. (Descendants of the soldiers placed in charge of the fortress were living in wooden houses around the castle until the twentieth century.) In contrast to the fifty-year-old fortress on the Asian side, the new construction had massive walls that took account of the recent developments in artillery. The two fortresses could control any traffic from the Black Sea heading for the port of the city or the Mediterranean. Cannon were placed on the new fortress to sink any ships that defied his embargo.

Mehmet spent the winter of 1452-53 based at Edirne. Meanwhile the villages outside the land walls of the city were cleared and a defensive ditch was built in sight of the defenders of those walls. Bursa and Edirne became the recruiting points for a massive Ottoman army of perhaps 100,000 soldiers, at least one soldier for each inhabitant of the city and well over ten soldiers for each man Constantinople was able to mobilize. Mehmet's army included mercenaries and individuals who were Greek, German, Latin, Hungarian and Bohemian. Serbs sent a detachment. It also included, in the words of one Turkish chronicler, "thieves, plunderers, hawkers and others following the siege for booty."

Mehmet had the insight to appreciate the new science of artillery. A Hungarian called Urban had built a particularly enormous gun but he was a technician and a businessman, not an ideologue. The Byzantines could not afford the price he wanted for his gun and his services so, in the tradition of international arms dealers, he found a market elsewhere. Mehmet saw the destructive value of the weapon and hired both gun and gunner at Edirne. In the months of February and March 1453 Mehmet had the giant gun transported from Edirne to the city. The convoy was unable to travel more than two miles a day, and sixty oxen helped to drag it along, with 200 men on either side ready to keep it steady. Fifty carpenters and masons went ahead to level the road and to build pontoons or wooden bridges over waterways in advance of the main convoy.

## THE SIEGE

Mehmet left Edirne on 23 March and arrived in the Constantinople area on 5 April and first camped slightly more than a mile away from the walls. Meanwhile, his opposite number inside the city, Constantine, made his preparations. The emperor was aged forty-nine, had been emperor for four years and had had experience as a soldier and administrator. He was the only emperor, outside the Latin occupation from 1204 to 1261, not to have been crowned in the Church of the Holy Wisdom. Like Mehmet, he was a pragmatic intellectual. He had gone along with the formal submission at the Council of Florence of the Church to papal authority in exchange for anticipated support from the west. In November 1452 a papal representative in the person of Archbishop Isidore arrived in the city.

On 12 December many priests accepted the idea of union, but opposition was articulated by one man, George Scholarius, who had become a monk with the name Gennadius: "Why put your trust in Italians rather than in God?" he argued. Support for the union was limited to some of the elite and those closest to the emperor. Neither the Church in Constantinople nor public opinion acknowledged what they saw as faithless surrender.

Although no armies came from the west, Constantine was supported by the Latin communities of the city. Venetians among the defenders included people from the best Venetian families such as Cornaro and Contarini. There was a troop of Catalans, and a charismatic Genoese soldier of fortune, Giovanni Giustiniani Longo, turned up in January 1453 with 700 fighting men.

The siege began with Mehmet's arrival. He first isolated the city by mopping up Greek outposts. A castle at Tarabya was taken and the defenders all impaled. The Princes' Isles were captured. On Prinkipos, Büyükada, one fort resisted. It was surrounded with brushwood and torched.

Mehmet placed the Great Gun to face the walls and established his base camp a few hundred meters to the west of the highest point of the walls between the Golden Horn and the Marmara. He was surrounded by his crack troops, the Janissaries. An elaborate modern statue of the sultan marks the site of where he placed his red and gold tent. The Great Gun was placed to face the gate that was afterwards called Topkapı, Cannongate.

Mehmet strung his main armies along the walls. A Bulgarian convert to Islam, Zaganos Paşa was to his far left. His area of control extended down to the Golden Horn and across to the northern bank, round Genoese Galata and down to the Bosphorus. Between him and the sultan was Karaca Paşa with soldiers from Europe. To Mehmet's right, as far as the Marmara were two *paşas*, İshak and Mahmud.

From the start the guns started pounding the walls. The defenders came down from the tallest walls and occupied the corridor between the inner and the middle walls. The Great Gun was so elaborate and complex that it was able to fire only five cannonballs a day. It had the backing of other smaller artillery and the besiegers battered at the wall with two or more cannons simultaneously. Mehmet arranged for fire to be concentrated on three parts of the walls which he thought were most vulnerable: the area between today's Tekfur Palace and Edirnekapı, the lowest point of the walls where the Lycus trickled into the city, and the area around Pege, Silivrikapı. Defenders rushed to make whatever repairs they could, filling damaged parts with earth and stones, and then suspending huge bales of wool over the walls to deaden the impact of the projectiles.

By 18 April Mehmet was confident enough to order an assault on the walls. But it was repulsed with a loss of two hundred Turks killed. This success raised the morale of the defenders. Their optimism was increased by a sea battle. Four Genoese sailing ships were seen coming in. Was this the beginning of relief from the west, relief that would vindicate the union of the churches? The ships faced the gauntlet of a fleet of a hundred and forty Turkish ships. They edged their way to the boom to gain access to the relative safety of the Golden Horn. The wind dropped and the sailing ships stalled. Smaller Turkish rowing boats moved in. These had the advantage of mobility but lacked height. Battle was joined with spectators lining the shores of both sides of the Golden Horn. The loftier ships were more easily able to fire down on the Turkish boats. There were too many smaller ships and inadequate communication among the Turkish vessels. When the wind moved again the Genoese were able to shake off the ships and reach the haven of the Golden Horn beyond the boom.

Mehmet was furious and had his naval commander, Baltoğlu, another Bulgarian, bastinadoed. He then carried out a ruse of genius. He was immensely practical and thought long about a problem. He never shared his ponderings, but when he made his mind up he was dynamic in executing his decision. Unable to break the boom or to take boats into the vulnerable Golden Horn, he decided to transport ships from his base on the Bosphorus through a ravine and up behind the walls of Galata to the Golden Horn at the Valley of the Springs near present-day Kasımpaşa. There were precedents for such a bold stratagem. In 1439 Venetians had transported boats overland from the Adige river to Lake Guardia. Mehmet may also have known of the transport of the Byzantine fleet from the Marmara to Lake Ascanius (İznik Gölü) in 1097 when, in collaboration with the Crusaders, Nicaea was taken in the First Crusade.

This audacious move was carried out at night with assiduous preparation. Mehmet's naval base was between present-day Tophane and Dolmabahçe. Galata was a self-contained walled township, and the landmark tower was the most northerly point of the colony. Beyond the walls behind the tower was open countryside covered by bushes and vines. The transporting of the Great Gun from Edirne had trained the troops in taking a huge unwieldy mechanism, unaccustomed to moving around on land. A primitive trackway with rollers and cradles for the ships was constructed. The oxen were brought back into service and barrels of lard were used to facilitate the task. All was meticulously planned and the transporting of seventy to eighty ships up eighty meters to the brow of the hill on today's İstiklâl Caddesi and down to the Golden Horn to Kasımpaşa was accomplished in twenty-four hours. The people of Galata were distracted by the feint of a naval assault on the ships moored to the boom, and the people of the city were forced to deal with a particularly ferocious bombardment of the land walls. Even so, there was a touch of good humor in carrying out the ruse. The crews boarded the ships, the sails were unfurled and the skipper walked along the plank among the rowers, as if they were rowing the boats overland. The boats were free to move around the upper Golden Horn on the morning of 23 April. The spirits of the besiegers soared as those of the defenders slumped.

Even so the defenders prepared to attack the boats. But because of delays and poor coordination among Greeks, Venetians and Genoese, the venture ended in disaster. The besiegers were able to build a bridge from a hundred wine barrels, securely lashed together and sealed by planks. Five men abreast were able to walk across the Golden Horn. The besiegers were now able to make an assault on the less formidable sea walls facing the Golden Horn.

April turned into May. On 7 May and again on 12 May the besiegers, using scaling ladders, made further attempts to assault the city.

From now on Mehmet chose to stay at his camp opposite St. Romanus Gate, while the Great Gun itself pounded away at the walls nearby. It was an unwieldy beast and was held together with giant hoops. In the spring rains it was hard to keep the gun stable and there was a ferocious recoil.

The rains of April gave way to the increasing heat of May, and there was the danger of disease. (It has been calculated that a besieging army of 25,000 men over six weeks produces a million gallons of human and animal urine, and 4,000 tons of excrement. Mehmet's army was at least three times that.) Three general assaults had failed. Mehmet continued to be innovative and was able to spring surprises. Serbs who had worked in silver mines at Novo Brodo were brought in to build a tunnel under the walls. They had to work through solid rock and propped up the wall with tree trunks. The defenders then produced a West European, perhaps a Scot called Grant—although it has also been suggested that he was a Welshman called Geraint. He led teams on countermining expeditions. There was hand to hand fighting underground and the defenders managed to burn down the props. The mining venture was abandoned. Then Mehmet produced another trick. Defenders woke one morning to see a huge turret outside the walls. It had been rapidly constructed overnight. But it was not a threat for long. With brushwood and barrels of gunpowder the defenders were able to destroy it.

Mehmet was waiting for the city to surrender, and as time went on he had moments of depression. In spite of an overwhelming superiority of numbers and materiel he seemed to be getting nowhere. His fears reflected the defenders' hopes. Was there a western army on the way? Rumors spread that a relief force was coming. On Saturday 26 May he held a council with his senior staff, and the possibility of withdrawal was seriously considered. But it was decided to launch a final assault on Tuesday 29 May.

The defenders had a sense that the end was at hand. But in terms of morale things did not go well for them during these last few days. The great icon of the Virgin Mary, the Hodegetria, was paraded to raise spirits. But it slipped and fell into the mud caused by recent rains. Unseasonable weather—a heavy fog—and the appearance of a great light shining on the Church of the Holy Wisdom were interpreted in different ways. But on Monday night, 28 May, the Church of the Holy Wisdom was packed—with Latins and Orthodox alike—for a final collective plea to God. Men left the church to go back to the defenses, to the space between the two parallel walls. The gates were locked behind them.

## Assault and Fall

The final assault was launched at half past one in the morning of Tuesday. The attack was made on the three areas of land walls that had been weakened by constant bombardment over the previous six weeks. There were also assaults on the walls along the Golden Horn and from the sea. On the land walls the first to attack were the *başıbozuk* irregulars. Behind them were *çavuşlar*, a kind of military police, armed with loaded whips and iron maces, whose job was to ensure that there was no backsliding. When Mehmet saw that resistance was weakening, he sent in his crack troops, the Janissaries. The besiegers broke through the walls, poured into the city and hand to hand fighting broke out inside.

The Turkish musicians beat their drums, blew into their trumpets, played their pipes and castanets and struck their tambourines. The defenders responded with ringing their bells and beating their wooden gongs. Cannon and muskets were fired. Every kind of weapon was used indiscriminately—arrows, arquebus, culverins, crossbows. To the din created by horses, donkeys and camels were added the screams, cries and sobbing of the defenders. It was not light until five and the dawn mist mixed with the smoke of gunfire. It was like an anticipation of the day of Resurrection, suggested one Turkish chronicler.

Mehmet enters the city

It was the festival of St. Theodosia, and people gathered at the church of that name. It is today Gül Camii, along the Golden Horn, near Fener.

Soldiers were permitted to do what they liked with the citizens for the first day. After that they could loot but that had to stop by nightfall of the third day. Many citizens were seized for ransom, sale or sex. Some managed to slip away on boats.

But Constantinople fell and with it the Roman Empire. The Emperor Constantine was killed in the general slaughter. Stories circulated about the circumstances of his death and what happened to his body, but nothing was definitely established. In the nineteenth century an enterprising coffeehouse owner attracted custom by claiming that a nearby unmarked tombstone was actually the final resting place of the last emperor. For the besiegers the main object of plunder was the Church of the Holy Wisdom where many citizens had fled in the confident anticipation of a miracle.

Mehmet made his entry in the conquered city later in the day of Tuesday 29 May. He rode to the Church of the Holy Wisdom and tried to curb excesses. He chastised one man who was attempting to remove some marble, but then he entered the church and instructed an imam give the call to prayer. The Church of the Holy Wisdom became a mosque and was to continue as a mosque until 1935 when Atatürk ordered that it become a museum. The sultan later on went to examine what was left of the imperial palace. Overcome by the deserted rooms and the sense of decay, he quoted a Persian poem on the transitory nature of fame:

The spider has become watchman in the Imperial palace, and has woven a curtain before the doorway; the owl makes the royal tombs of Afrasiab re-echo with its mournful song.

The invaders spread out to all parts of the city. Actually only four of the dozens of the churches were vandalized. In addition to the Church of the Holy Wisdom, the Church of the Savior in Chora near the walls (Kariye Camii today), St. John in Petra near the Golden Horn and the Church of St. Theodosia were looted. But the villages and hamlets inside the walls sometimes negotiated and surrendered without resistance. This happened at Hypsomatheia (Samatya), on the Marmara, which kept its churches, and continued to be center for Christian communities for another five hundred years.

## AFTER THE CONQUEST

Mehmet realized that, having conquered the city, he needed the skills and expertise of the Greek community. He sought out George Scholarius, the theologian who had attended the Council of Florence, repudiated the union and retreated to a monastery with the name Gennadius. In the aftermath of the siege, he had been captured and sold as a slave to a *paşa* in Edirne. The sultan located and liberated him and the two men seemed to hit it off. Scholarius was a scholar of European reputation and the sultan enjoyed discussing religious and philosophical issues with him, inviting him to drop in at the palace any time. The remaining Orthodox community was invited to elect a patriarch; they chose Scholarius.

Most churches survived the looting. Mehmet ordered the preservation of the Church of the Holy Apostles, which he designated as the mother church for the Orthodox community. Over the next two centuries most of the other churches were turned into mosques, but this mostly occurred after the reign of Sultan Mehmet II. Only the church of St. Mary of the Mongols has survived as a continuously functioning church since Byzantine times. Today, with the evacuation of the vast majority of the city's Greek community, some of the people attending the Orthodox churches in Istanbul are Arabic-speaking Orthodox from the region of Antioch (Antakya) and İskenderun.

The defenders had put up an amazing fight for survival. They faced an army five times the size of the army of the Fourth Crusade, but held out for six weeks, in contrast to just four days in 1204. Against overwhelming odds they never gave up. They threw back three direct assaults. The Genoese sailors achieved their purpose—entry into the Golden Horn—in spite of a much larger fleet of Turkish craft.

Still only in his early twenties, Mehmet, known after 1453 as Fatih, the Conqueror, showed military talent of an extraordinary quality. He had a creative, innovative strategic sense. He would brood and meditate in search of the solution to a problem. Once he had decided on it he saw to the detailed and speedy implementation of his answer. Sometimes it worked, as with the transport of the boats to the Golden Horn; sometimes it did not, as in his unfortunate experiment with the tower to combat the walls. He could be ruthless and cruel. His intellectualism, his curiosity and resourceful originality reminds us of Italian Renaissance princes. But for Mehmet the stakes were far higher and he won.

## HEIRS OF BYZANTIUM

Constantine had been one of four brothers. Two, Demetrius and Thomas, were jointly despots of Morea, forever quarreling with each other. A daughter of Demetrius became the wife of the Sultan Mehmet. The two brothers sent embassies of congratulation to the victorious sultan at Edirne and agreed to pay tribute. Six years later the sultan came to the Peloponnese to enforce arrears of payment. Thomas fled west. Demetrius submitted and for a while was well treated by the sultan. He took monastic vows and the name of David, dying in an Edirne monastery in 1470. Their daughter, Helena, had officially been taken into the sultan's harem, but it seems she died a virgin, leaving her property to the Church.

Thomas went to Italy, dying there. His son, Andreas, the claimant to the empire, transferred his rights to the King of France, Charles VIII, and fell on hard times, allegedly marrying a prostitute in Rome, running into debt and trying to flog off imperial titles and privileges. When he invaded Naples in 1493, Charles VIII regarded the campaign as a step towards claiming his imperial inheritance. Andreas died a pauper in 1502. Andreas's sister, Zoe, had better post-Byzantine luck. She was born after the fall of the city and was adopted and brought up a Catholic by the papacy. In 1472 Pope Sixtus IV negotiated for her to be married to the Tsar of Russia, Ivan III. Zoe sloughed off her Catholicism and became the Tsarina Sophia and a champion of Orthodoxy. Russia saw this marriage as sealing Moscow's claim as the legitimate successor of Constantinople, the third Rome.

## Chapter Three

# ISLAMIC EMPIRE

### CONSTANTINOPLE BECOMES KOSTANTINIYYE

Kostantiniye was the official Ottoman name for the city—as used on the coins that were minted—but we shall generally use the word Istanbul in referring to the Turkish Ottoman city. Europeans and the Christian communities continued to use Constantinople—and have done so to the present day.

There has been much debate about how far the Ottoman Empire replicated the Byzantine Empire. Distinguished historians such as Halil İnalcık have argued that there was a distinctive Near Eastern Islamic character to the Ottoman state. This is true, but the political, strategic and economic centrality of the city of Constantinople/Istanbul has probably determined the nature of political options for the management of empire. Moreover, there are scores of echoes of Byzantine and earlier Roman political attitudes and policies in the governance, internal and external, of their Ottoman successors. "Henceforth," declared Sultan Mehmet II, "my throne is Istanbul." Whoever had control of the city was in control of the empire, in Constantinople as in Istanbul. In each case, the death of an emperor/sultan far from the capital was concealed until a successor reached the city and was able to ensure the support of the military.

Mehmet, with his sense of history, saw himself as the successor of the universal Roman Empire. "The world Empire," he is reported as saying, "must be one, with one faith and one sovereignty. To establish this unity, there is no place more fitting than Constantinople." The one faith was Islam and, though no zealot, he was in a tradition of Muslim *gazis*, men who extended the boundaries of Muslim control. This did not exclude other religions, and he established an Armenian patriarchate and a chief rabbinate in the city, as well as maintaining a close personal interest in the affairs of the Greek Orthodox Church.

He also worked hard to repopulate the city. The villages outside were filled with prisoners of war in order to revive agriculture and therefore the provision of fresh food. He settled non-Muslim prisoners in the district of

Sultan Mehmet II

Fener and ordered his provincial governors to send families to the city. Whenever a new city was taken its artisans were brought to the capital.

## CHRISTIANS UNDER THE NEW REGIME

In the fifteenth-century Ottoman Empire Orthodox Christians formed a substantial minority, perhaps even a majority of the subjects. Before 1453 many Christians had already worked out a *modus vivendi* under the sultans in those parts of the former Byzantine Empire that had been conquered. Mehmet needed Christian merchants, craftsmen, farmers and sailors for the success of the economy. Accordingly he quickly came to terms with Christians in the city. Officially—and desperately—the Church had accepted union with Rome in the months before the siege. The patriarchate was vacant after the last patriarch of the old regime fled to Italy in 1451. The sultan, as we have seen, appointed the theologian George Scholarius (subsequently known by his monastic name Gennadius) as patriarch. From the sultan's point of view, this man owed everything to the new regime. His known principles and record meant that he would not be looking west for any salvation. In January 1454 the sultan presented him with the insignia of office, including a new specially made silver-gilt pectoral cross. The Church of the Holy Apostles was the venue for the patriarch's consecration and enthronement. From there he rode around the city on a horse, the gift of the sultan.

The new conquerors took possession of the Church of the Holy Wisdom, the symbol of the old empire. The Church of the Holy Apostles was assigned to the Christians but was in a state of dilapidation. Moreover, it was in a quarter newly colonized by Turkish Muslims. One morning the discovery of the body of a Muslim on the church premises sparked anti-Christian demonstrations. The patriarch asked the sultan's permission to move out. Permission was granted and he moved to the Church of Pammacaristos, now the Fethiye Camii in the Fener quarter. The sultan used to come and call on the patriarch in a side-chapel and discuss religion and politics. He took care not to enter the sanctuary itself, lest successors might use this as a pretext for turning the church into a mosque.

Under the new regime the patriarch was more than a religious leader. He became the head of the Orthodox Christian community, answerable to the sultan. He was responsible to him for taxation and for legal matters dealing with matters of personal law: divorce, wills, custody.

The city attracted the return of Greeks. The sultan forced all the Greeks of Trebizond, after that city surrendered to the Ottomans in 1461, to come to his new capital. The well-known Ypsilantis family, who claimed kinship with the Comneni, were forced emigrants from Trebizond. Other Greeks were brought in from Edirne, and from those Aegean islands that were absorbed into the Ottoman Empire. Some of the Greek families who returned to the Muslim city had been renowned in Byzantine times—Lascaris, Argyrus or Ducas—and prospered anew. In the following century, the head of one indisputable imperial family, Michael Cantacuzenus, became one of the richest men in the east Mediterranean world. Turks called him Şeytanoğlu, "son of the devil." Some Greek families converted to Islam. As well as occupying certain areas of the city, Greeks also settled in the Bosphorus villages. Therapia (Tarabya) became, for example, almost exclusively Christian. But, although freedom of worship was guaranteed, Christians had to accept the rule of the Muslim Turks and their own role as second-class citizens. They could not, without permission, build or repair churches. With the exception of the patriarch they were not permitted to ride around the city on horseback and they had to wear distinctive dress.

## Muslim Rule and the Fatih Mosque

Mehmet imposed Islamic rule, a blend of Turkish custom and precedent, based ultimately, and sometimes indirectly, on interpretations of the Qur'an and the Traditions of the Prophet Muhammad. These were interpreted by the mufti (*müftü* in Turkish), the principal religious figure in a locality. The Mufti of Istanbul was known as the *Şeyhülislam*, the Sheikh of Islam, and could in certain circumstances rule that it was legitimate to depose the sultan. The law would be implemented by an Islamic judge, a *cadi* (*Kadı* in Turkish). Interpretations were often benevolent. Ottoman statecraft might well have been based on the concept of the state, written for a Turkish ruler in central Asia in 1069:

> Control of the state requires a large army. To support the troops requires great wealth. To obtain this wealth the people must be prosperous. For the people to be prosperous the laws must be just. If any one of these is neglected the state will collapse.

Accordingly, Sultan Mehmet II encouraged trade and built the central market, the forerunner of the Kapalı Çarşı (the Covered or Grand Bazaar).

Mehmet took over the Church of the Holy Apostles, making it *vakıf* property—an inalienable endowment. The building was replaced by the Fatih Mosque, which became the model for major town mosques throughout the empire. The mosque was not simply a place of worship, but was a center for many other activities. The complex was known as a *külliye*. The Fatih Mosque was the central building, but attached to it were eight religious schools (*medrese*) with 600 students, a school for children, a library, a hospital, a refectory and two hostels that could accommodate 160 travelers. A large market with over three hundred shops provided an income for the *külliye*. The refectory provided free food for travelers, the students, the officials of the *külliye* and the poor of the neighborhood. Attached to the hospital were two doctors, who were Jews. There were also an eye specialist, a surgeon and a pharmacist. Two cooks prepared food under the supervision of one of the doctors. Later two more hospitals were added, one for women and one for non-Muslims. Musicians played to the patients.

The *külliye* was, in fact, one of the main contributions of the Ottomans to urban planning. Though characteristically Ottoman, the Byzantine monastery often had a similar function as a center for worship, education and welfare, relying similarly on a secular income. In the cities the Ottomans conquered, one or more *külliyes* were built. They integrated the regime into a wide range of social and economic activity. The *külliye* would include shops, the rent of which supported the foundation. The *vakfiye*, the basic deed of trust of the *vakıf*, was often quite elaborate. Sometimes the revenue of a particular *vakıf* might be assigned to another city or community of the empire, perhaps the birthplace of the founder or benefactor, or possibly a major city such as the capital or the holy cities of Mecca or Medina. The *külliyes* became focal points of a city and provided secular as well as sacred space. Today the areas around such mosques in Istanbul as Fatih and Süleymaniye are places for people to stroll around, for children to play in, for people to meet and for peddlers to sell their wares.

Mehmet's architect was Sinan, known as *Atik Sinan*, Old Sinan, to distinguish him from his prolific namesake of a century later. (There has also been a tradition that the architect was a Greek by the name of Christodoulos, but the style of the building developed from earlier

Dome of the Fatih Mosque

Ottoman rather than Byzantine models. Another story, current among Greeks in the nineteenth century, claimed that the architect was impaled after completing this work so he could not create another mosque that would rival this one.) The fifteenth-century Fatih Mosque was destroyed in an earthquake in 1766 and what we see today dates from 1771. Much of the rest of the complex has been restored. The *külliye* combined piety, economic sense and the shrewd politics of social cohesion. The combination of trade and religion was a feature common to both Byzantine and Ottoman Empires. It exploited the geographical location of Constantinople/Istanbul which became a magnet for traders and pilgrims.

Fatih Mosque today is in an area that is strongly and almost assertively Muslim. In the courtyard people sell video and audio cassettes and DVDs that draw attention to the issues that strongly affect many Muslims: Iraq, Palestine, Afghanistan, Chechnya. You can buy tapes of popular preachers. It is an old tradition. In the 1850s there was a particularly popular preacher from Trabzon, Hacı Pir Efendi, who would draw crowds to the Fatih Mosque to listen to his eloquence. He supported the Ottoman cause in the Crimean war and welcomed the British allies. He saw these infidels as different from other contumacious infidels (such as Greeks and Armenians) and who, as a reward for their goodwill towards the Muslims would, in the hereafter, be kept apart from other infidels until there was an opportunity to smuggle them into Paradise.

## CULTURAL DIPLOMACY

Sultan Mehmet II was a man of vision. He had a degree of self-awareness, and probably saw himself as a patron of the arts. He himself had been born in Edirne and brought up at Manisa in the west of Asia Minor. This city had strong cultural links with Foça, formerly the Byzantine port of Phocaea, and the island of Chios, both with strong Genoese connections. It is likely he became exposed to Italian cultural interests here. Certainly he had an informed interest and knowledge of Italian art. Like some of his contemporary Italian Renaissance contemporaries he was both a man of action as well as an aesthete and an intellectual. The library he built up in the new palace in Istanbul included the works of Arrian, the biographer of Alexander the Great and Homer's *Iliad*. He was familiar with the myth of the Trojan origins of Rome, and probably knew of current European theories that the Turks were the descendants of Troy. According to his contemporary Greek biographer, he visited the site of Troy and wondered where the tombs of Ajax and Achilles were. He claimed that he had vindicated the wrongs committed by the west against Troy.

The sultan also had a wide knowledge of Persian and Arabic Islamic culture. There is only one copy of the Qur'an known to have been in his library, but there were manuscript copies of heroic fiction as well as treatises on a range of subjects from mysticism to music. He possessed manuscripts in Hebrew, including a copy of Maimonides's *Guide to the Perplexed*, which may have been acquired for him by his Italian Jewish physician, Jacopo of Gaeta. A collector, he summoned calligraphers, bookbinders and artists from further east to work in his scriptorium. He tried and failed to entice the leading contemporary Persian poet and mystic, Jami, to abandon Herat for Istanbul. Some wandering scholars turned up in Istanbul and were awarded a pension and employment at Mehmet's court.

Culture was currency. He agreed to commute the payment of the ransom for a Turkoman prince to a presentation of manuscripts and pictorial albums. The albums in his library included paintings, calligraphy and sketches. Most of them were Persian work, from Herat and Tabriz, but some are of Chinese origin.

Mehmet was involved with aggressive wars for much of his reign—in the Balkans, against Turkish rulers in Asia Minor who had not yet accepted the hegemony of the Ottomans, and against the Italian states. With the conquest of Istanbul, the Ottoman Empire became the major maritime power in the eastern Mediterranean, replacing the domination of city states of northern Italy that had lasted for three centuries.

Mehmet built up an Ottoman navy, often relying on Greek and Italian manpower. Venice had, in the years up to the siege, been the ally of the Byzantine Empire and Genoa had officially been neutral. After the conquest Mehmet had his own Italian policy. He coveted Rome, and from 1463 to 1479 was at war with Venice, a war that was basically a struggle for control of the Aegean Sea. Turkish irregulars landed in Italy and fought against Italian forces on the outskirts of Venice. But in 1479 a peace treaty was negotiated. One of the most remarkable points in the peace negotiations was the sultan's request that Venice provide "a good painter," a bronze-worker, a maker of chiming clocks and an expert glazier.

The artist selected for this cultural mission was Gentile Bellini (1429-1507), brother of the more celebrated Giovanni Bellini and brother-in-law of the artist Andrea Mantegna. Gentile was familiar with the recent cultural and intellectual history of Constantinople/Istanbul. He had already painted a portrait of Cardinal Bessarion, the Greek monk who had accompanied the last Byzantine emperor to the Councils of Ferrara and Florence to negotiate a union of the eastern and western churches. Bessarion had stayed on in Italy, bringing a huge library of manuscripts and was one of the humanists who stimulated the revival of Greek learning in north Italy.

In 1479 Gentile was working on the decoration of the doge's palace, but he was released and set off for Istanbul in September of that year with two assistants. His mission was not just that of a hired artist, but was seen in Venice as being of diplomatic importance. Indeed, shortly afterwards Naples and Florence also responded to a request from the sultan for artists.

Gentile spent over a year in Istanbul, staying probably near the Hippodrome where there were workshops for painters attached to the new Topkapı Palace. His best-known work from this period is the portrait of the sultan that was acquired in about 1865 by Sir Henry Layard, later British Ambassador to Istanbul. It was bequeathed to the National Gallery, London, where it can be seen today. It seems that the sultan took time before he commissioned this picture, asking Gentile to do a self-portrait first.

There were several stories about Gentile's sojourn in Istanbul. There are reports that he got on well with the sultan who may have been mindful of the informal friendship Alexander the Great is said to have had with his favorite painter. Gentile is also reported to have drawn erotic pictures for the sultan, and to have painted some of the rooms of the Topkapı Palace.

The sultan had an informed interest in Christianity and had gathered together Christian relics which he had taken from churches in the city after the conquest. These included the stone on which Jesus had been born, some of Jesus' clothes and the corpses of the Prophet Isaiah, and one of the Holy Innocents. According to a Venetian Franciscan friar, he treasured these relics and stored them in a "precious cabinet in a room where there was nothing else except a Greek image of the Madonna, in the presence of which a golden lamp was always kept burning." The friar said that the sultan took Gentile into this room and showed him an icon he kept close to his chest and asked the artist to make another in contemporary style. These stories circulated in Venice, giving rise to the improbable story that the sultan was contemplating a conversion to Christianity.

The artist left Istanbul in early 1481, having been honored by a grateful sultan, and returned to Venice. Mehmet died later that year to be succeeded by one of his sons, Beyazit II, who did not share his father's wide ranging intellectual curiosity and enthusiasms. But he did make an inventory of his father's possessions. Many of the manuscripts and works of art that did not accord with his narrower and more religiously orthodox outlook were sold off. Beyazit's charismatic brother, Cem, however, went into exile and lived in Italy for the last thirteen years of his life.

Gentile Bellini was not the only Italian artist to come to Istanbul. Another portrait of Sultan Mehmet, now in the Topkapı Palace, was painted, possibly in about the same year as Bellini's portrait. This shows the sultan smelling a rose. It is believed to have been painted by an Italian who became a Muslim and took the name Sinan and is buried in Bursa.

Sultan Mehmet II's military expertise was acknowledged throughout Europe, and his interest in military matters was so well known that western authors of military treatises dedicated works to him. Other European princes wished to curry favor by sending their own military experts to Istanbul. The papacy and countries at war with the Ottomans tried in vain to place an embargo on the transfer of military knowledge to "infidels."

Mehmet II, as we have seen, made use of such western technology that served his purpose, and Istanbul became a strategic center for technological diffusion. Miners from the Balkans and Asia Minor brought their knowledge of metallurgy to the city. As the American historian of Hungarian origin, Gábor Ágoston, has written,

> Istanbul, with its Turkish and Persian artisans and blacksmiths, Armenian and Greek miners and sappers, Bosnian, Serbian, Turkish, Italian, German, and later French, English and Dutch Gun Founders and engineers, as well as with its Venetian, Dalmatian and Greek shipwrights and sailors, proved to be an ideal environment for "technological dialogue."

## MEHMET'S IMMEDIATE SUCCESSORS

Mehmet's successors were not so enlightened. The son who succeeded, Sultan Beyazit II, built his own mosque, which now stands near the University of Istanbul. Repudiating his father's cultural sensitivity, he took over the patriarchal Church of Pammacaristos (Fethiye Camii) and also the historic Byzantine monastery of St. John in Studios which became the İmrahor Camii, a seldom visited though impressive ruin to the west of the city. Other churches too were taken over.

Beyazit's son, Yavuz Selim, Selim the Grim, had his mosque built above Fener. Selim was the conqueror of Syria and Egypt, and also brought the southern coast of Anatolia under Ottoman control. His mosque is appropriately dark, forbidding and grim. Selim had seven grand viziers killed in the eight years of his reign and the proverbial saying of "a vizierate of Selim" indicated a job that was remunerative though hazardous. He was also the writer of melancholy Persian poetry:

Still alone, a lonely stranger, in strange lands I roam afar,
While around me march the sullen guards of grief and pain and care.
Till I've read life's riddle, emptied its nine pitchers to the end
Never shall I, Sultan Selim, find on earth a faithful friend.

Selim disliked Christianity and had the idea of forcing Christians to become Muslims. Dissuaded from that course, he then wanted to take over all surviving churches. The Orthodox patriarch found a smart lawyer who produced three ancient Janissaries who testified, on the Qur'an, that they had witnessed Sultan Mehmet allocating parts of the city to Christians—such as Fener and Balat and Samatya. Nonetheless more churches were annexed.

## FAMILY CONTINUITY AND SÜLEYMAN

Throughout its existence, the Ottoman Empire was in the hands of one family, a contrast to the British Empire and pre-Republican France. All the sultans were descendants of Osman, who, by defeating an Ottoman army and taking the city of Nicaea in the early fourteenth century, asserted his family's supremacy over his competitors among Turkish rulers in Anatolia: even so, it took the dynasty another two hundred years to establish its dominance throughout the lands that are Turkey today. Over the course of time, and especially in Istanbul in the late fifteenth and sixteenth centuries a certain Ottoman palace culture and practice emerged. During the sixteenth century the custom of eliminating rivals was established. Brothers of new sultans were killed. This secured unquestioned authority for the new sultan, reduced the risks of sedition and subversion and clarified lines of succession. The custom received religious sanction but the consciences of the citizens of the capital were not always at ease. In 1595 Sultan Mehmet III came to the throne and killed off nineteen brothers, some still in their infancy. "The angels in heaven," wrote a contemporary historian, "heard the sighs and lamentations of the people of Istanbul."

The Ottoman Empire reached its zenith under the Conqueror Mehmet's great grandson, Süleyman, known to Turks as *Kanuni*, the Law-Maker, and to Europeans as the Magnificent. There are curious parallels with the Byzantine Emperor Justinian. Both presided over empires that were successful militarily and also expansionist. Both codified existing laws. Both relied on able individuals who came from all parts of the empire.

Both had wives who had an influence on public and private policy.

In administration and culture the empire assumed the form that was not to change substantially for three hundred years from the sixteenth to the nineteenth century. Its main feature was Islamic autocracy. "I am the slave of Allah and the Sultan of this world," Süleyman declared on an inscription. "By the grace of Allah I am the head of Muhammad's community. The might of Allah and the miracles of Muhammad are my companions." The success of the emperor was—as it had been for the Byzantine Empire half a millennium earlier—a sign of divine favor. In the Ottoman case, its Islamic character was based on the theory that it was a frontier state pushing the boundaries of Islam. Implicitly, but not practically, the whole world was the objective. The sultan was also in theory the guardian of all Muslims. The Ottoman sultans used the title of caliph (halife) from the time of Selim the Grim, but it was only from the eighteenth century that the Ottomans began to insist on the ruler's role as protector of all Muslims, even those beyond the frontiers of the empire.

Economically, the empire seemed to be self-sufficient. But Istanbul continued to be the great center for trading throughout the Mediterranean, Black Sea and Indian Ocean worlds. Wool came from Europe. Hungarians brought in vast amounts of Kersey cloth from England. Textiles and spices came from India, silver from Persia and furs from Russia. The Black Sea trade also included caviar, flour, fish, iron tools, flax, walrus tusks and mercury. The Ottoman currency was stable, and throughout the sixteenth century Istanbul saw a steady growth in population, from 400,000 at the beginning of the century to double that by the end. It was, unquestionably, the largest city of Europe.

Strategically, the empire was the major power of the Mediterranean. Venice, also an east Mediterranean imperial power, was a commercial and military competitor. Venice had, since the twelfth century, been the main conduit for commerce and culture, between southeastern and western Europe. When relations were bad between Ottomans and Venetians, the former offered encouragement to the Adriatic port of Ragusa (Dubrovnik) and to the merchants of Florence. The Florentines had a colony in Galata, dominated by Genoese who were generally accommodating to the Ottomans.

A greater strategic threat in the sixteenth century was the emerging Hapsburg Empire, which, under the Emperor Charles V, spread across much of Europe, from Spain to Vienna. Sultan Süleyman would not acknowledge Charles as *emperor* and addressed him as king. This is an interesting point for it suggests that, in some ways, by possession of Istanbul, the Ottomans saw themselves as the heirs of the Roman Empire. The Ottomans followed the Byzantine policy of showing favors to their enemy's enemy. As the Hapsburgs were, in the age of the Reformation and Counter-Reformation, the champions of Catholicism in Europe, so the Ottomans supported Protestants in Europe, especially the Calvinists of Hungary and France.

But not always; in 1569 they concluded a treaty with France, a country that was safely distant. This was the introduction of "capitulations," whereby western Europeans were, over the next three centuries, to have a growing influence on the empire's economy. The word, capitulations, is misleading. The Ottoman Empire, in 1569, did not have to "capitulate" to anyone. The word referred to the chapters (*capitula*) in the Latin-worded treaty. This treaty, and others with other powers, offered commercial concessions and privileges and were actually based on Byzantine precedents. Foreign merchants came to be resident in the capital—and

Constantinople, 1572

other Ottoman trading cities—in their own quarters, having little contact with their Turkish hosts. Until the early twentieth century, foreigners were directed to Galata, and Pera, today's Beyoğlu, on the northern shores of the Golden Horn. Non-Muslims were not encouraged to stay in the central parts of the city, near the Topkapı Palace or the main mosques. Sultan Mehmet II had encouraged immigrant Jews to settle around Eminönü, but at the end of the sixteenth century, with the building of Yeni Camii, Jews were moved to neighborhoods on both sides of the Golden Horn. Henceforward Balat on the south of the inlet and Hasköy on the north became Jewish quarters.

The Ottoman state—again like its Byzantine predecessor—had an elaborate procedure for taxation and imposing customs duties. As well as maintaining an army and a navy, the state took on responsibility for constructing roads and canals, maintaining bridges and making drinking water available. It continued the pre-Ottoman Turkish practice of constructing caravanserais to promote trade. The state was efficient and quick to respond to events. After the Battle of Lepanto, when a Hapsburg fleet destroyed 200 out of 230 Ottoman boats, the shipyards of the capital were able to replace the stock within months.

## SLAVERY

By the sixteenth century slaves played a central role in the city's economy. Most senior officials were of slave origin, recruited through the practice of *devşirme*, the enlisting of provincial youths for service, both military and civilian, in the capital. The idea was to enhance the authority of the sultan by having a cadre who were totally loyal to and dependent on him. The sultan's officers used to go to Christian villages in the Balkans and Anatolia and summon all boys between eight and twenty to appear with their fathers before them. Urban youths were excluded as also were only sons. Boys were selected, brought to the capital and schooled at the Topkapı Palace. They learned Turkish, became Muslims and received training in horsemanship, archery, fencing, wrestling and other crafts. Cut off from their families and roots, they developed their own esprit de corps. Discipline was tough and the youths were under the authority of a white eunuch. But the system worked, insofar as it fulfilled the objectives of the exercise. After years of training, they went into the army or the civil service. Able youths rose to the highest positions in the empire. Some became pages and courtiers in the sultan's household. The official closest to the Sultan was nearly always a graduate of the *devşirme*.

The women of the palace, other than daughters of the ruler, were usually prisoners-of-war or purchases from the slave market. Most mothers of sultans over the centuries were of slave origin. Few sultans married—Süleyman was an exception—and the sultan would instead have acknowledged concubines, *haseki*. The Holy Qur'an permits (rather than stipulates or encourages) a Muslim to have up to four wives. In acknowledgement of this, four of the *haseki* were favored and were designated as *kadın*. The first to give birth to a male was designated *başkadın*, principal *kadın*, and given precedence over the others. Primogeniture only became the custom in the nineteenth century. Before then there were no clear rules for the selection of one of the sons (or indeed nephews) to succeed. But the mother of the sultan, the *Valide*, "Queen Mother," became, until the nineteenth century, a major figure in the politics of the court.

The palace was an institutional patron of arts. Slaves who had artistic talent—composition, calligraphy or engineering—were nurtured and encouraged. The great architect Mimar Sinan, originally from near Kayseri, was a product of the *devşirme* and showed skill as a military engineer. From designing bridges for the army he went on to buildings and mosques.

## THE GREAT SINAN

Sinan was well into middle age when he first started designing buildings. He was close to the court and his first work was the Şehzade Mosque, built to commemorate Mustafa, the son of Süleyman, who had been killed at the behest of the sultan's wife: he was an obstacle to the succession of her son.

Sinan was extraordinarily versatile and adaptable. Süleyman's daughter, Mihrimah, wanted a mosque in which worshippers would not feel they were indoors. He built the Mihrimah Mosque on the site of a former Church of St. George, by the Edirnekapı. Sinan had already built a mosque for the princess at Üsküdar, but the new mosque was constructed at the highest point of the city, where most visitors arrived. Around the Mihrimah Mosque is another *külliye*—with baths, schools and shops, though many of the latter were destroyed for road widening in the 1960s. The dome is built over a drum with vast clerestory windows that provide a flood of light into the body of the mosque.

Sinan also produced a mosque for Mihrimah's husband, Rüstem Paşa, a grand vizier renowned for being tight-fisted, commercially minded and an exacting tax gatherer. The Rüstempaşa Camii, near the Egyptian Bazaar, reflects his personality. It gives the appearance of having been built to a fixed budget. Sinan's genius gives the structure a grace but it is forced into a limited space above a row of shops which provided a rent for the upkeep of the mosque.

Sinan also built a caravanserai for Rüstem Paşa. This is near the Golden Horn in Karaköy, north of the Galata Bridge. It was built on the site of St. Michael's Church. Today arcades and balconies with offices and workshops above are filled with sacks of goods and spare parts and there is an atmosphere of busy scruffiness. It is in fact fulfilling to this day the function for which it was built.

Sinan's masterpiece in the city is the Süleymaniye Mosque, built in the 1550s. The mosque is at the center of a *külliye* that includes five *medrese*s, a hospital, a medical school, a public kitchen, a caravanserai, shops, fountains, a *türbe* (mausoleum) for Sultan Süleyman and a smaller one for his wife, Hürrem Sultan. The mosque impresses the visitor with both power and lightness. You enter the mosque courtyard through a three-story gatehouse, unique in Ottoman architecture. The whole vast site was built on sloping ground, the disadvantages of which are offset by terraces.

Sinan's work dominates the city, sometimes to the detriment of his successors. Pupils and immediate successors worked within the artistic framework he established, but none measured up to his genius. A generation after his death, the last great imperial mosque was built. Commissioned by Sultan Ahmet I, the Blue Mosque is ambitious and wonderfully ornate. It is at the center of another *külliye* and was constructed with six minarets, four around the dome of the mosque, and two more at the further corners of the courtyard. Semi-domes cluster round the central dome giving the whole mosque an impression of a cascade. It derives its name from the extensive use of blue tiles. Classical Ottoman architecture could develop no further.

## OTTOMAN BUREAUCRACY

By the end of the sixteenth century the city had been effectively Islamized. The number of *vakıfs* doubled between 1546 and 1596, from 1,594 to

The Blue Mosque

3,180. Most old Byzantine churches had, by the end of the century, been adapted for Islamic purposes. Some churches had fallen into ruin, while others become isolated from Christian communities that had been replaced by Muslims. The Ottomans required a mosque to be the focal point of each quarter and turned derelict churches into mosques.

The Ottoman bureaucracy became as elaborate and hierarchical, and also as educated, as that of the Byzantine Empire. Bureaucrats were trained and were expected to have a wide range of expertise: literature, language, geography, history, law, agriculture and calligraphy. There developed a "palace" culture—again parallel to Byzantine court culture. Senior officials were adept in practical matters and often able to deal in three languages—Persian for literature, Arabic for religious matters and Turkish for administration. Many slaves were of Balkan origin and the Serbian language lingered on in the palace. Greeks, Armenians and Jews were employed in dealings with foreigners. Jews were often the doctors in the palace.

During Süleyman's reign the bureaucracy expanded. There were eighteen "secretaries" in 1537, 222 by 1568. The Ottoman state also kept a close control of the markets and on local industry. The state aimed to protect consumers by controlling weights and measures and ensuring that there was no overcharging. The official in charge of the market inspector, the *muhtesib*, had the authority to bring violators before the *kadı*, the judge, and have them fined or flogged.

## THE GUILDS AND EVLIYA ÇELEBI

Craftsmen, indeed all the urban professions, were members of guilds. This provided the opportunity for further state control. The guilds looked after themselves and the interests of their members and were sometimes allied to religious *sufi* brotherhoods. They were usually conservative and hostile to innovation.

The most detailed account we have of the world of the craftsman guilds is in the writings of Evliya Çelebi, who was born in the Unkapanı quarter of Istanbul in 1611. His father had been a soldier and standard bearer to Sultan Süleyman I and later retired to become a jeweler. His mother was an Abkhazi slave. She and her brother had been bought in the Istanbul slave-market by Sultan Ahmet I, the builder of the Blue Mosque. The girl was given to the old soldier. The brother joined the pages of the palace and rose to become a confidant of Sultan Murat IV, grand vizier and son-in-law of the sultan: such was the social mobility, free of any racism, of the seventeenth-century Ottoman Empire.

Evliya Çelebi was deeply pious and believed in the significance of dreams. At the age of twenty-four the Prophet Muhammad appeared to him in a dream. Evliya wanted to ask the Prophet for intercession (*shafa'a* in Arabic: *şefaat* in Turkish). For some reason he was confused and asked instead for travel (*seyahat*). The Prophet said his wish would be granted and that he would be a great traveler—and so for much of the rest of his life he was on the move. The result of his labors was an extraordinary collection of observations, legends and stories. His journeys took him to Vienna in the west, the Hijaz on pilgrimage in the south, and to the Caucasus in the east. But first of all he wrote about the city of Istanbul. He went to each quarter, visiting first the mosques and tombs of holy men, and recorded the habits of the different communities. For a while he took service in the palace of the Sultan Murat IV and there are intimate word pictures of the sultan, a successful military conqueror. Murat's victories over the Safavid Persian Empire with the taking of Yerevan (Revan) in Armenia and Baghdad led him to build the Revan and Baghdad Pavilions in grounds of the Topkapı Palace. The sultan was—like most of that title— a poet, but also a sportsman, ready to wrestle with the champions of the time. When the sultan set off on the expedition to Baghdad, Istanbul saw a monster procession of the heads of the military, naval and civilian establishments, the clergy, the members of the guilds and students and schoolboys. Evliya claimed that there were a thousand guilds. Each guild had its patron saint, some being Companions of the Prophet Muhammad. One guild was for executioners. Evliya has a eulogy of the chief executioner, "a model hangman":

> ... girt with a fiery sword, his belt bulging with all the instruments of his craft such as nails, gimlets, matches, razors for scorching, steel plates, different kinds of powder for blinding people, clubs for breaking the hands and feet, hatchets and spoons. In his train followed his suite, carrying the remainder of the seventy-seven instruments of torture, and behind these yet another set of men bearing gilt, carved, greased and scented pails, with ropes and chains wound round their waists and

drawn swords in their hands. They pass with great vehemence but no light shines from their faces, for they are a sombre set of fellows.

Butchers, standard-bearers, the press-gang, *müezzins*, mosque-administrators, astronomers, soothsayers, schoolboys, beggars, physicians, oculists, keepers of the lunatic asylums, farmers, bakers, water-carriers, millers, court-footmen, sailors, caulkers, divers, book-sellers, mapmakers, bear-leaders, cooks, liver and tripe merchants, dried garlic merchants, sherbet-sellers, makers of sweetmeats, fishermen, silk merchants, slave dealers, armorers, firework-makers, goldsmiths, pearl-merchants, archers, fletchers, aigrette-makers, poulterers, sparrow-merchants, nightingale-dealers, tanners, shoemakers, bookbinders, musicians, tumblers, mimes, brewers and publicans are just some who took part in the procession. It indicates an inclusive, almost democratic, society. Evliya noted the numbers and described the participants as they marched past.

## THE "TULIP PERIOD"

In the two centuries after Süleyman power in the empire slipped out of the hands of the sultan and into the hands of ministers. Only occasionally did a sultan pull back authority. One was Sultan Ahmed III who reigned from 1703 to 1730. He was an assertive innovator in politics and fashion. In 1720 the first ambassador was sent to Paris. The envoy, Mehmet Çelebi Efendi, was asked, in his mission, to "visit fortresses, factories, and the works of French civilization generally and to report on those which might be applicable" to the empire. Mehmet took to the task with enthusiasm and in addition to sites of industrial and military importance also wrote enthusiastically about parks, palaces, the theater and the opera. As a result foreign artists and architects were invited to the city. The "Tulip Period," as it was called two centuries later, was a time of conspicuous consumption and the development of public entertainment. The area north of the upper Golden Horn became parkland with imperial pavilions where the upper classes retreated on Fridays. It became known as the Sweet Waters of Europe. Later in the century some of the mosques, such as the Lâleli Mosque near Aksaray, completed in 1763, and the Nuruosmaniye Mosque next to the Covered Bazaar, completed in 1755, have clear baroque influences: curving façades and elaborate curvilinear decoration.

## THE GREEKS IN THE CAPITAL

Over the seventeenth and eighteenth centuries, the Greeks of Istanbul became established, secure and prosperous. The wealthier families controlled much of the trade of the eastern Mediterranean. Wealth was won and secured by a policy of cooperation with the Ottoman authorities. Greek families settled in the area along the Golden Horn, known as the Phanar (Lighthouse) in Greek (Fener in its Turkish form), and were known as Phanariots. Sons of the wealthier families—about whom we have most information—were sent to Western Europe for their education, mainly to Padua but also to Rome, Geneva or Paris. Some studied medicine and became physicians to leading Turkish families, up to the imperial family. One young man, Panagiotis Nicousios, originally from Chios, became the doctor of the Ahmet Köprülü family. The Köprülüs, Albanian in origin, provided the sultan with a series of grand viziers in the late seventeenth century. Ahmet Köprülü noted Panagiotis' ability, his linguistic skills and his acquaintance with Europe, and in 1669 created for him the post of grand dragoman, in effect, the man responsible for the foreign affairs of the empire. After Panagiotis' death, a rich young Greek called Alexander Mavrocordatos, from one of the wealthiest Phanariot families, was appointed in his place. A tradition was created and the Greeks became integrated into the Ottoman system at the highest levels. Alexander Mavrocordatos was grand dragoman for a quarter of a century after which he was appointed private secretary to the sultan. Alexander had an international outlook and managed also to pick up a Habsburg title. He secured privileges and advantages for the Greek community in the empire.

In the eighteenth century the Orthodox Church was weak—few patriarchs lasted longer than a few years—but the Greek community flourished. The Phanariot families acquired landed bases in Wallachia and Moldavia—present-day Romania and Moldova—and sponsored education in the city. A patriarchal academy in Constantinople was revitalized to become a center for classical Greek studies. Seeds of a Greek separatism were sown.

Greek nationalism was fostered among Greeks beyond the bounds of the Ottoman Empire—in St. Petersburg and in Odessa—but they had embarrassingly close connections with the Greeks of the city. One Greek from Corfu, John Capodistrias, entered the Russian diplomatic service and was promoted to be the tsar's foreign minister. Another man, from one of the most established Phanariot families, Alexander Ypsilantis, served in the Russian army—losing an arm—and was a friend of Capodistrias. He became the military leader who was seen to have initiated the Greek War of Independence.

Such activities helped neither the Phanariots nor the Orthodox Church in the city. In 1821, when Greeks in the Peloponnese started a military campaign against the Ottoman authorities after the end of the Napoleonic wars, tension turned to catastrophic crisis. The patriarch, Gregory V was held personally responsible for those of his community who were literally up in arms against the sultan. He excommunicated the leaders of the Greek revolt, but still in April 1821 Turkish police entered the patriarchate compound and hanged him at the gate. Other bishops and clergy followed him to the gallows or were imprisoned. The grand dragoman and other leading Phanariots were killed. Life for the Greeks in the city was never to be the same again.

## CHANGES OF THE 1820S

In the nineteenth century sultans sponsored a new political-administrative class to run the empire, sharing decision making with bureaucrats. Some sultans like Mahmud II, who reigned from 1808 to 1839, his son and successor Abdülmecid (who reigned from 1839-61) and Abdülmecid's son, Abdülhamid II (1876-1909), were indisputably in control. Others were less proactive. Sultan Mahmud II was the first major western-leaning innovator, but his descendants and successors all had qualities that made them more like their contemporary monarchs in Europe than their Ottoman predecessors.

The decade of the 1820s was the turning point for changes in the Ottoman Empire, and its capital. The older regime had suffered a series of blows. First, the Greek War of Independence resulted in a gigantic cleavage in the multicultural social fabric of the city. The Phanariot Greeks no longer had a vested interest in the empire. With an independent kingdom of Greece to the west, could the state guarantee the loyalties of its largest and richest minority?

The second blow was the emergence of a modernized Egypt under Mehmet Ali Paşa, known in Egypt as Muhammad Ali. Born in Kavala (a port which today is in northern Greece), he was the son of an Albanian tobacco merchant who became a successful soldier and then Viceroy of

A group of Janissaries

Egypt, a major Ottoman province. His modern army saved the empire from humiliation in the Greek War of Independence, but while remaining technically a servant of the Ottoman sultan, in reality he became independent leader of his country and the creator of modern Egypt. His success showed up the inadequacy of the state's army based in the capital.

The Janissaries, the soldiers who had been the main fighting force in the rise of the empire, had by 1800 become a spent force. They were socially integrated into Istanbul and urban provincial society, operating protectionist deals with many merchants, and having religious support among popular *sufi* brotherhoods. But they had become useless and antiquated as an effective military force.

Mahmud's cousin and predecessor but one, Sultan Selim III, had failed to suppress the Janissaries. His attempt had ended up with his deposition. Sultan Mahmud was more cautious. He bided his time and made careful calculations, creating a separate new model army first with western uniforms and training more appropriate for the nineteenth century. In 1826 he struck. The Janissaries were cornered, captured and massacred. For days blood ran in the streets and bodies floated in the Bosphorus.

Greeks had dominated those areas where the Ottoman establishment had encountered Europe. After the Greek War of Independence the sultan realized he had to train Turkish Muslims to replace those Greeks who had negotiated with Europeans. The key training ground for the new elite was a Translation Bureau, *Tercüme Odası*. Bright young Turkish youths were sent to London, Paris or Vienna to serve in Ottoman embassies and to learn European languages. The bureau was established in the capital and translated texts from French and other European languages that would be of political, strategic and military importance to the empire.

The 1820s saw other very visible changes. The sultan started to wear a kind of western dress. The turban gave way to the fez. His officials adopted a high collared coat that became known as the *stambouline*. Stratford Canning, who first came to the city in 1809 (and hated it), was again there twenty years later when the Janissaries were suppressed. He kept returning until the 1850s and recorded the changes. Turkish officials became more approachable—and would even come to the embassy in Pera. The sultan received him at Topkapı, treating him with dignity and no longer as a piece of dirt.

## INTERNATIONAL INTEREST

As the Turkish elite began to take a committed interest in Western Europe, so Western Europe started to take an interest in the Ottoman Empire. At its height, the empire had controlled the northern shores of the Black Sea and the whole of the Balkans. In the eighteenth century parts of the Black Sea littoral, including the Crimea, were surrendered to Russia. European powers saw the empire as in terminal decline. The phrase "the sick man of Europe" has been attributed to Tsar Nicholas I when speaking to a British diplomat—although it is not certain that he said it. The European Powers—Austria, France, Britain and Russia—were less concerned about the health of the Ottoman Empire than about their rivals gaining strategic, economic and political advantages in Istanbul.

The urgency of the situation was brought home in 1828 when Russian troops swept down through the Balkan provinces, captured Edirne and were poised to attack the capital. The Treaty of Adrianople (Edirne) of 1829 saved the territorial integrity of the state.

Three years later a modern Egyptian army advanced into Anatolia, beating an Ottoman force at Konya and reaching Kütahya. Russia sent troops for the protection of the capital. They camped in the valley of Tokat Deresi, between Beykoz and Anadolukavağı on the Asian shores of the Bosphorus. A military threat to the capital was staved off by diplomatic intervention from European powers. But Ottoman vulnerability was underlined by an agreement with Russia that acknowledged the latter's "protection" of the empire. The agreement was signed at Hünkâr İskelesi, an imperial palace on the Asian side of the Bosphorus near Beykoz about twelve miles north of the city. (The word *iskele* means pier or jetty in this context, and is derived from the Italian *scala*.) The present palace on the spot was built thirty years later by Sarkis Balyan: it is now a children's hospital.

Outside interest punctured Ottoman self-confidence and accelerated the pace of reform, which was seen as the answer to external threats. The discrimination between Muslims and non-Muslims, it was thought, did not bind the non-Muslims to the empire. For centuries it had flourished as an explicitly Muslim empire with a population that included a very high proportion of Christians. Ideas of the European Enlightenment filtered into the city promoting the ideas of a commonly shared citizenship.

The reforms that were implemented between 1839 and 1876 became known as the Tanzimat.

## Sultans and Tanzimat Reformers

Although Sultan Mahmud II was the first to initiate radical changes in dress and the army, reform is more closely associated with his sons, Sultan Abdülmecid I (1839–61) and Sultan Abdülaziz (1861–76). Abdülmecid set the agenda for reform. He died in his early forties and was succeeded by his half-brother, Abdülaziz, a large man, by no means a workaholic, preferring practical jokes and physical pursuits to the routines of the office. Both sultans relied on the new breed of official and from the 1830s to the 1860s Ottoman politics were dominated by three youngish men, all of whom were francophone and eager for reform: all were from Istanbul. Their Istanbul origin is of significance for in previous centuries in both Ottoman and Byzantine times, many of the reformers were from the more outlying parts of the empires.

The oldest of the three was Mustafa Reşit Paşa (c1800–c1858). He had a mosque education and entered government service, advancing rapidly. In 1832 he was in charge of foreign affairs and in 1834 was appointed ambassador to Paris, where he perfected his French to the extent that he was able to converse with King Louis-Philippe without an interpreter. He went on to London as ambassador but in 1839 was back in Istanbul and made foreign minister to the new sultan, Abdülmecid I, then aged eighteen. For the rest of his life, he was regularly in office in Istanbul as minister of foreign affairs or grand vizier, or in London as ambassador. He was particularly close to the long-term British Ambassador Stratford Canning and was seen as a channel of British influence.

In November 1839 a gathering of notables, state dignitaries, diplomats, religious leaders and distinguished foreigners (including a son of King Louis-Philippe) gathered in the Rose Chamber, Gülhane, in Topkapı Palace. Mustafa Reşit Paşa read, in the sultan's presence, a decree that promised new laws to abolish discrimination between Muslims and non-Muslims. It was not a legislative enactment but rather a manifesto for action: new laws would be introduced in the following years. The language had echoes of French revolutionary rhetoric, but it is more probable that Mustafa Reşit Paşa's model was the epitome of nineteenth-century resistance to all *liberal* reform, the Austrian chancellor, Metternich. It was in the interests of both imperial and multi-ethnic capitals to have a strong state and for reform to be imposed from above.

The next few years saw the implementation of reforms proposed by

Mustafa Reşit Paşa in legal practice, with civil courts taking over many of the roles of religious courts, including the courts of the Christian and Jewish communities. The Ottoman state was asserting itself. Over the nineteenth century there was a fortyfold increase in the number of civil servants who managed the new state—from 2,000 to about 80,000. The empire was run by an Istanbul-based bureaucracy. Instead of being concerned largely with making war and collecting taxes, the civil service now took over responsibilities for education, hospitals and charitable institutions previously the preserves of mosque, church or synagogue. Opposition or resistance to these reforms came not only from the Muslim religious elite who lost their privileges and authority, but also from priests and rabbis who suffered in the same way. Christians and Jews, outside priestly ranks, also lost out. Before the supremacy of the state, Christian and Jewish women sometimes resorted to Muslim courts, where women's rights were more defined: a marriage had to take place with the consent of the bride and with respect for the bride's individual property rights.

The second young reformer was born in 1815, the son of an Istanbul shopkeeper. He became known as Ali Paşa, though his actual name was Mehmet Emin. He was all his life an autodidact. He obtained a civil service post when he was fifteen and taught himself French. Three years later he became an instructor at the Translation Bureau. At the age of twenty he was posted to the Ottoman embassy at Vienna where he made a study of the organization of the Habsburg Empire. He returned to Istanbul and was a protégé of Mustafa Reşit Paşa, who took him to London on his appointment as ambassador. When Mustafa Reşit Paşa returned to the city, Ali—at the age of twenty-four—was left in charge of the London embassy, and became ambassador the following year. On his return to the capital, Ali became one of the architects of the educational reforms. He also served as minister of foreign affairs during the Crimean War and grand vizier immediately afterwards.

The Crimean War brought the Ottoman Empire into the heart of European diplomacy. In 1856, immediately before the end of the war, a second major edict, known as the Edict of Reform or *Islahat Fermanı*, confirmed the ideas behind the Gülhane Edict of 1839, and announced further changes—in education, economic progress and administrative reform. It again emphasized the importance of the unitary state and of an efficient fiscal system.

Ali was very much a driven man, obsessed with reform. The Sultan Abdülaziz, was less of an enthusiast for reform than his brother and predecessor, Abdülmecid, and was often exasperated by Ali Paşa. But when Ali Paşa died—worn out at the age of fifty-six—surrounded by his books at his house at Bebek on the Bosphorus, the sultan is reported to have greeted the news with the words, "Thank God! I am free at last. Now I will reign as I please."

The third great reforming *paşa* of the central years of the nineteenth century was Fuat. Unlike Mustafa Reşit and Ali, he came from a more socially secure background. His father, Keçecizade İzzet Molla, had also been in public service and was an esteemed poet. Fuat was born, like Ali Paşa, in 1815 and studied at a newly established government medical school where he learned French. His talent was spotted by Mustafa Reşit Paşa, and he was diverted from a career in the army medical services and joined the Translation Bureau. Like Mustafa Reşit Paşa and Ali Paşa, he worked in Ottoman embassies in Europe and returned to Istanbul to serve—like them—as both minister of foreign affairs and as grand vizier. His expertise was in financial and educational reform. He was the principal negotiator for foreign loans, but also the man behind plans for the francophone Galatasaray Lycée. Fuat, like Ali, wore himself out and died in 1869 in France while receiving medical treatment. His body was brought back to the city and a mausoleum was erected in the grounds of a mosque he had commissioned in Klodfarer Caddesi two blocks to the west of the Hippodrome. The tomb is an eclectic mixture of Moorish and gothic themes.

All three reforming *paşas* knew Western Europe and sought examples and models from those countries. They presided over the expansion of the bureaucracy and raised the status of state service. A new expanded class of bureaucrats, well-informed, committed to public service and familiar with French, was to dominate the capital until the end of the Ottoman Empire. The huge expansion was not met by an expansion in the budget; salaries were poor and bribery was rampant. Nonetheless in spite of resistance, the reforms lasted and there was never any wish to reverse them.

The increased centralization of the state brought to the capital families that had been prominent in the provinces. In Çukurova (Cilicia) in southern Anatolia, for example, one clan with feudal authority was the Menemencioğlu family. The family had resisted being brought into the Ottoman official establishment in 1815, but after the Crimean War another more determined effort was made to bring them into line. The leader of the family, Ahmed Bey, had a private army of 1,200 horsemen and allegedly owned two thousand camels and an unspecified number of Nubian concubines. He accepted that he could no longer wield feudal power in the south of the country and in 1865 moved to Istanbul with his family and servants. He bought a large house in Beyoğlu and had his sons educated at French schools. The family, with remarkable agility, rapidly merged into the new class of Istanbul bureaucrats.

Ahmed Bey's son, Rıfat Paşa (1857–1935), a small boy when he left Cilicia with his father, became minister of finance three times. He married a daughter of Namık Kemal, who spent much of his life in exile as a founder of the Young Ottoman Movement, made up of young European-minded liberals. Rıfat Paşa became so much a part of the Istanbul establishment that Sultan Abdülhamid II wanted one of the *paşa*'s sons to marry one of his own granddaughters. The second son of Rıfat Paşa became a diplomat in Vienna, ambassador in Paris and ended up as minister of foreign affairs during the Second World War.

The Menemencioğlu family came from the provinces. By contrast, Osman Hamdi Bey was part of the Istanbul establishment. Born in 1842 in the city, the son of İbrahim Edhem, ambassador and grand vizier, Osman was sent by his father to Paris to study law, but he also went to classes in painting taught by Jean-Léon Gérôme, a specialist in "oriental" pictures. Osman himself exhibited his own work in Paris. He returned to Istanbul with a French wife and took up a number of posts within the imperial administration. Both a professional civil servant and an amateur painter, he was the founding director of the Archaeological Museum, near the Topkapı Palace, and presided over the 1891 construction by Alexandre Vallaury of the building that is still the main archaeological museum of the city. Osman Hamdi was also the founder of the State Academy of Fine Arts. As an administrator, he devised the antiquities laws and sponsored state archaeological expeditions in the empire. He supervised a range of digs himself, including excavations at Sidon in Lebanon in the 1890s, bringing to the museum the alleged sarcophagus of Alexander the Great and other massive Phoenician monuments still on display. He anticipated the change of script by signing his own paintings, in French, as "Hamdy." He received recognition in Europe and, among other honors, was awarded an honorary degree from the University of Oxford. In his personal relations he bridged the world of Ottoman bureaucracy and the cosmopolitan world of Pera and the international community. With his pince-nez and trim beard, his portrait might suggest a professor of the Third French Republic.

Elites of the empire were merging with a mobile European class of restive professionals. The late nineteenth century saw a flowering of artistic creativity in the city. Constantinople became part of a wider European community, with links through financiers, banks, diplomats, travelers and traders. This period has been called a Belle Epoque.

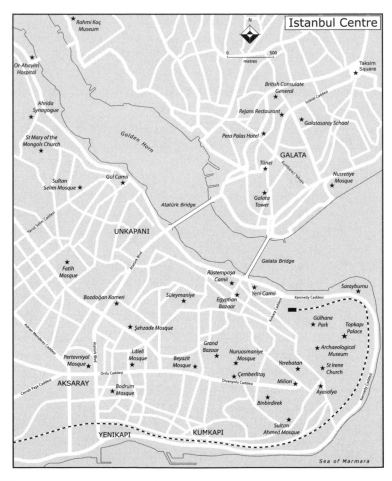

## Chapter Four

# MODERNITY AND FOREIGN INFLUENCES

Historians have often seen the Ottoman Empire in the nineteenth century as an economy in decline. But the city, during the century, saw considerable development in services and industry, both large and small.

During the earlier part of the century the state was the principal investor in industrial enterprises. The whole century saw a growth in the public sector, with—it has been calculated—over a million extra people working for the armed forces and the civil and local administrations. Industrial enterprises were heavily protectionist, with the public sector being the principal purchaser of the goods produced. At Tophane (which means arsenal) cannon and muskets were manufactured. In the 1820s spinning mills at Eyüp were founded. By the end of the century they had been transformed into the Imperial Ottoman Cloth and Material Factory employing five to six hundred men and women. The largely British equipment was steadily replaced by machinery imported from Germany.

It was at Eyüp that a state factory for the production of fezzes was established. In 1827–28, as part of the army reforms, the fez was introduced and made compulsory for all soldiers. It was to remain standard uniform until 1925. Hitherto the fez had been produced at small workshops, but the Imperial Fez Factory was built in the 1830s to designs by the Armenian architect, Ohannes Kuyumjian. It was burned down and rebuilt more than once. The shell has been restored and what has survived is now an exhibition center. At its zenith it was producing 200,000 fezzes a year. What was surplus to military requirements was sold to the public. A man in public was improperly dressed unless he sported a fez. The wearing of the fez spread with the influence of the Ottoman Empire, and died with the waning of that influence. Older men were still wearing it after the Second World War in Syria, Lebanon and Jordan. It was part of the official uniform of Egypt until the 1930s, and British officers and civilians in Egyptian and Sudanese service wore it. It even spread into East Africa.

The Galata Tower, c. 1870

Such was the demand during the nineteenth century that the country had to import fezzes. Over the years there were subtle changes in style. In the early nineteenth century the fez was tall and adorned with blue silk tassels. Ministers and members of the Ottoman imperial family ornamented their fezzes with diamond broaches. In the middle years of the century the fez became shorter. Sultan Abdülaziz designed his own. The colors varied from pomegranate red to dark violet. By the 1890s it was reckoned that the annual demand exceeded ten million.

One of the problems facing large-scale manufacturing was a labor shortage. Orphans and convicted criminals were drafted into the factories of Istanbul. The city also relied on migrant labor who usually received more favorable wages. The importation of laborers from the more industrialized parts of Europe guaranteed a transfer of skills. In the 1890s the Paşabahçe glass factory was founded on the Asian shore. The factory started with skilled workers from Austria and Bohemia, who were lured by the provision of housing, a German language school for the children and a Roman Catholic priest. On the eve of the First World War the factory employed four hundred Ottoman subjects as well as Hungarians, Germans, Italians, French and Greeks.

The dockyards were also full of foreign—many of them British— workers. In the 1870s there were, according to Sir Edwin Pears, two hundred British engineers, mostly Scots, working at Hasköy. Some had come with wives and relations, making a community of four hundred. There was a school, a literary institute and a Presbyterian minister. But the pace of internationalism and progress met obstacles. The boatmen of the Golden Horn and the Bosphorus, who were organized into guilds, objected to flourmills being built on the shoreline of the Golden Horn in a way that enabled ships to offload their grain on to the mill site. The boatmen saw their livelihood threatened and their concerted action succeeded in forcing the bigger ships to anchor slightly offshore so the boatmen could continue to transfer grain from the bigger ships to the mills.

Towards the end of the century there were stirrings of industrial action. Istanbul's first strike took place at the Beyoğlu Post Office in February 1872, in protest at the non-payment of wages. In January the following year some five hundred workers employed by the Maritime Arsenal at Tophane went on strike, asking for wages that had not been paid for eleven months. Soldiers were deployed, and there were skirmishes with the workers who plundered the bread that had been brought in for the soldiers. But the workers' wives showed greater militancy; they attacked the soldiers with sticks, calculating that they were unlikely to be beaten or imprisoned. Two years later the Arsenal workers staged another strike over the non-payment of wages—they were only six months in arrears. In the following years there was labour unrest among construction workers at Taksim, railway workers at Haydarpaşa railway station, foundry workers employed by the Şirket-i Hayriye, the Ferry Boat Company, and the cartridge factory. In the following decades workers' demands were mostly economic—more pay, or the actual payment of what was due.

The government encouraged and supervised the introduction of foreign technology which, it was calculated, had an overall positive impact on all aspects of the economy. By the 1850s Istanbul was in rapid touch with the rest of the world, thanks to the telegraph and underground cables. Steam power facilitated water transport on the Bosphorus and led to the expansion of the Asian suburbs as well as of the villages on both sides of the water.

Yet most productive enterprises throughout the century were virtually "cottage industries," employing between five and ten workers, perhaps members of one family. This was most common in textile and cloth making. Merchants bought up the finished work of such small businesses, where many workers were women, who could be paid less. The first textile factories that were built relied often on female labor. Conditions were not pleasant, as the poet Bedri Rahmi Eyüboğlu recorded in his poem, "İstanbul":

> Say Istanbul and a textile factory comes to mind:
> High walls, long counters, tall stoves...
> Tender slender girls toil all day long on their feet,
> Sweating blood and tears,
> Their faces long their hands long their days long
> In the factory the windows are near the ceiling
> Red-heeled fair-skinned girls—"No loitering, girls!"
> Out there the trees stretch row on row
> Walls walls endless walls

Innovations from overseas had a huge impact on these enterprises. For example, the import of artificial dyes stimulated a boom in carpet production, making those Istanbul homes lower in the social scale healthier and more comfortable. Another economically revolutionary import was the sewing machine, exported on favorable terms by United States companies. For the merchant, production costs could be kept down by making the machinery the responsibility of the cottage worker. The merchant might buy the machinery for the worker who would pay for it from his or her wages. These produced a vast sweatshop industry of garment and shoe manufacturing, with production for local consumption and a surplus for export.

## AN INDUSTRIAL FAMILY: THE DADIANS

Much of the growth of industrial Istanbul revolved around the Armenian family of Dadian. The first of the family to make an impact was Arakel Amira Dad, who was a civil engineer and entrepreneur at the end of the eighteenth century. A powder mill, to supply gunpowder for the Ottoman army had been set up at Makriköy, a suburb on the Marmara to the west of the city—Bakırköy today. Arakel impressed the sultan, Selim III, with his mechanical flair in carrying out a repair at the mill and the sultan put him in charge as Chief Powder Maker in 1795. The post was to be held by six members of the Dadian family for nearly a century, until 1882.

The Dadians created an industrial zone west of the city, spreading from Zeytinburnu to Makriköy (Bakırköy). Iron pipes, steel rails, agricultural implements, swords, knives and other metal objects were manufactured. Not far away were two-story barrack-like buildings that housed migrant workers. Makriköy had a boatyard for the construction of steamships. The Dadians were the main—but not the sole—drivers of the industrial innovations and became immensely rich.

Arakel's younger son, Ohannes Dadian, was a central figure in these developments. He learned Greek and French and studied the latest developments in European industrial technology. As well as his official position as Chief Powder Maker, he developed paper works, a spinning mill, an iron and steel foundry and a boatyard, all on the outskirts of the city. In 1835 he toured Italy, France, Austria and the United Kingdom, visiting gun foundries and researching textile production and arranging the import of machinery. Seven years later, he returned to Europe, taking two of his sons whom he placed in schools, one in France and the other in England. In the 1840s he built up a very good personal relationship with Sultan Abdülmecid I who came to stay with his family at the family home at San Stefano, today's Yeşilköy, to the west of Makriköy. Through his official position he obtained tax exemption for the family, and their servants, including "concubines." Ohannes translated technical textbooks from French and employed many Armenians from an orphanage he had founded. During the Crimean War the French commander in chief, Maréchal Pélissier, was so impressed by Ohannes Bey that he offered him brilliant prospects if he were to accompany him back to France. "I am a servant of Turkey," Ohannes replied, "born in my beloved country, and nourished by its blessings. No matter how insignificant my services may be, they must be paid to my country." The sultan, who was a witness to this exchange, was duly impressed and at a later meeting said to him, "Ask of me whatever you will," to which Ohannes replied simply, "Good health."

The Dadian family graves can be seen in the churchyard of the Armenian church at Yeşilköy.

The Ottoman government and the industrialists were very conscious of European habits, including the significance of international exhibitions, such as the 1851 Great Exhibition of London. In 1863 Istanbul hosted an exhibition in the Hippodrome. For five months local products and machinery from Europe were on display. Thirty years later another was planned, to be located at Şişli. The Italian architect, Raimondo D'Aronco, started his Istanbul career with his appointment as architect in chief of the exhibition. But the plans were abandoned after a major earthquake struck the city.

## THE IMPACT OF THE CRIMEAN WAR

In the middle years of the nineteenth century a succession of reform-minded sultans and officials transformed much of the physical appearance of the city, including such details as dress and household furniture. Political, social and economic reforms led to others during the century. Parts of the empire—especially the commercial centers and above all Istanbul—became culturally and economically an extension of Europe. The impact of the changes on the Ottoman Empire and on Istanbul was uneven, but Pera and Galata took off and acquired their distinctive cosmopolitan character. During the century Pera and Galata became the arenas for experimentation and innovation, from modes of transport to municipal government.

The Crimean War accelerated social and cultural change. The main action was on the Crimean Peninsula between September 1854 and February 1856, although the war was fought also in eastern Anatolia, and on the Danubian frontier of today's Romania and Bulgaria. Istanbul was a sort of base camp for 310,000 French, 99,000 British and 22,000 Sardinian troops, most of whom passed through the Bosphorus. Many stopped off in the city, which became a place for rest and recreation, and a refuge for the sick and wounded.

The western troops did not always behave well. The army commanders insisted that the soldiers respect local customs, but the message did not always get through. Some drunken soldiers were summarily executed when caught molesting Turkish women. There were complaints of French and British soldiers lounging around in mosques and mocking the müezzin's call to prayer, and shooting gulls over the water and pigeons in the streets. It must have seemed at times that the city was under foreign occupation, even if at a higher social level, the wives of senior officers were received in the Ottoman court.

From a reflex of hospitality or from a sense of deference, the Ottoman authorities provided major public buildings for their new allies. French troops were housed in the newly built barracks of Gümüşsuyu near Taksim and the Davutpaşa barracks west of the city walls. The latter barracks as well as the Military School near Taksim were burned down while French troops occupied them. They then took over the Russian Embassy—diplomatic relations having been broken off on the outbreak of war—on the Grande Rue de Pera, as well as Seraglio Point (Sarayburnu in Turkish), and the adjoining barracks of Gülhane. British troops were quartered in and around Scutari (Üsküdar in Turkish), on the Asian side of the Bosphorus. There were reviews of the British cavalry, but there were no Turkish spectators apart from the imperial suite. The Selimiye Barracks, built in the 1820s and still dominating the Asian shore opposite the Topkapı Palace, became the quarters for the British wounded—or more specifically, the other ranks among the British wounded. Sick and wounded officers were put up in an imperial *köşk* (pavilion) on a site now occupied by the Haydarpaşa railway station; the pavilion burned down while they were there. The Turkish sick and

"Sketch of a Ward at the Hospital at Scutari" by Joseph-Austin Benwell

wounded—and Russian prisoners of war—had to put up with outlying barracks and hospitals.

Other troops came from afar. Poles and Hungarians volunteered to serve in the Ottoman army. Tunisia, theoretically still part of the Ottoman Empire, sent forces. Their supplies were provided by merchants from the Tunisian island of Jerba who were already trading in the city. Some of the most wretched soldiers were those sent from Egypt. Most were veterans of earlier wars who had been seized for further service, chained in gangs and brought to Alexandria. They camped on the Asian side of the Bosphorus north of Anadolu Hisarı and were honored with a visit from the sultan, who never got round to inspecting his own troops.

The Crimean War was the first conflict to be recorded by war correspondents; Istanbul became their base. The influx of foreigners caused inflation and the city became one of the most expensive in Europe. Hotels opened catering for western tastes—all in Pera. Some commodities and consumer products were sold for the first time.

One innovation dating from that time was the naming of streets and the numbering of houses. Some British brought their own customs. Officers of a cavalry regiment camped behind Haydarpaşa introduced hunting. Regattas and steeplechases were held, with the sultan giving cups to the winners. French replaced Italian as the commercial and principal foreign language of the city, and the sultan's title changed from *Son Hautesse* to *Sa Majesté Impériale,* indicating parity with the European monarchs. Cultural influences worked the other way too. The Turkish commander, Ömer Paşa, became a popular figure in France and Britain, where people were, for the first time, taking a sympathetic interest in the Ottoman Empire. A French- and English-language literature of Turkey was launched. Soldiers took back to the west a card game that was a variation of whist. (The derivation of the word bridge is uncertain. One theory attributes it to the first Galata Bridge where soldiers would gather in a coffee house to play the game. Another presumed derivation is that it is from the Turkish, one-three, *bir-üç.*)

Inevitably there was a hostile reaction to the incomers. Turkish soldiers were expected to salute foreign officers, but foreign soldiers were not obliged to reciprocate.

The increased internationalization of Istanbul was reflected in its population growth. In addition to emigrants from Western Europe, political disturbances led to an emmigration of Muslims and Ashkenazi Jews from Russia and the Balkans. Most of the Muslims settled in parts of the old city within the walls. There Muslims formed 55 percent of the population in 1885. By contrast, in the Pera-Galata-Tophane quarters Muslims were in a minority.

Early in the nineteenth century local administration had been based on neighborhood mosques, answerable to Muslim authorities, at the head of which was the *şeyhülislam.* There were four municipal units in the city: Istanbul (within the old walls), Üsküdar, Galata and Eyüp. Each of these units was subdivided into quarters and neighborhoods. Where there was confessional homogeneity the religious leaders, priest, imam or rabbi, would take on local responsibilities. After the Crimean War the government was pressured to introduce municipal reform for the Galata unit. So a commission was set up with members from different ethnic communities and with men familiar with European models. The commission established rules for public health and planning, and was seen as an experiment that might be extended to the rest of the city. In 1857 the commission was replaced by a council with powers of local urban planning, and in time with authority over gas lighting, water and sewage. The commission gained a physical presence with the construction between 1869 and 1871 of the Department of the Municipality, which can be found today in Şişhane to the west of the upper Tünel station. The architect was an Italian, Giovanni Battista Barborini, and it is Istanbul's first town hall. With its neoclassical symmetry, it emphasizes the European face of Istanbul, with a yearning for order.

European influences also had an impact on ideas of town planning. The city had always been subject to fires. Wood had been a preferred material for construction. It was flexible, homely, attractive, and withstood the tremors of earthquakes better than stone. In 1864 the government decreed that all new buildings should be of brick or stone, but the nineteenth century still saw serious outbreaks of fire. In 1856 a fire in Aksaray destroyed over 650 buildings in densely packed winding streets. The fire provided the opportunity of imposing a grid plan on the devastated area. In 1870 a major fire destroyed over three thousand buildings in Pera, to the north of the current İstiklâl Caddesi between Galatasaray and Taksim. This disaster also offered opportunities for planners. There are no wooden buildings in the rebuilt quarter, and the streets are straight.

## INTERNATIONAL BANKING AND GALATA

Economic foreign interest and investment were mostly directed at infrastructural projects that would in effect stimulate international trade, such as ports and railways. But investment needed a sound system of banking and exchange, and the middle of the nineteenth century saw progress in this area.

Both Sultan Abdülmecid I (1839–1861) and his brother and successor Abdülaziz (1861–1876) were great spenders. During and after the Crimean War large amounts of credit were extended to the empire from Britain and France. By 1875 the empire was no longer able to pay off its debts, and in 1881 the Public Debt Administration was established. This was formed with representatives from lending countries and gave the administration control over many areas of the empire's procedures for taxation and expenditure.

Since late Byzantine times Galata had been the international commercial hub of the city. Within reach of warehouses on the banks of the Golden Horn was the Palazzo del Comune, the Genoese town hall. After the Ottoman conquest of 1453, the Genoese governor continued to have a special status. The governor was known as the *Voyvoda,* and the narrow road that went from the Galata Bridge up the hill to Şişhane became known as Voyvoda Caddesi. This street was the main street for wheeled and horse-drawn vehicles to gain access to Pera. The direct approach from the Galata Bridge to Galata Tower was too steep for all but pedestrians, sedan chairs and donkeys.

In the years after the Crimean War the main financial houses were built along this Voyvoda Caddesi. The streets and buildings on the steep slopes leading up to the Galata Tower were the homes of Jews who provided much of the workforce for the banking world. Indeed, Şair Ziya Paşa Caddesi, which branches off up the hill, used to be known as Yahudi Yokuşu, the Jewish Slope. Today financial services have moved out to the flashy area of Maslak and Levent, but for sixty years after the 1850s Voyvoda Caddesi (now called Bankalar Caddesi, Banks Street) was the financial heart of the late Ottoman Empire. During those decades the street must have resembled a huge building site. Many of these commercial buildings dating from late Ottoman years remain. Some have been transformed, others replaced. It is worth strolling along the street, preferably at the weekend or very early in the morning. It is not pedestrianized and one needs to stand back—often in the middle of the road—to savor the glory of some of these buildings.

It was not only banks that lined the street. This was also the street for those in insurance services, exchanges, commercial houses and departmental stores and professionals practicing law and architecture. The area provided the commercial and financial nexus between the city and the rest of the world. The professionals were serviced by smaller shops and kiosks, often in the lanes leading on to the street—small restaurants, tobacconists, barbers' shops, coffee shops and grocers' stores, and also brothels. But for the last half century there have also been shops stocking white goods. As the banks moved out, electrical goods moved in. Often they were in a one-building unit called a *han,* large nineteenth-century commercial buildings which were the successors of the *kervansarays* (caravanserais) built by the Selçuks and Ottomans.

The word *han* persisted from the sixteenth to the nineteenth century. The function was much the same, but the structure changed. No longer were there courtyards or gateways big enough to admit laden camels. The later *han* would now not be out of place in Western Europe or the United States.

Banking developed rapidly after the Crimean War. The first bank, the Banque de Constantinople, had been started by the government and two private bankers in 1845 but this did not last long. The Ottoman Bank was founded in London in 1856, with British capital, with the objective of promoting commerce with the Ottoman Empire. It became an international syndicate with the name Banque Impériale Ottomane in 1872. Three years later the sultan gave it the authority to manage the state's budget and expenditures. Although there were depositors from all parts of the empire, there was a widespread suspicion that it was a foreign bank. The first headquarters of the Ottoman Imperial Bank was in a small street parallel and above Voyvoda Caddesi, called Bank Sokağı. It occupied part of the eighteenth-century St.-Pierre Han, built in the 1770s by a French ambassador for French traders in Galata. The building still stands, albeit in poor condition. The upper storey was added in the 1860s for the use of the bank.

## THE WHITE SLAVE TRAFFIC

Lower Galata acquired another reputation between the 1880s and the First World War as a center of prostitution and the white slave traffic.

Pogroms in the parts of Eastern Europe under Russian control led to a displacement of Jewish families and communities. Girls were lured to Istanbul, with the promise of a good marriage or a job in service, given single tickets either for the boat from Odessa or for the train. They were met at the port or at Sirkeci station and brought to the brothels of Galata and Pera, where they found themselves trapped. Sailors from the port nearby were often touted by sellers of postcards.

The city became a port for the trans-shipment of girls to Alexandria and Buenos Aires, the other major global centers for the traffic. In the years before and during the First World War, charitable organizations—both Jewish and non-Jewish—in Western Europe reported on the scandal. Locally, the United States Ambassador, Henry Morgenthau Sr., led a campaign with local religious communities, Turkish authorities and interested residents (including one lady, embarrassingly called Madame Fucks) to combat the traffic. Their work succeeded and the city's role in the white slave traffic was largely a thing of the past by 1930.

Prostitution was under government surveillance in late Ottoman times. Prostitutes were registered and were obliged to receive regular medical checks. Registered prostitutes had to be at least eighteen years old, but it was reckoned that many were younger, some as young as thirteen or fourteen. Few carried on after the age of twenty-five, but one woman was found in a Scutari (Üsküdar) brothel to be thirty-six. Outside the international traffic, some girls were recruited locally. After the First World War, a report on 2,123 prostitutes in the city found that 774 were from Muslim backgrounds, 691 Greek, 194 Armenian, 124 Jewish and 171 Russian. Local servant girls pushing prams in Taksim Square were sometimes propositioned with offers of better prospects.

The trade operated in a wide spectrum. At the grimmer end were the brothels of Galata, where, as the report of one London Jewish charity put it in 1914, the women

> … are seated on low stools or on boxes or on low couches, with almost nothing on in the way of clothes. Their faces are painted and powdered, but the haggard look in their eyes cannot be hidden. In almost every case, each prostitute sits in a small compartment not more than 20 to 24 inches wide with a wire netting in front facing the street. Some few have small windows. These wire nettings are apparently placed there to prevent the girls being molested by the men in the street, but they permit the girls to call out to passers-by. In every house the "Madame" sits near the door or close at hand to watch over the inmates.

Sailors were the main clients in Galata. Private houses in Kasımpaşa, on the northern shores of the Golden Horn, catered for poorer Muslims. Further up the hill the sex trade was a little more upmarket. The principal red light district was around Abanoz Sokak, a few blocks west of the Grande Rue de Pera—now an area of good, reasonably cheap restaurants. In Pera the girls would walk the streets, frequent the cafés or go to the

> … so-called music-halls. They are chiefly the "flash" prostitutes with whom the better class Turks and foreigners go. Many of the "artistes" too, that sing and dance at these variety performances are nothing more nor less than prostitutes, and after their "turn" go among the audience to seek out other means of earning money. At one house in particular

where the performance commences near midnight and goes on till 4.30 in the morning, the scenes are really disgraceful.

Şişli, north of Taksim, was even more upmarket. Şişli also had the hospital in which diseased prostitutes ended up. There were also red light districts in Kadıköy and Moda.

## MID-CENTURY PUBLIC TRANSPORT: STEAMERS, BRIDGES, TRAMS AND TRAINS

One of the new civic amenities that developed apace following the Crimean War was public transport. The present-day system is largely based on nineteenth-century foundations.

The first public transport reflected the priorities and interests of cosmopolitan Istanbul. In 1851 a company was founded, Şirket-i Hayriye, that dominated public transport on the Bosphorus and Golden Horn until the First World War. It was a public company and all Ottoman subjects were able to be shareholders. The first shareholders included the Sultan Abdülmecid I, his mother the Valide Sultan, the grand vizier, Mustafa Reşit Paşa, and the Jewish banker, Camondo. Foreign vessels were banned from carrying passengers, and the company started with six boats but rapidly expanded to scores. Boats would ply between Eminönü and Üsküdar and the Bosphorus villages every twenty minutes or so. The comfort of passengers was stressed, with seats, heating and gas-lamps, and separate sections for men and women. Boats were ventilated and cleaned daily. Vessels were imported from England and foreign engineers were required to maintain them.

The first bridge over the Golden Horn was built in 1836 near the shipyards at Azapkapı. This did not survive and the first Galata Bridge, from Karaköy to Eminönü, was built under the patronage of the mother of Sultan Mahmud II in 1845. It was replaced in 1863 by a timber structure—wood was permitted for bridges but smoking was banned—which lasted for twelve years. Another bridge was constructed in the same year, further up the Golden Horn, between Ayvansaray and Hasköy, but this bridge conflicted with the interests of the owners of rowing boats who tore it down after ten days. In the 1870s a third Galata Bridge was constructed of iron and wood: the central section could be raised for the passage of sea traffic. This lasted until 1912 when it was replaced by a floating bridge constructed by a German company.

Galata Bridge, c. 1890

One traveler in the 1890s, Edmondo De Amicis, observed that, standing there,

> ... you can see all Constantinople pass by in the course of an hour. The crowd surges by in great waves of color, each group of persons representing a different nationality. Try to imagine the most extravagant contrasts of costume, every variety of type and social class, and your wildest dreams will fall short of the reality; in the course of ten minutes, and in the space of a few feet, you will have seen a mixture of race and dress you never conceived of before.

He then catalogs those he saw:

> Turkish porters, an Armenian lady in a sedan chair, Bedouins, Greeks, a dervish in a conical hat and camel's hair mantle, a European ambassador with his attendants, a Persian regiment in towering caps of black astrakhan, a Jew in a long yellow garment open at the sides, a gypsy with a baby on her back, a Catholic priest, ladies of a harem wearing green

111

and violet in a carriage decorated with flowers, a Sister of Charity from a Pera hospital, an African slave carrying a monkey, and finally a storyteller in the garb of a necromancer.

The 1912 bridge lasted for most of the twentieth century; I remember it from my first visit in 1962. There used to be a walkway and shops below the road—as there are restaurants today. Stalls for drinks and ice cream and small restaurants were packed beneath the drone and hooting of the traffic. The boards of the bridge creaked as the water splashed against it, causing the lower level to rise and fall, but not always in harmony with the waves. Rowing boats were moored to the bridge below the pedestrian level. From these boats fishermen caught mackerel which they cut up and grilled over a primus stove. They then stuffed the cooked fish into a large wedge of bread and sold them to pedestrians for 75 *kuruş*, or about a nickel. I used to lean over with my money and listen to the waves smacking the bridge and wait for the moment when the rise and fall of the rowing boat and the fall and rise of the bridge provided a moment's opportunity for fish and cash to be exchanged. In 1992 fire destroyed much of the bridge, and a Turkish company built the bridge now in use. What was left of its predecessor was towed up the Golden Horn and is now used as a pedestrian bridge linking Sütlüce and Eyüp.

Horse trams were introduced in 1872. In July that year the first line ran from Azapkapı along the waterway through Karaköy and Tophane to Beşiktaş. Five months later a second line connected Eminönü to Aksaray. More lines followed, from Karaköy to Şişli, but the line from Unkapanı to Fatih, where there were no foreign interests, was delayed. Attempts were made to keep the trams clean and comfortable. Each tram was preceded by a man who wielded a stick to keep the dogs away. But standards slipped for those trams that operated in the inner parts of the city within the walls. "The Tramway Company operates its most rotten cars on this line," observed the novelist and social critic, Hüseyin Rahmi, in 1896: "The dust and mud of the street hid the green paint of the cars... The four horses were so weak and lifeless that they could very well be used for a course in skeleton structure while still alive."

Railways developed in Anatolia before they linked Istanbul to European capitals. Turkey's first railway was built in 1856 from İzmir to Aydın—and was formally opened by the British Ambassador, Stratford

Canning, by now Viscount Stratford de Redcliffe, as his last public act in Turkey. The first railway in Istanbul was on the Asian side and linked Haydarpaşa to İzmit and opened in 1873. From the 1860s there were proposals for a line on the European side. The Ottoman government gave a concession to a Belgian banker, Maurice de Hirsch, in 1869, and a line to Sofia in Bulgaria was opened in 1874. There was some unhappiness about the proposed track having to be laid along the Marmara shore and cutting into the gardens of Topkapı Palace, but Sultan Abdülaziz was an ardent enthusiast for new technology. The Topkapı Palace was no longer the principal seat of the sultan, and the line began to operate a suburban route with stations at Küçük Çekmece, Yeşilköy, Bakırköy, Yedikapı, Kumkapı, with the terminus being then, as now, at Sirkeci. Greeks, Armenians and Jews, and some foreigners, built homes in the villages of the Marmara suburbs, and the commuter line boosted the development of those villages. Sixteen years later an international line brought expresses from the Ostbahnhof in Vienna. The Orient Express was born.

The two railway termini of the city have been built in contrasting styles. Sirkeci station was built between 1888 and 1890, after the first Orient Express arrived. The architect was a German, August Jasmund, who mixed his styles. Brick banding suggest Moorish influences, while the octagonal towers remind us of contemporary barracks. The main entrance, facing the Golden Horn, is monumental and is like a Seljuk portal. Stalactite capitals and the use of steel and glass display the eclecticism typical of that era. Yet unlike some of the exotic buildings of Pera it does not quite convince. The building has to be seen from the Golden Horn side, but this aspect is ruined by the insensitive construction of a petrol station. Sirkeci station has a railway museum and a 1930s-themed restaurant. In its heyday the restaurant and bar opened on to a terrace towards the water, but car fumes and pollution have ruined that idea.

Haydarpaşa station, the terminus of the lines to Anatolia and Asia, was built between 1906 and 1908 to the designs of two German architects, Otto Ritter and Helmuth Cuno. If Sirkeci is built in an idiosyncratic orientalist style, Haydarpaşa makes few concessions to the architectural traditions of the Islamic world. It is of solid, no nonsense, Teutonic neo-Renaissance appearance, typical of German architecture of the reign of Kaiser Wilhelm II. By contrast, the pier, where passengers from Europe would have arrived, is a gem. The architect was Vedat Tek Bey and was a conscious attempt to create an authentic Ottoman style. There are plans afoot to turn Haydarpaşa station into a luxury hotel.

## BELLE EPOQUE ARCHITECTURAL ECLECTICISM AND THE WORK OF THE BALYANS

The cosmopolitan eclecticism of the architecture of Galata and Pera was repeated throughout the nineteenth-century city. New kinds of buildings—theaters, shops, banks, department stores and hotels—reflected a variety of experimental architectural styles. Gothic, classical, Islamic and Byzantine revivals were mixed up with neo-Renaissance and Art Nouveau. Many individual buildings sprung out of text-book academicism, which can be seen also in the classical revival. It is western Paladian classicism that is reproduced, not the classicism of the sites of Asia Minor, few of which had, in the later part of the nineteenth century, been surveyed and drawn. Similarly, the Islamic revival buildings were introduced by non-Muslim architects such as Vallaury and D'Aronco, sometimes with Renaissance revival or Art Nouveau flourishes. At the end of the century, Turkish architects such as Kemalettin worked on a neo-Ottoman style, in reaction against the eclecticism of the nineteenth century. But even the schools for the production of Turkish architects, the Academy of Fine Arts founded in 1881, and the School for Civil Engineering, founded in 1883, had as its principal architectural instructor, the prolific Alexandre Vallaury, responsible for some of those buildings from which Turks wanted to be emancipated.

Many, if not most, of the major public buildings that were erected in the nineteenth century were the works of one remarkable Armenian family, the Balyans. They were responsible, as the late Godfrey Goodwin wrote, "for as many acres of building as Sinan." The family were originally from a village near Kayseri and over four generations were responsible for mosques, palaces and barracks in the city. They operated at the heart of the Ottoman establishment, under the patronage of a state and a sultan that showed not a glimmer of prejudice against infidels or Christians. The family was also responsible for some of the major buildings of the Armenian community in the city: churches, schools and the Armenian hospital beyond the walls, which today houses a museum of the social life of well-to-do Armenian families before the disasters of the twentieth century.

The first of the Balyan architects was Krikor, or Kirkor (1764–1831). He slowly gained the confidence of the ruling family. Twice banished and twice restored to favor, he was the architect of three major imperial buildings during the 1820s.

The first he designed was the Nusretiye Mosque, built for Sultan Mahmud II to celebrate—*Nusretiye* means Divine Victory—the suppression of the Janissaries in 1826. It was significantly built at Tophane, by the parade ground attached to the gun foundry. On the shores of the Bosphorus it is seen by anyone approaching the city by sea—which was how most did approach it in the 1820s. Although in some ways it followed the pattern of some eighteenth-century mosques such as Nuruosmaniye near the Covered Bazaar, there are the first signs of Balyan bold and shameless exuberance. Instead of geometric shapes, there are shells, fronds and swags adorning the vertical surfaces. The minarets are particularly slender, with baroque turrets and a blend of woodwork with the stone. The inscription in relief on the marble inside is the work of Mustafa Rakım, who gave lessons in calligraphy to Sultan Mahmud II.

A second monument was also associated with military reforms. Wooden barracks built by Sultan Selim III (1789–1807) were destroyed by fire, and Krikor was the initial designer of the vast complex known as the Selimiye Barracks on the Asian shore opposite the Topkapı Palace. They form a huge square around a courtyard. Krikor was responsible for only one flank: the three others were added between 1842 and 1853. The barracks, when built, were the largest in the world. It was the symbolic headquarters of the new European-style army: power in masonry. There are over 1,100 windows. The whole complex was built on a slope, and so one flank has three stories, another four. It is an assertion of military power and, like the Nusretiye Mosque, is a visible reminder of that power for any who approach the city by sea. The North West Tower is dedicated to a museum in honor of Florence Nightingale. The barracks were restored in 1963 and reverted to their original military function, having in the meanwhile served other functions; after the First World War the complex served as a tobacco warehouse.

Krikor Balyan also designed a palace on the Bosphorus at Beşiktaş, but this was later demolished to make way for Dolmabahçe Palace.

Krikor's son, Garabed (1800–66), was perhaps the most prolific of the family. He was appointed Chief Imperial Architect and followed his father in the construction of two major barracks in the city. The first was the Kuleli Barracks, built for the cavalry from 1837 to 1839. This became the Constantinople base for the French army during the Crimean War. The second was the Gümüşsuyu Barracks, overlooking the Beşiktaş football stadium. Originally of timber, the barracks were rebuilt between 1852 and 1862. Krikor also built the Dolmabahçe Mosque for Bezmiâlem Valide Sultan, the mother of Sultan Abdülmecid. It is a relatively restrained neoclassical composition, with Corinthian capitals below the minaret balconies, but by far his most important work was the neighboring Dolmabahçe complex, described by Godfrey Goodwin as "the first of his notorious palaces." In this there is no restraint, either architecturally or financially.

The palace is designed to face and to be approached from the Bosphorus. To enter formally by land you may go through one of two monumental gates that are extraordinarily ornate. Godfrey Goodwin claimed that there were all manner of styles. This is true to some extent, but there is such eclectic originality in the work that it is creating its own distinctive style, the climax of Balyan exuberant inventiveness. Foliage motifs and medallions inset with vegetation predate Art Nouveau. The materials used are marble, plaster and stone.

Like the new barracks, the whole complex is an assertion of power. Dolmabahçe became the residence of Sultan Abdülmecid, and also the seat of his government, while the Topkapı Palace became obsolete. Dolmabahçe evolved into one of the series of palace-cities that has characterized Istanbul between the time of Constantine in the fourth century and Abdülhamid's Yıldız complex at the end of the nineteenth century. To the south and north there are two classical wings, respectively, the *selamlık*, the public quarters, and the *haremlik*, the private quarters. Between is a vast domed room, the Throne Room, twice the height of the rest of the building. The decoration of this room was undertaken by Garabed's son, Nicogos. The hall measures 130 by 145 feet (40 by 45 meters) and is surrounded by fifty-six columns. Filling up much of the space is a magnificent chandelier with 750 candles and weighing four and a half tons. The room is overlooked by four spacious balconies, supported by groups of four Corinthian columns. These balconies were allocated to guests, the diplomatic corps and the palace orchestra. The women of the household were able to peer down through grilled and latticed windows.

Dolmabahçe Palace

In spite of the seclusion of the women and the division into public areas (for men) and private areas (for women), the palace was architecturally and culturally a turning point in Ottoman history. In contrast to the Topkapı complex, it was built as one unit. The Balyans perhaps had the idea of a European palace—Schönbrunn or Versailles—in mind. Although there had for centuries been smaller palaces along the Bosphorus, the building of Dolmabahçe emphasized the European personality of the nineteenth-century Ottoman Empire. Galata and Pera were, in contrast to the city within the walls, the more European districts, and the Bosphorus villages were always the homes of the non-Muslim communities.

The costs of the palace helped to bankrupt the empire, but it has also played more positively symbolic roles in the modern history of the country. Soon after the completion of the construction, the Throne Room became the venue for major political meetings and ceremonies. A banquet in honor of the French commander during the Crimean War was held here. The room hosted a reception for the Hapsburg Emperor Franz Josef in the same year. The room was used for the first Ottoman parliament in 1876. During the thirty-two year reign of Sultan Abdülhamid II the palace was not greatly used, but in 1918 his successor, Sultan Mehmet V Reşat, entertained the successor of Franz Josef, the Ottoman emperor's wartime ally, the Emperor Karl and his wife, Zita (who died in 1989). The last caliph, Abdülmecid II, lived in the palace, and his library can still be seen. His daughter, Dürrüşehvar Sultan, was brought up in the palace, and several portraits of her painted by her father still hang on the walls.

The palace was neglected after the First World War. It had little relevance to the concerns of the new Republic, but Atatürk, when he started returning to Istanbul, saw the potential of the building. "This Palace," he declared, "no longer belongs to Sultans described as the 'Shadow of God.' It is now the Palace of the People, a real living being and no shadow." He arranged for the palace and the Throne Room to be the setting of conferences—ideologically on language and history and economically on tourism. The palace certainly impressed foreigners. Atatürk hosted foreign visitors, including King Edward VIII, and his friend, not yet his wife, Mrs. Wallis Simpson. In 1938, physically broken, Atatürk came to the palace and occupied a small room in the *haremlik*, dying here on 10 November 1938.

The luxury of the palace was an embarrassment to Atatürk's successors when most people in the country were facing austerity. But by the 1970s the tourist potential was exploited and the palace was cleaned, restored and opened to the public.

Garabed had four sons who followed him in the family business: Nicogos, Agop, Sarkis and Simon.

Nicogos (1826–58), in spite of his short life, designed several imperial buildings. In his early twenties he was the architect for the Ihlamur Kasrı, today in a small park, in the valley tucked among hills covered with blocks of flats. In the eighteenth century the valley was a venue for picnics and hunting expeditions. The small palace *(kasr)* was built by Sultan Abdülmecid I as a pavilion for these outings. There are no bedrooms and limited service areas, but the gem of a building displays the Balyan style of exuberant decoration. Abdülmecid's son, Sultan Mehmet V Reşat, who reigned from 1909 to 1918, used Dolmabahçe Palace as his residence but was somewhat overawed by that building and preferred to spend the days here at Ihlamur. In the following years of his life, Nicogos as well as being in charge of much of the internal decoration for Dolmabahçe Palace, undertook the design of two similar pavilions on the Asian shores of the Bosphorus. Beykoz Kasrı was actually commissioned by Mehmet Ali Paşa, Viceroy of Egypt, as a present for Sultan Abdülmecid I. And Küçüksu

Kasrı, another gem, is full of Balyan extravagance. It was used and retained for ceremonial purposes—King Edward VIII came here in 1936—but has been a museum since 1983.

One of Nicogos' works has become part of an iconic image of modern Istanbul. In the mid-1850s he designed the mosque at Ortaköy, which is now often photographed with the first Bosphorus Bridge as background. The mosque was built on a site jutting into the Bosphorus, and abuts a relatively small imperial pavilion. Both are best seen from the water.

A second son, Sarkis (1831–99), was sent to Paris to study for two years before working with his father and succeeding him as Chief Imperial Architect. In addition to his public work, Sarkis was also an entrepreneur and developed the docks at Beykoz. Sarkis was responsible for the Çırağan Palace, designed in 1862. He also designed the palace at Beylerbeyi on the Asian side of the Bosphorus, to the north of the first Bosphorus Bridge. Commissioned by Sultan Abdülaziz, it invites comparisons with Dolmabahçe, diagonally across the water, but is slightly smaller and is less ornate. Dolmabahçe was built at great speed and Beylerbeyi has the impression of a more leisured design. Sarkis also worked on two other palaces, pushing the empire even further into debt.

The Çırağan Palace has had a checkered career. It was built soon after the accession of Sultan Abdülaziz, to replace previous, more modest, palaces along the European shores of the Bosphorus. Older buildings were destroyed to make way for the new palace. One building destroyed was a lodge attached to the Mevlevi sufi order, with tombs of Muslim saints. In 1865 Istanbul suffered one of its most destructive fires. The sultan had a conscience about building an extra luxurious palace while so many others were destitute and homeless. Like Beylerbeyi and unlike Dolmabahçe, it comes across as an integrated creation with the Balyan extrovert quality kept in control. Inhibitions over the cost were overcome, and the interior decoration is extravagant. The sultan had a study assigned for his use. One French visitor was expected to admire the tassels on the curtains, "each one of which cost six thousand francs. An amount of money that would allow a whole family of ordinary people to live in comfort for a year is here enclosed in the tassel of a curtain."

Sultan Abdülaziz did not use the palace for long. For reasons that seem uncertain he preferred Dolmabahçe. Beylerbeyi and Çırağan were abandoned.

In 1876 Sultan Abdülaziz was deposed as the new political classes could no longer tolerate his extravagant idleness. On the morning of 30 May he was woken up in Dolmabahçe Palace, told he was no longer sultan and taken by boat to be detained at the Topkapı Palace. He requested a transfer to a small house in Beşiktaş but was transferred to Çırağan. There, a few days later, he apparently committed suicide, slashing his wrists with a pair of scissors he had asked for to trim his beard. In spite of the overwhelming probability of suicide, some entertain the belief that he was assassinated.

His successor and nephew, Sultan Murad V, lasted only three months. He too was deposed, on the grounds of mental instability, and was succeeded by his half-brother, Abdülhamid. Çırağan became the gilded prison and home for most of the rest of Murad's life.

Sultan Murad V was seen as a progressive. He enjoyed beer or wine with his meals, and was a lover of western classical music. He had traveled to London with Sultan Abdülaziz in 1867, and made an impression on Queen Victoria. He spent his thirty-year incarceration enjoying the company of his children and grandchildren, reading and playing music. The piano on which he composed music, which included marches and polkas, has survived and is in the villa of a descendant in Beylerbeyi.

The ex-Sultan Murad V died in 1904. Four years later Çırağan was brought again into service to be the venue of the newly restored parliament. More money was spent on the building of a conference hall and committee rooms. The new parliament assembled there in 1909, but at the beginning of the following year, fire broke out in the attic and most of the building was gutted.

Çırağan seemed ill-fated, and there were some who saw the palace's grim history as God's answer to the sacrilege of building on the tombs of Muslim saints. The building remained a shell for nearly eighty years. In 1987 it was bought by the German Kempinski chain and has been meticulously restored. It is now a five star luxury hotel. Each guest has his or her own butler.

Sarkis also did work for the brother and successor of Sultan Murad V, Sultan Abdülhamid II. His most interesting work, mocked by architectural historians, is the Hamidiye Mosque by the Yıldız Palace. The mosque has Gothic windows and classical and Persian features. Some carvings in the women's section are believed to have been the work of the sultan himself.

By instinct a recluse, Sultan Abdülhamid II used to make one public appearance each week. Following the pattern of his Ottoman and indeed Byzantine predecessors, he would visit a place of worship for weekly devotions. Each Friday there would be a procession from the palace a hundred meters away. The sultan arrived in a landau drawn by white horses and accompanied by male members of his family. "The carriage was pursued on foot," recalled an eyewitness, "by fezzed eunuchs in black coats and a posse of fat Paşas in full uniform, panting and puffing, treading on one another's heels and tripping over their own swords." He entered the mosque, surrounded by bowing officials. Attendant troops cried, *Padişahımız çok yaşa!* ("Long live our Sultan!"). After the prayers, he reviewed the troops from a balcony and returned to the palace.

The third son was Agop (1837-75), otherwise Hagop, the Armenian form for James or Jacob. His best-known work was the Pertevniyal Mosque, built for the mother of Sultan Abdülaziz. It has the family stamp, but lacks the conviction of some of the work of his brothers and father. It has suffered from the pollution of traffic in recent years. Hilary Sumner-Boyd and John Freely describe it as "garish." But then, most commentators have not been kind to the work of the Balyans.

## Fin-de-Siècle Dragomans

Until the second half of the nineteenth century the British Embassy, and other embassies, relied on dragomans from the city—Greeks and Armenians, Jews and Maltese—to deal with the Ottoman officials. The special tasks of the dragoman were honed over generations, and there emerged families of dragomans, who might serve several European embassies. Dragomans often acquired a foreign passport as a result of their labors, and there were families whose members might be nationals of several European countries. As Philip Mansel suggests, nationality became a career. During the nineteenth century the loyalty of the dragomans became suspect, and the British Embassy changed its policy of relying on local dragomans and started to bring out talented young British men to study the Turkish (and other useful) languages. In 1877 a modest language school was set up at the Bosphorus village of Ortaköy, three miles from the embassy, near enough for convenience but far enough away, it was thought, for students not to be distracted by "the charms of the city." A senior second secretary from the embassy supervised the training of student interpreters who studied Turkish, Arabic, Persian, modern Greek and in some cases Russian, Bulgarian and modern Islamic law. Teachers were recruited locally. For law, students went to the Galata chambers of Edwin Pears, who spent forty years in the city, practicing law, though never mastering Turkish.

One of the most interesting of those who went through Ortaköy in the early years was a young Irish Catholic, Gerald Fitzmaurice. He was twenty-three when he arrived in 1888, having given up on a possible career as a priest, and was to remain in Constantinople, in the embassy, until a few months before the First World War. He acquired a huge reputation as a man of influence. He achieved fluency, regarded as unsurpassed, in colloquial Turkish. He did this by spending time in the cafés. Language competence was essential for the effective functioning of the embassy, but the student interpreters were seen as middle-class swots. "The merits and defects of the scheme," observed one Foreign Office official,

> resemble those of the Indian Civil Service under open competition. Many young men of the middle or lower middle class, indefatigable workers in grammar schools, examined at high pressure, obtain appointments: and come out without the moral and physical training of the best public schools, the social habits of the upper classes, or the active habits of country gentlemen.
>
> The natives do not look up to them: they marry early and go about on wheels instead of on horseback, so seeing little of the back country: they have often little bottom and in many cases go off their heads.
>
> Less exam and book learning: and more saddle and savoir faire would serve the state better.

Fitzmaurice had to work for several "country gentlemen" who served as ambassadors, and was at odds with most of them. But he also acquired a huge network of acquaintances at all levels, "from Pashas to porters," *The Times* correspondent, Philip Graves, observed. His role was that of a kind of superior servant, clearing goods through customs and escorting royal and titled visitors around the sites of the city. Fitzmaurice spent years in Constantinople without leave. By contrast, in the summer after the embassy at Tarabya was burned down, the ambassador went on a cure at Marienbad, on the pretext of relieving pressure on accommodation. The ambassador might receive up to £10,000 a year, whereas Fitzmaurice would have been lucky to receive £1,000. Fitzmaurice's political judgment was fallible—he did not anticipate the 1908 Young Turk revolution—but many saw him, perhaps exaggeratedly, as a man of influence in Turkish politics. His status and salary reflected his social standing, rather than his actual usefulness. But in the early years of the twentieth century, the embassy, with its yacht, its billiard room, ballrooms and social life, became a kind of finishing school for wealthy young men, who were designated honorary attachés. Three of the most remarkable became Conservative politicians, each one of whom fell under the spell of Fitzmaurice's personality.

One was George Lloyd who later became high commissioner in Egypt and chairman of the British Council. Lloyd was perhaps closest to Fitzmaurice. Both were middle-class Celts. Fitzmaurice wrote long, affectionate, gossipy letters to Lloyd, laced with Turkish and complaints about his bosses. Another was Mark Sykes, the travel writer and eponymous negotiator of the Sykes-Picot Treaty carving up the Middle East during the First World War in the event of the collapse of the Ottoman Empire. The third was Aubrey Herbert, author and poet. Another attaché was the nineteen-year-old Lord Vernon, "quite youthful and fond of jewelry and scents," Fitzmaurice sniffily told Lloyd. "God knows we are decadent enough."

Another young man attached to the embassy was George Young, the heir to a baronetcy. He was at the embassy for only three years but became an authority on Ottoman law, and produced the seven-volume *Corps de Droit Ottoman*, which provides an intriguing picture of the prescriptions of the final Ottoman years. Young went on to become a foreign correspondent for *The Daily News* in Berlin, Professor of Portuguese at the University of London and parliamentary Labour candidate at the General Elections of 1923, 1924 and 1929. He also wrote one of the best books on Istanbul.

Others who passed through Istanbul were similarly impressed by Fitzmaurice. Harold Nicolson who worked at the embassy later wrote an evocative novel, *Sweet Waters*, about the life of a young British diplomat in Constantinople, flitting by boat from his home at Kanlıca across the Bosphorus to his office at Tarabya during the summer and to Pera during the winter. Fitzmaurice gave Nicolson high marks for fluency in colloquial Turkish. Another visitor, the novelist Marmaduke Pickthall, thought Fitzmaurice should have been British Ambassador, such was his influence with "the reactionary Turkish party." Others who served in the embassy, such as Reader Bullard and Andrew Ryan, wrote warmly and affectionately of the gruff Irishman.

## GOOD YEARS FOR ARMENIANS

Well-to-do Armenians flourished during the central years of the nineteenth century. Some families produced generations of outstanding individuals who had important roles in the private sector, building up hotels and also industry. Others combined prominence in the private sector and influence in politics, even in the court. The Duzians were hereditary controllers of the imperial mint. The Dadians combined business and courtiership. The Balyans, as we have seen, produced generations of architects.

In the middle of the nineteenth century there were about 150,000 Armenians in Istanbul. They felt an affinity with France. As Migirdich Dadian put it in an article for a French readership in 1865, there were "age-old memories of fighting side by side on the battlefields of Syria during the Crusades and the alliances formed with the French nobility abroad." This may not have been very tactful, and over the following decades such attitudes built up barriers between Armenian and Turk. The first Armenian newspaper dated from 1836 and after a generation there were over a dozen Armenian periodicals. Armenians were often more familiar with the Turkish than the Armenian language; three Armenian periodicals were written in Turkish, though using Armenian script. One of the sons of the entrepreneur, Ohannes Dadian, Artin, had known the future Sultan Abdülhamid II when they were both children. Artin studied at the Sorbonne in Paris and became a government official and rose to be a *paşa* and the Ottoman minister for foreign affairs. His daughter, Yevkine or Eugenie, became the official interpreter for the imperial harem, interpreting between the wives and daughters of Sultan Abdülhamid II and royal visitors such as Princess Victoria Augusta, wife of the Kaiser Wilhelm, on their visits in 1889 and 1898.

Other members of the family were skilled professionals. One Dadian translated Oscar Wilde's *A Woman of No Importance* into Armenian, while others held professorships at the Imperial College of Medicine.

THE JEWS OF ISTANBUL...

Among the people whom the Sultan Mehmet II invited to repopulate Istanbul after 1453 were the Jews. A Jewish community had existed in Byzantium. They were mostly in Galata and were part of the Italian-speaking community, with links to Genoa and Venice. The Jews who came in the years after the conquest were largely from former Byzantine territories in Greece and the Balkans. They were known as Romaniots, or popularly as *gregos*. But this community was overwhelmed in the following century by the immigration of Jews from the Iberian Peninsula, following their expulsion after the Reconquest. Mehmet's son, Sultan Beyazit II, encouraged Jewish immigration, sending boats to bring the Jews to the city and offer them refuge. It is reckoned that some 40,000 Jews expelled from Spain in 1492 came to Istanbul. In early Ottoman times Eminönü had a large Jewish community, but in 1660 a large fire destroyed many buildings in that area, and the mother of Sultan Mehmet IV decided to construct the mosque, now known as the Yeni Cami, the New Mosque. Jews were moved to Hasköy and Balat. Balat lies on the Golden Horn, near the old Byzantine Blachernae Palace. The word *Balat* is derived from the Greek, *Palation*, Palace. The Balat Gate in the sea walls survived until 1894 when it was destroyed by the earthquake of that year.

The culture of the Spanish Jews became the dominating characteristic of Istanbul Jews. The first two chief rabbis under the Ottomans were Romaniot, but afterwards they were descendants of emigrants from the Iberian Peninsula. They brought their language, Ladino, sometimes called Judaeo-Spanish, to Istanbul, and this became the principal Jewish language until the twentieth century. It still survives, and there is a new interest in Ladino language, literature, music and culture.

The Jewish community was frequently divided. The movement of Sabbatai Zevi, a messianic Jewish preacher, took many Jewish followers into the bosom of Islam in the 1660s and created a permanent schism. The followers, called *dönme*, were rejected by the Jews and not fully accepted by Muslims, and remained outsiders to both. In the nineteenth century there was an Ashkenazi/Sephardic divide which was reflected in the use of either Yiddish or Ladino. Istanbul has also always had a strong Karaite community, composed of Jews who base their religion on the Torah and reject rabbinical Judaism. The Jews of nineteenth-century Istanbul were further divided, politically, between those who supported a modern secular education and those who felt the religious teachings were sufficient.

During the nineteenth century the Jewish population was around 50–55,000, with forty synagogues. Emigrants, mainly to the United States, were replaced by immigrants from Eastern Europe, including Karaites from the Crimea.

The relatively high status held by Jews in Istanbul and elsewhere in the early Ottoman Empire suffered in some ways during the nineteenth century. Jews had had a close financial relationship with the Janissaries. With their dissolution in 1826, Jewish interests lost out, even if this was offset by the liberal reforms of the Tanzimat, and the interest and patronage of successive sultans. The liberalization led to some friction with other non-Muslim communities, especially with Greeks. Istanbul witnessed some blood libels—accusations that Jews were kidnapping Christian children, killing them and using their blood for their traditional bread, *matzot*. The instigators were nearly always Christians, and Jews found protection with the police and sometimes refuge with Muslim families.

Liberal education also improved the status of the Jewish community. In the nineteenth century the Jews of Istanbul and the Ottoman Empire became of interest to outsiders. Christian missionaries, in particular from Britain, France and the United States, sought the conversion of Jews, founded schools and published books in Ladino and Hebrew. The Alliance Israélite Universelle (AIU), founded by Adolphe Crémieux in 1860, established one modern Jewish school in Hasköy. Today, the school is a Jewish Old People's Home. Another was founded in Galata, at Dibek Sokak, at the back of the Galata Tower. Altogether ten AIU schools, five for boys, five for girls, were founded in what is now the Greater Istanbul area. Both groups of schools opened up the rather closed Jewish communities to the world, encouraging knowledge of European languages, especially French. By the end of the nineteenth century French was the main foreign language spoken by Turkish Jews.

In 1858 the most distinguished of the Istanbul Jewish community, was the banker Abraham Camondo (1785–1873). Born in Ortaköy, though a citizen of Austria, he founded and funded a modern school in Hasköy, later known as the Camondo Institute. It lasted thirty years and provided instruction in French, Turkish, Hebrew and Greek. There were technical branches as well as a rabbinical college. Camondo paid for it all.

The broader education facilitated Jewish social mobility, and led to the emergence of a middle class that preferred to live with their social peers of other confessions than with their co-religionists, in the newer suburbs of Şişli and Nişantaşı. Balat and Hasköy were left to the peddlers, tailors, shoemakers, butchers, tinkers, boatmen and producers of bread and wine.

Jews became active in journalism, publishing and bookselling. They took their place in the cosmopolitanism of Pera, and were addressed as *Efendi* or Madame, instead of the more offensive *cifut*. One traveler in the middle of the century was shocked to see a Jew reading the Scripture, wearing a fez. Later in the century Jewish reformers such as the historian Abraham Galante urged Jewish schools to include the teaching of Turkish, on the grounds that a lack of proficiency in this language had been a constraint on the emancipation of Jews.

By the beginning of the twentieth century Jews were attending the modern secondary schools alongside Muslims and Christians. The reforms of the Tanzimat had allowed Jews to enter the public sector professions such as the diplomatic service and the home civil service. They were strong in the telegraph offices and the Treasury, the army medical services and the universities. They encountered some resistance, as did Christians, to their service in the armed forces as combatants. Muslim soldiers objected to serving in mixed units, for part of the ethos of the army was that any war the Ottomans were involved in was a *jihad*, with exclusive Islamic implications. Some Jews overcame this prejudice, and indeed there were three Jewish generals by the end of the empire. Sultan Abdülhamid II encouraged Jewish enrollment and assured the acting chief rabbi, Moshe Levy, that kosher food would be available to Jewish soldiers. This sultan was regarded particularly as a friend of the Jewish community, and he encouraged Jews to call on him. In 1899 Jews of Haydarpaşa faced objections to their opening a synagogue from the local Christian congregation. The sultan gave his support to the Jews and the synagogue was gratefully named Hemdat Israel after him.

## . . . AND OF BALAT

Certain areas of Istanbul became distinctly Jewish, in particular Balat and Hasköy. Balat was a jumble of minority communities—Greek and Armenian as well as Jewish—and traces of their presence have survived. The Sultan Mehmet II settled *gregos* there, and the names of their synagogues indicate the places of origin of their founders: Ahrida (Ohrid) and İstipol (Štip), now in the former Yugoslav Republic of Macedonia, and Kastoria and Saloniki (Thessaloniki), both now in Greek Macedonia. Over the centuries Romaniot and Ladino-speaking Jews were joined by Jews from Italy and, in the eighteenth and nineteenth centuries, Ashkenazi Jews fleeing persecution from east and central Europe. In the last 150 years many Jews moved out of Balat to other parts of the city, in particular to Galata and to some of the Bosphorus villages. Even so, in the nineteenth and early twentieth centuries Balat was a fairly self-contained area, where the language of the streets was Ladino. Even those who could not claim a descent from the immigrants from Spain and Portugal adopted Ladino. Turks, Greeks and Armenians also lived in Balat, as minorities. The majority of the population was, however, Jewish and the *muhtar* of the quarter, the man who negotiated with the municipal and national authorities, was usually a Jew.

The decline of the Jewish community of Balat started in the earlier part of the twentieth century. Those who could move out did so—to Nişantaşı, to Ortaköy or across the Bosphorus to Kuzguncuk. Between the wars many immigrated to Latin America. The property tax, the *varlık vergisi*, a vicious imposition that was targeted at non-Muslims during the Second World War, encouraged many to emigrate. Many of those who could afford it, or had the right contacts, moved to Europe or America, North and South. Others responded to the activities of Zionist organizations and immigrated to Palestine/Israel. This reflects the pattern of Jewish emigration from other Middle Eastern countries.

Until the 1940s there was a distinctive popular culture in Balat. Today the Ahrida Synagogue is Balat's only functioning Jewish place of worship. It is the oldest of the city, and, though there is not enough of a community to sustain weekly services, it is the preferred location for weddings and funerals. Originally built in the fifteenth century, it has been repeatedly restored. The tapestries were presented by the heirs of Isak Babani, from one of the wealthier families of Balat. In the 1650s the chiliastic Sabbatai Zevi proclaimed his mission as a Messiah to the local community from this synagogue.

During the Second World War this synagogue was requisitioned, as were other Jewish institutions of the quarter, for use by the Turkish army. To celebrate the five hundredth anniversary of the Jews from the Iberian

Street scene in Balat

Peninsula coming to Istanbul, the Ahrida Synagogue was thoroughly restored in 1990. The restoration work uncovered eighteenth-century pointed arches that had been concealed by rounded arches of the nineteenth. Plasterwork was removed to disclose ornamentation that went back to 1694.

Most Jews of Balat were poor, clung to their festivals and were meticulous in their religious observances. Indeed, on Friday evenings, before the sunset that marked the beginning of the Sabbath, the *gabay*, a synagogue official, used to tour the area, ordering shops to close. He would be accompanied by a Turkish policeman to enforce the Jewish rule. Non-Jewish shops also closed for the Sabbath, partly out of solidarity, partly because there would be no customers.

The tight-knit Ladino-speaking community was undermined, paradoxically, by the good work done by the schools of the Alliance Israélite. A modern education through the medium of French was free for those who could not afford the fees, and this meant most of the children of Balat.

Much of Jewish Balat has gone since the emigration of its traditional inhabitants. The improved highways heading for Eyüp have transformed the area between the sea walls and the Golden Horn. Until the 1970s and 1980s it was an overcrowded slum, which older Jewish wits used to call ironically Balat-les-Bains. There used to be a pier here and busy traffic across the Golden Horn to Hasköy. An old Jewish cemetery at Eğrikapı, on the land walls above Balat, was full and the Jewish dead were taken to the cemetery at Hasköy. One major survival of Jewish Balat outside the walls is the Or-Ahayim Hospital, still functioning, established as the only Jewish hospital in the city in 1899. The Baghdadi Jewish family, Kedoori, gave a generous donation in 1922, and a small synagogue in the grounds has been named after them.

Inside the walls there used to be several synagogues, and traces of some can still be seen. The spacious Yanbol Synagogue in Ayan Sokak was named after the Bulgarian town Yambol from where many of the first congregation came. The wooden İstipol Synagogue, on Salma Tomruk Sokak, was founded in the early Ottoman period but is today abandoned and rapidly falling into ruin. Nearby, the Kastoria Synagogue, up against the Byzantine land wall, dates from the same period. Opposite the gateway to this synagogue are houses that belonged to one of the wealthier Balat

Jewish families, the Paltis. One nineteenth-century Palti was a doctor to the sultan, and another had a small factory for making fezzes. A Palti was *muhtar* of the Balat quarter. The house had a large garden full of roses and rue, the latter plant having a role in religious ceremonies. There used to be a local Ladino saying, *a tomar aver la kozina de Palti*, meaning "He's gone to take the air in the Paltis' toilets." It was said ironically about someone having made some marvelous journey and alluded to the fact that the sweet-smelling flowers climbed up the walls to the toilets' windows.

Other houses have signs of former Jewish ownership, with a decoration incorporating the Star of David or the Jewish date of the last restoration. One house, across the road from the Ahrida Synagogue at 14 Kürkçü Çeşme Sokak, was the home of Haim Nahum Efendi, Istanbul's chief rabbi from 1908 to 1919. He was more involved in Ottoman politics than his predecessors. He had been educated in France and identified with the Young Turks. He was part of the negotiation team that signed the Ottoman surrender at the end of the First World War at Mudanya in 1918. Perhaps he was too close for his own and his community's good, for he then left Istanbul and went on to be chief rabbi in Egypt, becoming an intimate of King Fuad. The house is of brick, with grey roughcast rendering, and with Art Nouveau ironwork, in which Stars of David can be identified.

The wealthy Babanis, who gave the tapestries to the Ahrida Synagogue, used to live in the house behind the Çana Synagogue at 186 Çiçekli Bostan Sokak. In the 1860s Aaron Babani was the manufacturer of uniforms for the Ottoman army. His house was destroyed to make way for the Milli Cinema. His son, İsak, exported textiles and became *muhtar* of the quarter during the First World War. His house was built in 1913 and was the first in the area to have electricity. The Babani family had to sell off this and other properties to pay the property tax in the Second World War.

Many buildings in the Balat were restored in 2007 and 2008 with funding from the European Union, and it has been anticipated that the area may undergo a process of gentrification.

## THE ROMA

Another community, located alongside Balat, played a minor but persistent role in the kaleidoscope of the Belle Epoque. Like others it has endured, but in recent years has been under threat.

The Roma of Istanbul go back a thousand years. The first reports of Roma in the city date from 1050 when gypsies, allegedly from India, camped outside the walls. After the Ottoman conquest, Sultan Mehmet II gave them permission to settle. The main Roma quarters are in Ayvansaray beyond Balat, not far from the walls and the Golden Horn, and in Sulukule—and, in particular, the areas of Neslişah and Hatice Sultan—a little over a mile (two kilometers) to the southwest. Many of the popular musicians and dancers of the early twentieth century were from this community. In the second James Bond film, *From Russia with Love*, and in the novel of that name by Ian Fleming, the gypsy dancers have their encampment just outside the walls. Fleming had been a journalist in the mid-1950s and had a reasonable acquaintance with Istanbul. Gypsy dancers were hired by households for special entertainments, including bear shows. The chief dancing girl would lead her team, each member carrying veil, yellow boots and fans.

Until the early 1990s Sulukule was an area of popular entertainment, providing a source of income for many Roma. In the process of making Istanbul the European City of Culture in 2010, much of the Sulukule quarter has been demolished on the grounds that the area was rife with drugs, prostitution and illiteracy. As well as popular entertainers, Roma have provided the city with street hawkers, knife grinders, flower sellers and shoemakers. In contrast to many other districts, the Roma people of this area were almost all born in the neighborhood. A network of marriages has made the community one extended family, and they are largely self-sufficient. They have no big protectors, and they are politically weak and vulnerable. The area is potentially valuable, with land values soaring. Some people have sold up. But others do not wish to leave an area that has been home for Roma for centuries.

## Chapter Five
# WALKING THROUGH BELLE EPOQUE ISTANBUL

Istanbul is best explored on foot. The traffic is horrendous, but there are some quarters that have been pedestrianized. Others have very little traffic and it is possible to walk along and admire the buildings without too much risk of being knocked over. This chapter looks in some detail at the legacy of the Belle Epoque period in Istanbul.

### İSTIKLÂL CADDESI/GRANDE RUE DE PERA

The street leading from Taksim to Tünel is called İstiklâl Caddesi. It has for 150 years been a symbol of the city's cosmopolitanism, both its current and its previous names reflecting internationalism. İstiklâl Caddesi means, in Turkish, Independence Street, but it was long known by the French name, Grande Rue de Pera. In the early nineteenth century it was called Cadde-i Cedide, meaning New Street in Ottoman Turkish.

The tramway has been revived, and occasionally a police vehicle cruises through hundreds of people—mostly under thirty—who amble, chat, flirt, look into shop windows or watch other people. It is a very mixed

crowd, mostly Turkish, but foreigners mingle and adopt the slow and sedate pace of *Istanbullus*.

In the last ten years Istanbul has enjoyed an economic revival. Shops with familiar international brand names line the street. There are two Starbucks cafés, but Burger King, McDonalds, United Colors of Benetton, Body Shop and Accessorize all look on to İstiklâl Caddesi. They bear witness to the continued international character of the street.

Mosques and churches also stud the street. The synagogues are just beyond Tünel, discreetly veiled after terrorist outrages in recent years. Several large consulates lie just off the street, bearing the appearance of country houses in spacious grounds. Those belonging to Russia, Britain, the Netherlands and Sweden were built as grand embassies in the middle of the nineteenth century. They are now reduced to being consulates general, since the capital (and the embassies) shifted to the new-old city of Ankara, in the 1920s.

İstiklâl Caddesi's multicultural character goes back to the middle of the nineteenth century. Between the Crimean War and the birth of the modern Republic, the street became the axis of Belle Epoque Constan-

İstiklâl Caddesi

tinople. The shops were not "outlets" of multinational companies, but were owned and managed by people of a score of nationalities; both from the kaleidoscope of communities within the Ottoman Empire—Turk, Arab, Greek, Armenian, Jewish, Balkan and so on—but also from the rest of Europe. Today, the shop fronts, the brand names and the posters reflect contemporary concerns. But when the stroller looks up at the upper storeys and gazes at the buildings as a whole he or she sees a wonderful display of architectural and social history of the last century and a half. Belle Epoque Istanbul begins and ends in İstiklâl Caddesi. If this thoroughfare was the most public face of the internationalization of Istanbul, other districts also reflected profound social economic and financial developments.

## TAKSIM TO TÜNEL

Let us take a walk from Taksim Square along İstiklâl Caddesi, the Grande Rue de Pera, towards Tünel and experience something of the cultural history of the street.

Taksim means distribution. To the right as you enter İstiklâl Caddesi you see a polygonal stone structure. From here water used to be distributed from a tank, linked by stone pipes to reservoirs to the north in the Belgrade Forest. Originally built in the reign of Sultan Mahmud I in the early eighteenth century, the building was restored in 1839. Next door is the French Cultural Center. The building was originally constructed in the seventeenth century as a French hospital for plague victims. It became a building attached to the French Consulate General in 1926.

Just beyond Zambak Sokak on the right are the Fitaş-Dunya Cinemas. It is today a seven-screen complex, with the Fitaş complex upstairs and the Dünya below. This site has been devoted to pleasure for nearly a century, from 1868 housing an observatory and a government meteorological station under the direction of Aristidi Kumbari Efendi, with extensive grounds as an amusement park. Then a cinema was built, called first Kozmograf, then Nuvo ("nouveau") and later Halk Sineması (the People's Cinema). For a short time in the 1930s it became a cabaret with the name Mulen Ruj ("Moulin Rouge") before becoming a cinema again in the late 1950s, doubling also as an operetta stage. The present cinemas were built in the 1960s.

On the other side of the street is the Lale Cinema, first built as a cinema in the 1930s but much restored since. It was the place for the showing of Istanbul's premier films. Further down, just before Kücükpar-makkapı, is Kadri Han, the site of another cinema that was called Yıldız ("star"), but better known as Etual ("étoile"). Long running films used to be shown here. Beyond Kücükparmakkapı Sokak was the Russo-American Cinema. This had a short life and closed in 1925. It owes its name to the fact that, although it used to show American films, it was much frequented by White Russian refugees.

On the right, on the junction of İmam Adnan Sokak, is the ornate Art Nouveau building, designed by A. J. Karakaş, early in the twentieth century for Ragıp Paşa, the court chamberlain of Sultan Abdülhamid II. Just opposite is Hacı Bekir's confectionery, the history of which goes back to 1777 when Ali Muhiddin Hacı Bekir provided sweetmeats for the Sultan and opened a shop in the city. The shop is still celebrated for its *lokum*, Turkish delight.

On the right, the Rumeli Pasajı is another investment of Court Chamberlain Ragıp Paşa. The ground floor is a shopping arcade and at the entrance is the Rebul pharmacy, the successor of one founded by Jean César Reboul at the end of the nineteenth century. Reboul was the President of the Association of Ottoman Pharmacists. Opposite is the Bahçeli Bath house, originally designed by Davut Ağa in the early seventeenth century. It was taken over by Court Chamberlain Ragıp Paşa and was a public bath until 1951.

In the first decade of the twenty-first century İstiklâl Caddesi lost another historic cinema building, the Saray on the right between Sakıza-ğacı Caddesi and Yeşilçam Sokak. The structure occupying the site was known as the Deveaux Apartment Building. On the ground floor the Gaumont (spelt Gomon in Turkish) company opened a cinema. The Gomon specialized in the best of the silent films. In 1930 it was renamed Glorya, and four years later, Saray, and operated under that name for fifty years, closing in 1986. It also served as a concert hall. Louis Armstrong played there.

Opposite was another cinema, Alkazar. It was opened in the early 1920s as the Ciné-Salon Electra and specialized in showing westerns. It ceased to be a cinema in the 1960s, and the lower hall was converted into a beer hall and billiard parlor.

On the left before Ayhan Işık Sokak is the site of the Della Suda Pharmacy. The original founder in 1847 was François Della Suda, who was the pharmacist for the Ottoman army. In 1859 he became a *paşa* and renamed himself Faik. Members of his family opened other Della Suda pharmacies in Istanbul. These lasted well into Republican times.

At the corner there used to be a pastry shop—Nisuaz ("Niçoise")—much favored by writers and artists. It flourished from the 1920s to the 1950s. A bust of Atatürk sculpted by Kenan Yontunç used to be displayed in the window. Atatürk himself came to see it in 1931. Diagonally across the road is the magnificent Emek Building. The French architect Alexandre Vallaury was commissioned to build this in the late 1870s. Vallaury was born in Istanbul and studied architecture in Paris. He was a founder of the Academy of Fine Arts, designed its building and taught there from 1883 to 1907. The Emek Building is in a heavy though confident neo-Renaissance style with statuary on the façade. The most celebrated social club of Istanbul, the Cercle d'Orient or, in Turkish, Serkldoryan, occupied the first floor. The national and foreign elites of the city were all members. Before the First World War Cemal Paşa, Enver Paşa, Talat Paşa and Ferit Paşa, the leaders of the Young Turks, were members. The club features in the novel, *Sweet Waters*, by Harold Nicolson, who, as a young diplomat before 1914, used to eat at the club.

Another member in the first twenty years of the twentieth century was Ali Kemal Bey, a liberal journalist educated in France and married to an Englishwoman. He fell foul of the Young Turks and evaded capture and probable execution in 1909, but, under the Allied occupation after the war became minister of the interior just when Mustafa Kemal was raising the standard of revolt against the Ottoman Imperial regime. Ali Kemal Bey issued a decree that acknowledged Mustafa Kemal's patriotism but suggested that he did not understand politics. Mustafa Kemal was dismissed and people, Ali Kemal said, were under no obligation to follow his instructions. Because of his clear-cut repudiation of Mustafa Kemal at such a crucial moment, Ali Kemal later became a marked man. In November 1922, shortly after the triumph of the nationalist forces under Mustafa Kemal, Ali Kemal Bey was seized from near the Cercle d'Orient and taken to a boat and on to İzmit where he was interrogated by a court. When he left the court a crowd tore him to pieces and his body was hanged from a lamppost. The son he left by his English wife, Osman Wilfred, assumed the surname Johnson after his English grandmother and became a farmer on Exmoor. His grandson is Boris Johnson—like the great grandfather, a journalist and politician, currently Mayor of London.

After the Republic was founded the club was renamed Büyük Kulüp.

Just beyond Fuat Uzkınay Sokak is the Anadolu Pasajı, another mall. It was built on more land owned by Ragıp Paşa, and used to house smart furnishings and fabric stores. It was also the site of the Brasserie de l'Orient but was renamed, after a change of ownership, the Anadolu Birahanesi (Anatolian Beer-saloon) in 1934, another favorite haunt of artists.

Almost opposite is Halep Pasajı (Aleppo Mall), commissioned by an Aleppo merchant called Haccar. On the ground floor there used to be a pastry shop and a beer hall. The rear parts were burned down in 1904 and a theater was constructed that had various successive names—Varyete, Fransız Teatrosu and Ses. It now houses a theater company.

Across the road is Atlas Pasajı, built in 1870 for the Köçeoğlu family. Sultan Abdülaziz used to have a suite of rooms here. It now is the home of the State Gallery of the Fine Arts, a small but lively theater and some antique and gift shops.

Just before Zurnacıbaşı Sokak on the left was the site of one of the oldest cinemas in Istanbul. Sigmund Weinberg brought the cinema projector to the city and the cinema here was first named Sine-Palas, then Eden and then, until it closed in 1954, Chic.

On the right is the office of the Istanbul Foundation for Culture and the Arts. This foundation organizes the Istanbul Film Festival in April, the Istanbul Theatre Festival in May, the Istanbul Music Festival in June and the Istanbul Jazz Festival in July. Another of the street's famous pastry shops was here. It opened as L'Orient in 1923, changed its name to Baylan under the pressure to Turkify business, and was another popular resort for the leading writers of the Republican period. It closed in 1967, but another branch of Baylan is still in business today in the Kadıköy market on the Asian side.

The grand building on the right, surmounted by a dome, used to be one of the smartest hotels in town. Some pastry shops—one with the name Café-Restaurant de Paris—were owned by an Armenian, Migirdich Tokatlıyan. Many of these were destroyed by a fire in 1892 and Tokatlıyan commissioned Alexandre Vallaury to build a hotel on the site. Like the Emek Building it is in a Renaissance revival style. The hotel was completed in 1897, with 160 rooms. All the furnishings and fixtures were imported from Europe. Huge fashionable balls were held here. Fashionable writers used to gather in the lobby. Guests who stayed included Leon Trotsky, on his way to exile on one of the Princes' Islands, and Agatha Christie. Tokatlıyan also opened a hotel in Tarabya (Therapia), for the summer season, when the Pera embassies migrated for the season to the Upper Bosphorus.

At the end of the block is Çiçek Pasajı (Flower Arcade). One of Istanbul's earliest theaters, the Naum Theatre, was opened here in 1840, was burned down in 1847 but reconstructed the following year. It then became the major theatrical venue in the city and companies came from Europe to put on classical plays. The sultans were patrons, and the court assisted the theater financially. The Prince of Wales, on his ten-day visit in 1869, came to this theater three times to see popular light operas, just a year before it was destroyed in the fire in 1870.

The theater was replaced by the Cité de Pera, built for the owner, Christakis Zographos, by the architect, Kleanthes Zannos, in 1876. It became one of the most remarkable buildings of the street. It was from the beginning provided with gas and running water and all the amenities of modern European life. The ground floor housed shops, but a marble staircase led up to apartments on three upper floors. An Istanbul French-language newspaper at the time wrote, "We can confidently say that Pera has been adorned with a monument that gives honor not only to its owner, but also to the entire city, and which marks the beginning of a new era for the architecture of the country." It became the reference point for later malls, and for other multi-functional, multi-story buildings around the city. After the First World War flower auctions were held here and it became popularly known as Çiçek Pasajı. After the 1917 Russian Revolution it was the haunt of impoverished refugees. During the Allied occupation of the city up to 200,000 Russians turned up. "Those who had brought a few valuables with them," reported George Young,

> took over every cabaret, cookshop, and café in Pera. The less fortunate ladies hired themselves out as waitresses or worse. The men hawked their clothes on Galata bridge or sold their useless swords to any service. The gay courage shown by these mayflies was only equalled by their improvidence. The best of them, men and women, suffered the most. A Russian ambassador and his wife, whom I had last seen in semi-regal state, ruling Pera and the Porte, I found living by teaching. A com-

Cité de Pera

mander-in-chief upon a war-front, who had made history, was growing cabbages, and not even his own cabbages.

During the 1920s and 1930s the Degustasyon restaurant on the ground floor of the Cité de Pera was a fashionable meeting place for writers. But after that the building was neglected and the arcade collapsed in 1978. It was rebuilt and reopened in its present form in 1988: much of its former distinct grandeur is preserved. The original name can still be read below the ornate cornice over the archway, flanked by caryatides.

The building that became the Galatasaray Post Office, from 1907 to 1998, was built as a block of apartments in 1875. It is another classical revival construction, solid and stately rather than distinguished.

Galatasaray, the Palace of Galata, is the school behind the lofty iron railings on the left. In the sixteenth century there were barracks here, and a school was founded to induct fresh soldiers. Three centuries later, in 1868, the school was recast with a European curriculum, and renamed the Imperial School. It became a medical training center in 1873 but the buildings reverted to a school three years later. It became the Eton of

Turkey, its graduates having been among the elites of business and the professions. The famous soccer team was a spinoff of the school and was founded in 1907.

The road running down on the left is Yeniçarşı Caddesi. On the right is a restaurant owned by the octogenarian photographer, Ara Güler. Güler, who is Armenian, has been taking haunting and evocative pictures in black and white of the quarters and people of the city since 1950. Some of his photographs, enlarged, adorn the walls of the restaurant. Others can be seen on the menus and table settings.

The very first cinema in the city was set up on the right, just beyond Meşrutiyet Caddesi. A beer hall, called Sponeck Birahanesi, was where in 1897 Sigmund Weinberg set up a projector with films supplied by Lumière Frères from Paris. Weinberg was a Romanian and came to the city as the representative of Pathé and sold photographic equipment. He also opened a cinema at Tepebaşı near the Pera Palas Hotel. In 1915 he became head of the Central Army Cinematic Office but was dismissed when Romania joined the Allies against the Ottoman Empire. He returned after the war, however, and ran the Ciné-Palas movie theater. The beer hall was closed in the 1930s.

The Galatasaray Meydanı, the square between the old Post Office and the school, has since 1995 been the site of demonstrations every Saturday by relations of people who, for political reasons, have been taken into police custody. Meşrutiyet Caddesi winds off to the right towards the British Consulate General. İstiklâl Caddesi takes a left turn.

The Aznavur Pasajı, on the right has a narrow entry and can easily be overlooked. But the Art Nouveau ironwork over the entrance and on the upper balconies is worth contemplating, as well as the mosaics on the floor of the entrance. At the end of the nineteenth century this mall used to house some of the most fashionable stores in town—Zapontis for clocks, Vitalis for footwear and Nomismaditis for musical instruments: all had Greek owners.

On the left is the grand façade of the Mısır Apartment Building. *Mısır* means Egypt, and it was built in 1910 on the site of a theater as a town house for the Egyptian *hıdiv* (viceroy, usually spelt *khedive* in English), Abbas Hilmi, later deposed by the British in 1914. Originally one unit, it has since been divided into apartments. Its unique feature is the triple façade of balconies overlooking the street.

The Hacopulo Pasajı is named after a Greek tailor who had his premises here. The mall is not all enclosed, and boasts a somewhat minimal garden. Number 13 used to have a printing press that issued the liberal newspaper of Namık Kemal and Ahmet Midhat Efendi in the early 1870s.

To the right is a turning into Emir Nevruz Sokak, which is some fifty yards long, with a Greek Orthodox church at the end. Turning left into Olivya Geçidi, we come to the Rejans restaurant on the right. It was founded in 1932 and replaced the Turquoise restaurant. The proprietors were Mikhail Mikhailovich and Abdürrahman Şirin, and the place had a White Russian ambience and clientele. The waiters were allegedly grand dukes in reduced circumstances. As well as chicken Kiev, boeuf Strogonoff, bortsch and vodka, a feature of the place for decades was the piano music played by the Baroness Valentina von Klodt Jurgensburg, who later simplified her surname to Taskin. She used to wear orange slippers and black silk dresses. A fire caused the place to close in 1976 but it reopened, refurbished, the following year. Abdürrahman Şirin bequeathed his share of the restaurant to his nephew and the place still preserves a tang of the 1930s.

Russians have continued to find a home in the city, which has sustained its millennium-old reputation as a mart for traders from the northeast. The rich Russians buy clothes in Nişantaşı, the poorer buy white goods and cheap clothes in Aksaray. Russian girls find questionable jobs in night-clubs between Taksim and Tünel.

Across the road is the Church of St. Antony of Padua, the premier Roman Catholic church of Beyoğlu. It was built in 1906 replacing a theater, the architects being two Italians, Giulio Mongeri and Edoardo de Nari. The parish traces its history back to the thirteenth century when Franciscans built a chapel in Galata. This was destroyed in 1696, and a small chapel was built further up the hill on what became İstiklâl Caddesi. Two more churches were built and then destroyed before the present brick Italian gothic pile was built. Shops between the church and the road were rented out to help fund the building.

Diagonally across the road is Elhamra Pasajı. This wonderful building was designed in 1920 by a Turkish architect, Ekrem Hakkı Ayverdi and contains an eclectic range of styles; gothic arches frame the windows and the first and second floors on the right hand side. Slender classical columns between the rectangular windows rise to a neo-Islamic *muqarnas* blind archway. It is well worth while to pause and contemplate this example of multiculturalism frozen in stone. The building marks the site of a French theater dating back to 1827. In 1861 a ballroom called the Crystal Palace was added. Those buildings were torn down in 1920 for the present construction. Kallavi Sokak on the right is named after an Italian family, Glavani, who in the nineteenth century owned much property in the area, including the site that became the Grand Hôtel de Londres.

On the left between Eski Çiçekçi Sokak and Nuru Ziya Sokak is the site of the shop and residence of Ernest Commendiger. The family were piano makers and had two musical instrument shops in Pera. They provided the sultan's family with sheet music and instruments, and in 1847 Franz Liszt stayed with them for a month—as a plaque on the wall of a building now belonging to the freemasons thirty meters down Nuru Ziya Sokak bears witness. The last caliph, Abdülmecid II, was a lover of music and entertained plans in the early 1920s to transform this site into an arts center, making use of the piano that Liszt had used.

Music was an enduring passion with the Ottoman imperial family during the last century of the empire, encompassing listening, playing and even composing. The Sultan Abdülaziz, otherwise fairly relaxed, exerted himself to compose dances that were published in Lucca, Italy. In 1867 he paid a state visit to Britain—the first Ottoman Emperor to visit Europe with peaceful intentions. The Prince of Wales hosted a reception a Marlborough House, and a smart courtier arranged for the band of the Grenadier Guards, under the baton of the fashionable conductor Sir Dan Godfrey, to play the sultan's *La Gondole Barcarolle* as part of the evening's programme.

Beyond Nuru Ziya Sokak is the Beyoğlu Anadolu Lycée. The school has an interesting history. Originally a girls' secondary school was established here in 1842, with support from the wife of the British Ambassador, Stratford Canning. Catering initially for the daughters of resident British diplomats, it closed during periods of crisis and war but opened as the English High School for Girls in 1920. In 1979 it was nationalized to become part of the state system of English medium schools—the Anadolu schools.

On the other side of the road and back from it is the Armenian Catholic Church of Surp Yerrortutyun (Holy Trinity). The site had provided Catholic churches from 1699 but Napoleon III persuaded Sultan

Abdülaziz to reassign the site to Istanbul's Armenian community, and this church was designed by Garabed Balyan.

The cul-de-sac to the right, Deva Çıkmazı, leads to a building with a dusty plaque indicating that it was the Istanbul headquarters of the Società Operaia Italiana di Mutuo Succorso, the Italian Workers' Association. The present construction was designed by Alexandre Vallaury on the site of an earlier building where Garibaldi stayed in 1831. The society was founded in 1863 with the purpose of caring for the widows and orphans of the Italian community and also of promoting Italian culture in the city. In the 1920s and 1930s Mussolini aimed to galvanize Italian communities in the Levant. The communities found the Rome government was ready to fund community hospitals, schools and cultural associations and membership of the Fascist Party was a useful leverage for the securing of funds. The interior decoration has a faded imperial grandeur, with sash reliefs on the wall over the stairway and above a bust of Garibaldi.

There are a number of former embassies in and off İstiklâl Caddesi. Five are of outstanding architectural interest. On the left in its own grounds is the Netherlands Consulate General. It occupies a site that was originally a "factory" belonging to the Dutch community—a commercial center, houses and warehouses. The present building was constructed in 1854 and designed by two brothers, Giuseppe and Gaspare Fossati. They had worked in Russia earlier. Gaspari was brought to Istanbul in 1837 to build the Russian Embassy. Giuseppe then joined him. They stayed on and, in addition to designing many buildings, restored the Church of the Holy Wisdom, the Ayasofya Mosque.

Another grand Roman Catholic church, Sancta Maria Draperis, lies to the left, approached by descending a flight of steps. The site has been in the hands of the Church since the seventeenth century. The present building is the third on the site, basically eighteenth-century but heavily restored in 1904.

Number 201 on the left can be easily missed. It houses an old-fashioned shop selling clocks and antiques. The iron grill gateway portrays a giant beetle in an Art Nouveau style, and the wall and windows have decorations that suggest Charles Rennie Mackintosh. The architects are named in a stone by the doorway: Yenidunia and Kyriakides, a Turkish-Greek partnership.

Across the road just before Gönül Sokak is the Cité de Syrie or Suriye

Çarşısı, originally built as three separate buildings in 1908. They were later amalgamated to form an arcade. It housed a downmarket cinema, with ancient films and cheap seats, which started as Ciné Centrale in 1911 and over the course of the decades was named Şafak ("Dawn"), Cumhuriyet ("Republic") and finally, if inappropriately, Zafer ("Triumph").

In well-tended gardens behind a barrier on the left is the Russian Consulate General, designed by Gaspare Fossati and built between 1838 and 1845. The soil on which it was built, legend has it, was brought from Russia. It was built as the Russian Embassy and is not, as a sequence in the James Bond film *From Russia with Love* suggests, built above one of the Byzantine cisterns. It was one of the first major diplomatic constructions in Pera, but, because of rocky relations between the Ottoman Empire and Russia, closed down periodically.

The Markiz Pastry Shop is worth a visit. One of the most celebrated cake shops Le Bon's, dating back to 1840, was previously on this site. It 1940 it relocated across the road and its replacement here became the most famous café in Pera. Alexandre Vallaury designed the two Art Nouveau

Art Nouveau Markiz Pastry Shop

tile panels, depicting two of the four seasons, spring and autumn. Summer and winter were destroyed en route from Paris, and the cut-glass replacements were designed locally by Mazhar Resmol. It recently reopened and serves cakes for chocoholics and ice creams for the gourmet. It also serves a drink called *salep*, usually regarded as a winter drink. *Salep* is a powder made from the resinous roots of an orchid and is added to warm milk, brought to a boil and stirred vigorously. Cinnamon or pistachio nuts may be added. The derivation of the word is curious. *Salep* is from the Arabic *tha'lab* meaning fox, but the full name for the root is *khusa tha'lab*, meaning fox's testicles, for this apparently is what the orchid root looks like. The *salep* at the Markiz Pastry Shop is a work of art.

Kumbaracı Yokuşu is a steep and narrow road to the left. It is believed to follow the route taken by the ships transported overland by Sultan Mehmet II from the Bosphorus to the Golden Horn during the 1453 Siege of Constantinople.

Just beyond Kumbaracı Yokuşu on the left is the Hıdivyal Palas. This is on the site of the first "European" hotel in Istanbul, opened by a man called Missirie in 1841 as the Hotel d'Angleterre. Over the years it had many changes of name—Hallas Brothers, Egypt Hotel, Hıdiv Hotel—before it closed as a hotel in 1950, assumed its present name and became a business center. It used to be the center of Levantine and international social life for half a century. The balls were glittering and the French cuisine sumptuous. The author Pierre Loti stayed here several times.

Next door but one is the Botter Building. Jean Botter, a Dutchman, was Sultan Abdülhamid II's tailor. This building is the work of that sultan's favored architect, the Italian Raimondo D'Aronco. The ground floor was designed for a shop and a workshop, with the residential quarters upstairs. Built in 1900, this is the first Istanbul example of Art Nouveau, typified in the wrought iron balconies and the decoration around the doorways. Decoration is part of the façade, not added to it: the wall was a malleable two dimensional surface, integral to the construction of the building. There is a flow, a plasticity, in the building and the metallic elements—the ironwork of the balconies and the small columns—are in no way concealed. D'Aronco (1857–1932) was born in northern Italy and was sent by the Italian government to Istanbul in 1893 to design an Ottoman National Exhibition, on the model of the great European exhibitions. A devastating earthquake in 1894 put an end to that project. D'Aronco was a restless soul, studied Byzantine and Ottoman art and architecture and was an early user of glass and iron in large constructions. The Ottoman government and, in particular, the Sultan Abdülhamid II, gave him other commissions in the city.

Botter sold the building to an Egyptian *paşa*, Husni Hasan, whose heiress daughter, Zeyneb, died in 1993. Since then there has been a dispute over the ownership, and although one floor is occupied, nobody has any incentive to invest in the upkeep or improvement of the place. Inside there are niches on the staircases with a few remaining Art Nouveau ironwork lamp holders. The whole building has a sad and neglected appearance.

A little further down on the left is the Swedish Consulate General. This was designed by an Austrian architect, Pulgher, and built in 1871. Fashionable shops lined the pavement until the 1970s.

On the right, just before Mücyyet Sokak, is the Narmanlı Hanı. It is not the most exciting building in the street artistically, but its history reflects some of the social changes to Pera before it became the highway of Belle Epoque Istanbul. It was built at the beginning of the nineteenth century and owes much to the tradition of the early modern caravanserais. There is a courtyard off which rooms might have been used for merchants, their goods and their animals. (The gateway is tall enough for a laden camel.) But before and even after the Russian Embassy was built, Narmanlı Hanı provided consular offices—and stables—for the Russian diplomatic mission. Russians occupied parts of the building until 1932, while other parts of the building have housed a jail. Until recently one of Turkey's oldest surviving newspapers was published from this building. The Armenian language *Jamanak* was founded in 1908 by two brothers named Koçunyan. It was renamed *Jamanak-Türkiye* in 1935 and today is issued from the basement of the church, a couple of hundred meters up the road.

If we double back and turn left along Asmalımescit Sokak we enter an area of cheap hotels, indifferent buildings with exceptional bits of decoration. Some twentieth-century writers lived in apartments facing the street and one, Fikret Adil, lived at number 47. His house was a rendezvous for artists and writers and he wrote a book on the area, called *Asmalımescit 74*.

But let us continue to the end of İstiklâl Caddesi to a little square at the entrance to Tünel, the underground railway station. The roads and alleys from the Golden Horn to İstiklâl Caddesi are very steep. Yüksek

Kaldırım, the road from Karaköy Square up the hill to İstiklâl Caddesi, is still a long series of steps. In the 1870s it was reckoned that 40,000 pairs of feet used it each day. Sedan chairs for the fashionable continued in use.

Sedan chairs in Istanbul were just contemporary with the underground railway that runs from Karaköy to this point, known as Tünel. An Imperial decree of 1869 awarded the contract to build an underground funicular to a Frenchman, Eugène-Henri Gavand. He formed a company, the Metropolitan Railway of Constantinople, and work from Galata to Pera started in 1872. Delays were caused by disputes with property owners on the route, but the service began in January 1875. The line is just over a third of a mile (570 meters) in length, and is the third oldest underground line in the world—after London (1863) and New York (1868). Two-car trains operated on each of the parallel lines. The first cars were divided into one compartment for men, and one for women. A third compartment carried goods, animals and sometimes horse-drawn carriages. There was a grand opening with champagne and choice wines, served by a French confectioner, the father of the architect, Alexandre Vallaury. The streetcars have been periodically replaced. The railway was nationalized in the early days of the Republic and since 1939 it has been managed by the Istanbul municipality. The journey takes a minute and a half.

Religion, pastry shops, cosmopolitanism, consumerism and entertainment—these have been persistent themes in and around the Grande Rue de Pera/İstiklâl Caddesi since the Crimean War. From the 1990s there has been a revival of the street. A greater awareness of the extraordinary artistic and cultural heritage of its buildings, an economic boom that has affected the whole city, the increase of cultural tourism: all have helped the street and its neighboring areas to adjust and adapt, without any sacrifice of its integrity or its historic identity. There have been reverses. Buildings have been lost. Others are in dire need of tender loving care. But its character remains what it was and it is one of the great streets of the world.

## From Tünel to Pera House

Opposite the entrance to the underground station is Tünel Pasajı, flanked by tall apartment buildings. It is possible to walk back through the café to Asmalımescit Sokak which runs from İstiklâl Caddesi down to the Pera Palas Hotel.

This was the grand hotel of Istanbul. The first owner was the company that owned the railway lines to Western Europe. This company formed a subsidiary to manage the hotel—the Compagnie Internationale des Grands Hôtels. The subsidiary also provided catering for the Orient Express when it left Istanbul for Europe. Built to designs by Alexandre Vallaury, construction began in May 1892 and the hotel was opened in October the following year. It was a pioneering establishment, with an electric lift and its own generator. Much of the décor, including the lifts, and atmosphere date from before the First World War.

Its rival was the Tokatlıyan Hotel which, with its dances and shows, was older and had a reputation for frivolity. The Pera Palas, with its bar, was more intellectual.

The state took over the hotel in 1923, and a Syrian, Misbah Muhayyeş, first managed and then five years later bought it. His family managed the hotel through a trust until the 1970s, when a businessman from Gaziantep, Hasan Süzer, bought out the Muhayyeş interest and undertook major restoration. Hasan Süzer appreciated the historic importance of the hotel without diminishing the quality of the services. He collected old documents relating to its past: menus, guest lists, letters and photographs.

Some of its former guests are commemorated by bedrooms named after them, such as Agatha Christie. The room, number 101, occupied by Mustafa Kemal Atatürk, has become a museum with several of his clothes and personal possessions. These were not carelessly left behind by an apparently absentminded guest whose attention was focused on higher things, but acquired by Hasan Süzer, from one of Atatürk's bodyguards.

To the north of the hotel on the left is open space, with an exhibition hall and a terraced café looking down onto the Golden Horn. Below is an underground car park. It all looked very different a hundred years ago. In the late nineteenth and early twentieth centuries the road north of the Pera Palas rivalled the Grande Rue de Pera as a highway of chic fashion. In place of the open space and hall there was a small public park known as Les Petits Champs des Morts, after a former cemetery that occupied the site. (Les Grands Champs des Morts was at Taksim Square.) The terrace was built up from earth excavated from the tunnel made for the underground railway nearby. The small park had a theater, designed by a Greek assistant to Raimondo D'Aronco, which opened in 1880, and programs included

"Tortoise Trainer" by Osman Hamdi

French comedies, Italian operas and Viennese operettas. Sarah Bernhardt played here. In 1972 the theater was destroyed by fire, the gardens of the park were razed and the site took its present form. Today, alas, it is a place where alcoholics and drug addicts congregate.

Across the road is the Casa d'Italia, formerly the Italian Embassy and now the Italian Cultural Center. The architect was Alexandre Breschi, who completed the building in 1867.

The street used to have three smart hotels. The Pera Palas was the first. The second was the Bristol Hotel, designed by another Greek architect, Achille Manoussos, in 1893, his work and that of other Greek architects rarely departing from neoclassicism. The Bristol Hotel has been taken over by the Suna and İnan Kıraç Foundation and completely renovated by the architect Sinan Genim, since 2005 operating as the Pera Museum. As well as a museum of Anatolian weights and measures and a collection of Kütahya tiles, it houses one of the most enjoyable collections of paintings in the city. There are splendid portraits of the sultans and ambassadors as well as of social scenes of elite Istanbul of the eighteenth and nineteenth centuries. These are of enormous historic and artistic interest. The portraits of the Count and Countess of Vergennes, French ambassador and ambassadress in 1766, make them seem distinctly uncomfortable in Turkish attire.

Several paintings are by the Italian, Fausto Zonaro (1854-1929), who came to Istanbul in 1891. He was fascinated by "the orient" and was a prolific painter of daily scenes, and of portraits of ordinary men and women. He sold paintings to a book stall and gave art lessons—one of his students became the mother of Nâzim Hikmet, Turkey's most accomplished twentieth-century poet and a committed communist who died in Moscow. He had several paintings commissioned by members of the diplomatic community.

There are several iconic Zonaros in the Pera Museum. One is of a girl at Göksu (the Sweet Waters of Asia), the fashionable resort on the Asian shore of the Bosphorus. A fair faced girl takes center stage (or center canvas) on a boat on the water. In the background can be seen Anadolu Hisarı among smart villas, and pleasure boats are being rowed. This painting may actually have been painted after Zonaro left the city.

Another wonderful Zonaro is entitled "The Daughter of the English Ambassador Riding in a Palanquin." The young lady, whose face can hardly be seen, is in a palanquin being borne by two uniformed bearers whose heads are lowered. Counterbalancing them, two tall proud swordsmen walk, one in front and one behind. The bearers shuffle and the swordsmen stride through a garden, actually the garden of the British Embassy, two hundred meters from this museum. The painting was commissioned in 1896 by the British Ambassador, Sir Philip Currie, and the young woman portrayed is actually his step-daughter and was on her way to her wedding. Beyond the garden perimeter Stamboul can be seen in the distance, beyond the invisible Golden Horn. It may seem slightly excessive for four servants to escort a young lady round her own garden, and according to Zonaro's memoirs, the group posed for the artist over several days. In the same year Zonaro presented one painting of cavalry crossing Galata Bridge to Sultan Abdülhamid II. The sultan liked the gift and appointed him court painter, providing him and his family with a studio and a home in the Akaret apartments in Beşiktaş, built as a terrace of homes for palace workers and now transformed into luxury flats and shops. Many of his paintings commissioned by the sultan line the corridors of Dolmabahçe Palace. Zonaro remained in favor until his patron was deposed in 1909. After that he retired to San Remo.

A third Zonaro, "Woman Playing a Stringed Instrument," has a woman in daily attire, strumming a lute (*ut*). Playing music was a popular pastime among upper-class women. What is particularly interesting is that this painting is an echo of another painting in the same room, "Two Musician Girls" by Osman Hamdi Bey. In this picture one girl is standing, strumming a lute, and another is sitting on the floor, apparently tapping a tambourine. Both paintings—the Zonaro and the Hamdi—might be defined as "orientalist." There is much that is similar in the work of Hamdi and Zonaro in the portrayal of women. Zonaro's girl is more realistic—she is absorbed in her music—while Hamdi's girls are a little more stylized. But in both cases they are not objects, seen from the outside, but participating creative individuals, seemingly unaware of being observed.

There are several other paintings by Osman Hamdi in the Pera Museum. The best known is perhaps "Tortoise Trainer," portraying a dervish—based on a photograph of Hamdi himself—thoughtfully looking at four or five tortoises at his feet, surrounded by bits of greenery, presumably food. He holds a reed flute behind him and has a kettledrum over his shoulder. The location of the scene is an upper room of the Green

Mosque in Bursa. It is a compelling picture—and you can buy a copy on a mouse pad in the museum shop—but what is he training the tortoises to do?

The third fine old hotel of Belle Epoque Petits Champs is the Grand Hôtel de Londres, otherwise Büyük Londra Oteli. This is another fine neo-classical pile, with caryatides replacing columns to support the entablature on the second floor. Originally called the London Hotel when it was first opened in 1891, it was renamed the Belle Vue before acquiring its present portmanteau name. The comfortable bar is full of dead junk and live parrots.

## THE BRITISH CONSULATE GENERAL

A little further north on the left are the tall walls of the British Consulate General, previously the embassy to the Ottoman Empire. The first embassy on this site was built in 1801, but a devastating fire destroyed this and other embassies in Pera in 1831. The sultan offered a house at Tarabya, twelve miles up the Bosphorus, and this offer was accepted. In 1841 W. J. Smith of the Department of Woods and Forests in London came out to Istanbul and made plans for a new building on this site, 120 by 160 feet (36 by 50 meters) with a marble staircase dominating one of the shorter sides. Sir Charles Barry, the architect of the Houses of Parliament that arose from the ashes of the fire of 1834, inspected, modified and approved the plans.

Smith settled in Istanbul to execute the building. It took thirteen years to complete. The construction coincided with the building of the Dolmabahçe Palace, and the sultan was in a position to commandeer supplies of stone as well as available stonemasons. When Smith did recruit a dozen masons, the sultan sent soldiers to pressgang these for his own work. One slipped back to the embassy, was recaptured by the sultan's troops and received a public flogging. For this building stone had to be brought from further afield.

As the building went up, it was realized that the foundations were weak and extra stone had to be laid down, sometimes to a depth of twenty feet (six meters). Consequently, the building has no cellar.

Meanwhile Smith, although a paid official of the British government, was receiving profitable commissions to design other buildings in the city. Two of his masterpieces survive. He designed a School of Medicine, now the Faculty of Architecture of the University of Istanbul, today overlooking the Beşiktaş soccer stadium. (The writer Orhan Pamuk started to study architecture here in the early 1970s.) He was also responsible for the nearby Gümüşsuyu Military Hospital, which had the innovation of central heating.

By 1848 the ambassador could occupy the upper residential floor and six years later the whole embassy was able to take up permanent occupation. The original estimated costs of $55,000 had risen to an actual expenditure of $130,000.

Known as Pera House, it is another example of Renaissance revival and can remind the viewer of the Travelers' Club and the Reform Club in Pall Mall, London—both Barry works. The classical style was no longer fashionable and, like the Pall Mall clubs, the source of inspiration was the Palazzo Farnese in Rome. It surrounds a court, closed by a glass roof. The opening was celebrated by a Christmas ball in December 1855 during the Crimean War. One of the guests was Florence Nightingale taking time off from her work with injured soldiers across the Bosphorus at Üsküdar (Scutari).

Twenty five years later, the wife of a later ambassador, the Marchioness of Dufferin and Ava, described her first impressions of the building:

> You enter through big doors into a great court, with a marble floor, which originally was open, but is now covered with a glass roof... All round this, with windows opening on to it on each storey, is a great wide corridor, on to which the rooms open. From the court you go up a fine marble staircase, and, after looking at the gallery, you visit the reception rooms; two sitting-rooms and a waiting-room for his Excellency, two drawing-rooms and a waiting-room for me. I was pleased with these rooms; they are well-furnished, and not too gigantic. Then come a big ball-room, a dining-room, a billiard-room. This is only two sides of the square; a third side is taken up by staircases (even the back-stairs are marble), and the secretaries' rooms. Upstairs we have eleven bedrooms, out of which I have to get school-room, day-nursery, and a boudoir for myself; for as there are eighty-seven high steps up to this floor, I must have a sitting-room at the top of them.

In a prominent position on the ground floor is a bust of Stratford

Canning, later Viscount Stratford de Redcliffe, who presided over the opening of the building. Stratford Canning served four times in the city, the first time in 1808. He has become the epitome of the British Ambassador: cool, omniscient, domineering, detached, hard-working and conscientious.

A cousin of the prime minister George Canning, Stratford Canning really wanted a political career, but he came out to Constantinople as secretary to the mission at the age of twenty-one in 1808. "The environs of Constantinople," he recalled in memoirs, "were at that time infested with robbers; the danger was however not sufficient to prevent excursions into the country. A member of the Embassy rarely went out to any distance without the protection of the Janissary or armed attendant, and the ambassador was always preceded by a bodyguard even in the streets." His first ambassador rented a house in a Greek village in the Belgrade Forest. On his first posting to the city Canning was unimpressed by the people he met:

> With the exception of the few English who are here, and of the Austrian, Spanish, and Swedish missions—all very meagre—the Christian population of this city is an *omnium gatherum* from all the dunghills of Europe. Equally destitute of education, manners, and common-sense, with no oppressive load of honesty, they are not fit company for our servants. With the Turks we can have but little intercourse in the way of society. A lady according to our English notions is here an unknown animal. One might as well talk of a red goose. The French, headed by a chargé d'affaires of the name of Maubourg, are the vilest scum that ever fell from the overboilings of the pot of Imperial Jacobinism.

He did meet Byron on this first posting of whose good nature and varied conversation he retained sixty years later "a most agreeable recollection." Yet his memories of another well-connected visitor were less happy. The eccentric Lady Hester Stanhope, niece of William Pitt, hired a house at Tarabya for the winter of 1810–11. She fraternized with the French Ambassador, the despised Maubourg, from whom she wanted a visa to visit France. France and Britain were then at war and the young Canning rather prissily told her she should get permission from the British government to visit enemy territory. She wrote at once to the secretary of state for foreign affairs, a withering letter of complaint: "Mr Canning is young and inexperienced, full of zeal but full of prejudice… as he is both a religious and political Methodist, after having appeared to doubt my love for my country, he will next presume to teach me my duty to my God!"

At the age of twenty-four he spent his last year as head of mission. He did learn some Turkish but was otherwise uninterested in the Turks, and was happy to leave what he called "this vile hole," "that semi-barbarous capital," expecting never to return.

Postings in Switzerland and America followed. He returned to the city in 1826, as part of the negotiations for the independence of Greece. Like many of his class and generation, he was soaked in the classics and in his extreme old age amused himself translating English nursery rhymes into Greek iambics. He always saw himself as one of the liberators of Greece, though was disappointed with the actuality of the Kingdom of Greece—"disunion, and party hatred, and political intrigue carried to the worst extremes." He was no more enamored of the Imperial capital: "These rascally Turks continue as impracticable as ever," he wrote to his cousin, then prime minister. "They are much worse than when I was here last." His temporary stay in Constantinople coincided with the suppression of the Janissaries by the Sultan Mahmud II, and he was a witness to the terror that haunted the streets of the capital. During the 1830s he withdrew from his diplomatic career and spent some years as a member of parliament, first for the rotten borough of Old Sarum, then for the slightly less rotten borough of Stockbridge and finally for King's Lynn.

Foiled in his hopes of a ministerial career, he reluctantly accepted appointment again as ambassador to Constantinople in 1842. The expectation of becoming secretary of state for foreign affairs or ambassador in Paris eluded him in 1852 and he stayed on until 1858, when he was over seventy. He became reconciled to the city, and charitably observed changes, sartorial and ceremonial, that reflected the reforms. "Very few years more," he wrote,

> and not a turban will exist. Grand Vezir, Reis Efendi, Ulema, employees of every description, now wear the red cap, cossack trousers, black boots, and a plain red or blue cloak buttoned under the chin. No gold

embroidery, no jewels, no pelisses. The Sultan wears a blue jacket, Cossack trousers, black boots, and the red cap like the others.

Canning's influence on many aspects of Turkish society, from ministerial appointments downwards, was allegedly formidable. He was regarded as a friend of Turkey and could be prolix in his reports. Although he lived into the age of the telegraph he was instinctively a plenipotentiary, in pursuit of British interests without having to consult Whitehall. For most of the time he got away with it. He fully supported Turkish reforms that improved the legal status of non-Muslims. In his last sixteen years he dealt with only one sultan, Abdülmecid, thirty years his junior. For many years the grand vizier was Mustafa Reşit Paşa, who had been ambassador in London. Canning had a very good working relationship with both men. ("By birth and education a gentleman, by nature of a kind and liberal disposition," Canning wrote in his memoirs, "Reshid had more to engage my sympathies than any other of his race and class.") Outside work, Canning took exercise by boar-shooting in the Belgrade Forest or attending the opera (which "bad as it looks, is really very tolerable. But we do not go often, though we have a box, which is the envy of all the diplomatic corps"). He was a good entertainer, and his residence became a kind of constant guest-house. Mustafa Reşit Paşa used to come with his children—but not, one suspects, with his wife.

After the 1848 uprisings in the Hapsburg Empire, the Hungarian nationalist Lajos Kossuth found refuge at the embassy, which became even more of an international venue during the Crimean War. Canning was the personal hinge between the British allies and the Ottoman Empire.

When he finally left he looked with satisfaction on the changes he had seen. In 1856 he had invested the sultan with the Order of the Garter. (The previous year, the French Ambassador had invested the sultan with the Légion d'Honneur: the sultan saw this honor as a sign of the Ottoman Empire's admission to "the great family of Europe.") Later in the year, the sultan attended a *bal costumé* at the newly built embassy. As the sultan alighted from his carriage an electric wire communicated the fact to the British fleet in the Bosphorus. They fired a salvo of cannons, and the band in the palm court played national anthems.

This building was damaged in the great fire of Pera in 1870, although Smith had claimed that the building was incombustible. The ballroom has a magnificent chandelier, intended as a present from Queen Victoria to the Emperor of Russia. The trans-shipment of the chandelier through the Dardanelles coincided with the outbreak of the Crimean War and the chandelier was taken for the British Embassy: such is the story told. The ballroom has, amid heraldic shields, wall friezes of dolphins and tridents emerging from the waves, symbols of Britain's naval domination of the world in the 1850s, and has survived the retrenchments of the last thirty years. Today it is hired by British companies as a show room, and is used for receptions and recitals.

Pera House was used for formal occasions. It was built to be seen from a distance, but is so hemmed in by walls and other buildings that this has never been possible. Much official business was conducted from consulate buildings elsewhere. At the same time as the embassy was being built, a cluster of buildings was acquired just below the Galata Tower, on the steep road going down to the bridge. This site included a consulate, a consular court, a seamen's hospital and a jail, used until the Allied occupation of the city after the First World War. The jail still survives, and has been transformed into a restaurant by a Turkish architect, Mete Göktuğ. Diners can still eat in the cells to the accompaniment of music provided by Mete's Crimean wife.

On 20 November 2003 the consulate general was the target of a terrorist attack. A white van loaded with fertilizer explosive detonated outside the gates. The consul general, Roger Short, who had just gone out to have his shoes cleaned and was in an office in a Portakabin inside the walls, was killed instantly, along with twenty-one others, British and Turkish, who worked in the consulate general. Hundreds in the vicinity were injured, and buildings were damaged, including the consulate and the chapel of St. Helena. The attack was one of four terrorist outrages in early November. Two synagogues, including Neve Shalom Synagogue, the biggest in the city, were attacked five days earlier, and the buildings of the HSBC bank in Levent on 25 November. Altogether sixty-five people lost their lives, including four suicide bombers. The identity of the planners was soon identified. The brains behind the attack was alleged to believed to be a man from Mardin in southeast Turkey, who had been in Pakistan and Afghanistan with other terrorist groups and was later, it is believed, killed in a United States assault on a base in Iraq in September 2004.

A garden has been dedicated to the memory of the victims just inside where the gate used to be.

The chapel that was damaged was dedicated to the mother of Constantine the Great and lies in the embassy enclosure though detached from the main building. In the early years of the present century there were reports that the British government was planning to sell the chapel to a hotel. A vigorous campaign frustrated any such plan. The site had originally been presented to the British government by the sultan and there were ethical and legal reasons against making money out of a gift. But the chapel is still closed.

The man who led the fight to save the chapel was Ian Sherwood, the head of the Anglican community. He had already saved another Anglican building in the area, Christ Church, the Crimean Memorial Church. This had been designed by G. E. Street, the architect of the London Law Courts, and was constructed between 1858 and 1868. The foundation stone was laid by Stratford Canning in October 1858: it was his last public act in the city as British Ambassador to Turkey. The church can be reached by going down the steep Şahkulu Bostanı Sokak, on the other side of İstiklâl Cadddesi. A declining Anglican community in the area had led to the deconsecration and abandonment of the church in 1976, but ten years later Ian Sherwood arrived. Sherwood occupied the crypt with a sleeping bag, and campaigned successfully for re-consecration. It is now attended by a small number of British and American Anglicans, a handful of Istanbul Greeks and Armenians and a larger number of refugees—from Sri Lanka, Sudan, Rwanda and elsewhere—who have ended up in Istanbul and have enjoyed the pastoral care of Ian Sherwood. In January 2006 I attended a morning service, and a Burundian was baptized by total immersion with the name Claud William Laud.

## THE BUILDINGS OF BANKALAR CADDESI

About eight hundred yards to the west and sixty below Tünel station is Bankalar Caddesi, otherwise Banks Street, which a century ago was the commercial heart of the city.

Ownership of most buildings in Bankalar Caddesi was in the hands of non-Muslim Ottomans or of foreigners. In Republican times buildings were renamed to reflect a Turkish authenticity. Thus Noradounghian Han became Nur Han and Lazaridi Han became Güzin Han.

Like the rest of Istanbul, Bankalar (formerly Voyvoda) Caddesi seemed to be in an irreversible decline during the first generation of the Turkish Republic. Immigration to Palestine before and after the foundation of the State of Israel lured many of the poorer Jews away from the streets between the Golden Horn and the Galata Tower. Greeks, increasingly marginalized, also left in large numbers. But the buildings remain, eloquent survivors in stone of another world.

Let us walk along the street from the Karaköy Square, which was cleared for traffic by the Menderes government in 1958. The process involved the destruction of a small mosque designed by Raimondo D'Aronco, which can be admired today only in old photographs. The building housing the Vakıfbank today was built in 1966 and replaces the Cavafian Han, which went back to the 1860s. Then on the left we have the Jeneral Han. The road slopes upwards, and, in order that the upper three floors are at right angles to the walls, the shop fronts become lower as you walk up the road. The middle three floors are in a solid, restrained classical style, constructed in 1904 by an unknown architect. It used to hold offices of the Banca di Roma. Like other buildings in the street— and elsewhere in the city—additional floors have been added, framing and accentuating the impressive classical rectangle of the middle storeys

Opposite is the Minerva Han, built between 1911 and 1913, it is believed, by the Greek architect, Basile Couremenos. It was originally the headquarters of the Bank of Athens and occupied the site of Crespin Han, the property of a French family who settled in Istanbul in the eighteenth

The Camondo Steps: unexpected Art Nouveau

century. There are sculptures of the goddess Minerva on the façade.

The building that dominates the street is the Ottoman Bank on the left. But before we get there we pass three other bank buildings, each an impressive construction. The first is occupied by the Sümerbank. Built in the 1880s, it simultaneously housed the Deutsche Bank and the central management of the Anatolian railways. Next door is the Türkiye İş Bankası: this building was constructed in 1918 for an insurance company in a neo-Ottoman style. The flanking fifth floor windows are below panels of tilework, and a projecting awning shades the central bays of the fifth floor.

The architect of the third building is known—Giulio Mongeri. He designed it for the Assicurazioni Generali Insurance Company in 1909. He also designed the first purpose-built cinema in Istanbul in 1914, the Majik, now the State Theatre on Sıraselviler Caddesi, off Taksim, and was also one of the two architects of the Church of St. Antony of Padua on İstiklâl Caddesi. Across the road is the Ankara Han, built in 1911–12, seemingly inspired by the Assicurazioni Generali building. In both buildings, three huge arches cover bays of three upper floors.

We come to the biggest building of the street, now the Ottoman Bank and the Central Bank of the Republic of Turkey. It replaced a building known as Glavany Han, which had housed the offices of bankers and lawyers, and was built between 1890 and 1892 as the headquarters of the Ottoman Imperial Bank and the Ottoman Tobacco Monopoly. The architect was Alexandre Vallaury. The plan consists of two symmetrical parts: one for each of the commissioning businesses. Although the façade facing Bankalar Caddesi is severely classical, the façade facing the Golden Horn is quite different, with oddly Ottoman revival features such as stone lattice work and overhanging eaves. Vallaury was responsible for other iconic buildings in the city including the Pera Palas Hotel and the Ottoman Public Debt Administration Building, now a school, which occupies a commanding position, overlooking the Golden Horn above the railway station.

The Ottoman Bank was opened with great ceremony. In the words of the newspaper, *Sabah*,

> an eloquent prayer was said for an increasing of the life, prosperity, abundance and glory of His Imperial Majesty, the Sultan, and after all present

had said amen to this prayer, and following the speech delivered by the General Manager, the Honourable Sir Edgar Vincent, and the words of the Minister of Finance, His Excellency and the Most Benevolent Nazif Efendi… all present visited various parts of the beautiful building, and… ice cream, sweets and a quantity of delicious drinks delighted all guests.

Four years later, in the early afternoon of Wednesday 26 August 1896, the bank was stormed by a group of Armenian nationalists, led by a seventeen-year-old called Babken Siuni. Many staff were out for lunch when two well-dressed men came in and asked to withdraw some cash. The bank clerks agreed. The men gave a signal to others at the door and suddenly twenty-five armed men burst in, closed the main doors and barricaded themselves inside. Security forces arrived and a battle raged in the narrow street outside. Sir Edgar Vincent escaped through a skylight to the roof, but bank employees were held as hostages and bombs were hurled at troops from inside the bank. The Armenian nationalists were ready to negotiate, however, and made demands for the improvement of conditions of Armenians in eastern Anatolia, threatening, if they were not met, to blow up the building, including themselves. Later in the evening of the same day, the first dragoman of the Russian Embassy came to negotiate and early in the morning, thirteen hours after the start of the crisis, an agreement was reached. The nationalists were granted amnesty. It emerged that they had targeted other sites, including a police station and a Greek church. Armenians throughout the city suffered reprisals on the following two days. Shops in Galata were looted, and individual Armenians were butchered in the streets. The massacres were especially ferocious in a poor Armenian quarter in Hasköy. It was reckoned that over five thousand Armenians were killed. In the following months tens of thousands emigrated from the city.

The building continued to be the head office of the Ottoman Bank until 1998. Since 2001 the Ottoman Bank has been part of Garanti Bank, and this building was opened as the Ottoman Bank Museum in 2002. At the time of writing, the museum is closed for refurbishment.

Diagonally opposite the bank are the Camondo Steps. The designer of this unexpected piece of Art Nouveau in the midst of brash commerce is unknown, but the steps date from the 1880s. The Camondos were a family of Jewish financiers and philanthropists who flourished in the early and middle of the nineteenth century and owned a neo-classical *han* and residence adjacent to the steps. In 1913 the Istanbul Municipality had a project for thirty public lavatories (or "toilet parlors"), one of which was to be in the space below these steps. The project, which would have added function to the grace of the steps, was not implemented.

Next to the steps as we walk up the road is the Demirbank Building, another work designed by Vallaury. It was built for the Ottoman Exchange and Stocks Company—the inscription can still be seen in the stonework above the front door—in the 1880s. The company went into liquidation in 1902 and a British consulate office occupied the premises until the 1940s. Further west on the same side, the tallest building is Şark (Orient) Han built in 1918 by an Armenian architect, Michel Nouradjian. In the 1890s the previous building had been the headquarters of the Streetcar Company of Constantinople, the ground floor being stables for the horses that used to draw the cars. The façade was replaced under the supervision of Giulio Mongeri. It was owned and occupied by the Şark Insurance Company until 1997.

Back on the side of the Ottoman Bank but further to the west is Akbank. It has an undistinguished façade, reminding us of central European architecture of the 1930s. Indeed the façade was imposed in that decade on a building that was built, as Baltazzi Han, in about 1890. In the years before the First World War it provided offices for German and Italian banks as well as offices of a cement factory, a brewing company and the Norwich Union.

The lower building—only three floors—next door is called Burla Binası (Burla Building), and may date back to 1883. It was built for the Economic Cooperative Society which ran one of the leading department stores in the city until it went into liquidation in 1923. The building was then bought by the Jewish Burla brothers who specialize in the sale of electrical equipment. They started business in 1911 elsewhere on this street and are among the oldest establishments in the street.

The front of Bereket Han on the northern side of the road was built in the 1880s but the building is on the site of the Palazzo del Comune, the official headquarters of Genoese Galata, built in 1316. The walls at the back belong to the fourteenth-century building, and the Genoese coat of arms—unlikely to be as old as the building—can be seen sculpted on the rear door.

Across the road is Hezaren Han, with its projecting central bay. Dating from 1902, the architect was Alexandre Vallaury. It was built on the site of a tiled wooden building. This had served as a wood and coal store and stables for the bank that had been located at St. Pierre Han behind.

## Chapter Six

# END OF EMPIRE

### SULTAN ABDÜLHAMID II

The years from the 1870s to the First World War were a time of creativity, and of economic and political expansion. For most of the period the ruling force was the last proactive sultan, Abdülhamid II, who reigned from 1876 to 1909. He wrested back a number of levers of power that had slipped from of the hands of his immediate predecessors into those of ministers in the Ottoman government. In 1876 he proclaimed the first Ottoman constitution, which led to the summoning of the first parliament in the Muslim world, in 1877. This was against a background, however, of a disastrous war with Russia. The following year the Russian army was on the outskirts of the city and Abdülhamid prorogued parliament indefinitely. There was not to be another parliament until 1908. Decision-making became concentrated in the sultan's office in the Yıldız Palace, and the ministers in the traditional headquarters of the Ottoman government, the Babıali (Sublime Porte), were marginalized. From a distance the sultan controlled ministries and the military with a secret service that reported to him directly. Although Istanbul had a press that was as not as free as that of Paris or London, but was more diverse than that of Vienna or St. Petersburg, the censorship was capricious, paranoid and often absurd. The British Embassy was asked to ban the singing of "Onward Christian Soldiers" at the English church, on the grounds that it was provocative.

Sultan Abdülhamid II has often been portrayed as reactionary and illiberal. He never understood this, but rather saw himself as concerned with efficiency and reform, a kind of Ottoman Peter the Great. Nor was this self-perception unreasonable. He founded schools for civil servants and initiated bureaus for the collection of official statistics. He encouraged support for the regime through symbols such as the imperial coat of arms that appeared on all official publications including school text books. His predecessors had awarded honors, but he expanded the sultan's role as the fount of honors. Medals and decorations went to all classes. He even

A young Abdülhamid II at Balmoral, 1867

introduced the Şefkat Nişanı (the Order of Compassion) for women. The twenty-fifth anniversary of his accession was marked by celebrations, an echo of Queen Victoria's jubilees.

Politically repressive, Sultan Abdülhamid was nonetheless a patron of the arts. The Yıldız Palace became most closely associated with the sultan whose understandable paranoia—in 1876 his two predecessors were both deposed within a few months—made him retreat behind the high walls surrounding the gardens. All the major architects of his reign contributed to the palace buildings. Unlike Dolmabahçe, but like the Topkapı Palace, Yıldız is a complex of separate buildings scattered over extensive grounds. The 125 acres (half a million square meters) of the park are enclosed within a fifteen feet (four-meter) high wall. Yıldız was the last of the imperial city-palaces, although some of the design of the gardens went back to the 1850s. A romantic English park was the theme, but the effect is eclectic, with pavilions surrounded by formal gardens. Streams, lakes, ornate bridges and winding paths provide an ordered informality. Abdülhamid at one stage had plans for a miniature railway that could take passengers across viaducts over the lakes.

The entry to Yıldız Palace for the visitor today is by the Yaveran Building, a long, two-story timber construction designed by Sultan Abdülhamid's favourite architect, the Italian Raimondo D'Aronco.

Abdülhamid followed a tradition of the first successors of the Prophet Muhammad. A ruler should be a craftsman or a professional. His uncle, Sultan Abdülaziz, had been a calligrapher. Abdülhamid was a carpenter and joiner, and escaped from the cares of running an empire into his workshop, designing furniture, characterized by his initials, that can be seen today in Yıldız and other palaces. His carpenter's tools are on display in the workshop in the Yaveran Building.

Detached from the main building and facing the bosky park is the Şale Köşkü ("Chalet Pavilion"). A large annex was added to this building by Sarkis Balyan in 1889 on the occasion of the first visit to Istanbul of the German Kaiser Wilhelm II. Nine years later Kaiser Wilhelm paid a second visit. The Şale Köşkü was again enlarged and transformed by D'Aronco.

D'Aronco was also responsible in 1895 for the reconstruction and expansion after a fire of the Imperial Porcelain Factory in the grounds of Yıldız Park. He also constructed the small family theater and the greenhouse with its extraordinarily realistic plaster-cast palm trees.

Istanbul, c. 1895

Abdülhamid loved the stories of Sherlock Holmes, which he read in French translations. He also loved western music, and especially the operas of Offenbach and Verdi. He was a competent and expressive pianist. He had a resident theater company, a family concern, which performed in his private theater seating an audience of a hundred. The Belgian diva, Blanche Arral, and the French tragedienne, Sarah Bernhardt, both performed there.

Abdülhamid, however, did not like unhappy endings, and—like with some eighteenth-century productions of *King Lear*—insisted on changes. For example, he was not happy that Verdi's *La Traviata* should end with the death of Violetta, so the opera was edited for Yıldız productions to end with the visit of a gifted doctor who cures Violetta of her tuberculosis. Her final aria is not a prelude to death but a triumphant return to vigor and health.

The sultan was also charming to visitors. When he received the governor of the Constantinople branch of the Imperial Ottoman Bank, Sir Hamilton Lang, he used an interpreter. Lang was among the foreign guests invited to productions at the Yıldız theatre. Lang spoke in French, the international language of business and diplomacy. The sultan understood the language but by employing an interpreter allowed himself twice as long to give a considered answer. Lang found Abdülhamid kind and courteous. They shared stories of gout from which both suffered. "It was in the family," the sultan said.

## Arab Courtiers: Arap İzzet

The fifty years before the First World War saw a weakening—and at times a severing—of the ties between the Christian provinces of the empire and the city. It made sense to reinforce links with the Arab Muslim world. The Sultan Abdülhamid pursued this policy proactively. Some writers have seen something sinister in the way he surrounded himself with particular Arabs. One in particular, known as Arap İzzet Paşa—Arab Izzet—has been portrayed as a kind of Rasputin. But things were not quite like that.

İzzet Paşa was born Ahmed İzzet al-Abid, in 1851 into a Damascus family that was regarded as pro-French. There were strong links between the leading Sunni families of Damascus and Istanbul. These families provided governors and leading officials of the empire. Ahmed İzzet went first to a Muslim school in Damascus and then to Christian-run schools in Lebanon. He was fluent in Arabic, Turkish and French and knew some English. In his twenties he became secretary of the administrative council of the Syrian province and then head of the commercial court in his city and edited a local newspaper. He mediated between Turks and Arabs in an intellectual way, translating the first volume of the work of a leading Ottoman historian, Ahmet Cevdet Paşa, from Turkish into Arabic. He moved to Salonica and then in 1885 to Istanbul, where he became president of the Mixed Court of Appeals, a court dealing with cases between citizens of the empire and European foreigners. He was an ally of another Arab, a Palestinian, Abu'l Huda al-Sayyadi, who had a base at Yıldız. In 1895 Abdülhamid, who had heard of İzzet's talents, summoned him to the palace where he became one of the sultan closest advisers.

İzzet acted as a liaison figure between the sultan and Arab dignitaries, religious and civil. With his knowledge of French he was also a link with foreign embassies from whose governments he received a number of decorations. He was on all committees dealing with financial matters. His closeness to the sultan inevitably earned him enemies.

İzzet's main contribution to Ottoman affairs was to persuade Abdülhamid to promote the Hijaz Railway from Damascus to Medina to facilitate pilgrims on their way to meet their religious obligation of visiting Mecca. Each year his home town of Damascus used to see the assembly of thousands of Muslims from Anatolia, Central Asia and the Fertile Crescent, who then set off in a huge caravan to travel for two months overland to the Holy Places of the Hijaz. There were obvious commercial benefits for Damascus. The sultan and the Ottoman authorities accepted İzzet's recommendations and launched an international appeal for funds. The Ottoman army was employed in the construction of the railway.

His closeness to the sultan—some people saw him as "the second Sultan"—meant that he was targeted by the reaction against Abdülhamid after the sultan was toppled in 1909. İzzet had sustained his contacts with France and escaped to exile in Nice. During the First World War he was sentenced to death *in absentia*, but he returned to Syria after the war and assisted members of the imperial family in exile.

Arap İzzet's life and career shed light on many aspects of late Ottoman Istanbul. Although Istanbul was providing many of the new civil servants, the city, the capital of the empire, was still open to non-Turks of ability, energy and intelligence. His career as a discreetly loyal—albeit shadowy—courtier could have been replicated in the empire at any time in the previous four or five centuries. He owned property in the capital, including a villa on the island of Büyükada, which was confiscated along with the rest of his Istanbul assets. Between 1929 and 1933 the villa became the home of the exiled Leon Trotsky.

## From Abdülhamid to the Great War

In July 1908 the sultan restored the constitution after over thirty years and the city witnessed an outburst of popular feeling. The Yıldız system of government was replaced by a new parliament that met in December that year in a building on the Hippodrome. The authority of the grand vizierate was restored, and an elderly Anglophone and Anglophile, Kâmil Paşa, headed a government of pro-British reforming liberals who aspired to a federal empire. They were opposed by younger, more abrasive men in a party, the Committee of Union and Progress, who wanted greater centralization, spearheaded by a Turkish *Kulturkampf*. But not everyone was enthusiastic for reform and liberalism.

In the spring of 1909 a mutiny broke out against the reformers. Riots spread in the city and ministers fled for their lives. One minister, Mahmud Muhtar, a son-in-law of the deposed Hıdiv İsmail of Egypt, fled to Moda—a smart area of Kadıköy—and was sheltered by the *grande dame* of the British community, Lady Whittall. He was able to escape, disguised as a stoker, in a yacht belonging to one of his Egyptian in-laws. Under Mahmud Şevket Paşa, the "Army of Action" marched on the capital at great speed from Macedonia and camped menacingly outside the walls. It was believed that the sultan was behind the mutineers. Yıldız was surrounded. Palace guards, sensing which way the wind was blowing, deserted their posts. The sultan then surrendered to the army. The *Şeyhülislam*, the leading Muslim authority on matters of law, issued a *fetva* (legal opinion) permitting his deposition, and a commission consisting of two senators and two members of the lower house of parliament, headed by an Albanian and including a former minister for the navy, a Jew from Salonica and an Armenian Catholic, called on the sultan at the Yıldız Palace. The sultan accepted his fate with serenity. Later, another delegation informed him he was to be exiled in Salonica; he was duly escorted to Sirkeci station, where he boarded the imperial train and went into exile. Three years later, Salonica fell to the Greeks in the First Balkan War and the ex-sultan was brought back to the capital and spent his last years in dignified retirement at Beylerbeyi Palace.

The sultan's brother, Mehmet Reşat, was proclaimed Sultan Mehmet V, but he was not allowed any powers to rule. These were taken over by the parliament and the new "Young Turk" government, a triumvirate of Talat Paşa, Cemal Paşa and the charismatic Enver Paşa. Enver's wife was from the imperial royal family.

The Young Turks received military assistance from Germany and brought the Ottoman Empire into the First World War. For Turks, the international conflict did not start in 1914, but earlier in 1911 with the Italian invasion of the North African Ottoman territories that are now Libya, to be followed by Balkan wars in 1912 and 1913. These saw a further reduction of Ottoman lands in Europe and brought thousands of Muslim refugees from the Balkans to the capital. Turkey formally entered the First World War on 30 October 1914, joining Germany, Austria-Hungary and Bulgaria.

## HASHEMITES IN ISTANBUL

Those who have seen the film *Lawrence of Arabia*, directed by David Lean and released in 1962, will remember the portrayal of the Emir Faisal by Alec Guinness. Faisal is presented as a wily *Bedu*, a contrast to the international world of the clumsy British who have come to rescue the Arabs from Turkish oppression. It is a totally false image.

Faisal was certainly the most politically astute of the four sons of the Hashemite Hussein, Sherif of Mecca in the Arabian Hijaz. The Hashemites of the Hijaz, who had wielded local authority under the Ottoman sultans, were among the aristocrats of the Ottoman Empire. As such they had their base in the capital. Indeed, the man in whose name the "Arab Revolt" was launched, Sherif Hussein, was born in Constantinople. In 1891, when Faisal was about five years old, the family was exiled from Mecca. Hussein and his three eldest sons—Ali, Abdullah and Faisal—moved to the capital. The family had a villa at Emirgân, and the boys were brought up by the Bosphorus. Constantinople was their home until 1908, the year when Faisal became a member of the Ottoman parliament, representing Mecca. In the parliament he would have operated in Turkish. Faisal and his brothers received a private education from a Turkish army officer. They became fluent in the language. His brother, Abdullah, loved the city and in his memoirs recalled that

> We found Constantinople itself fascinating beyond description, a city of great beauty enthralling in every season, summer and winter alike. How pure are its springs, how fine its fruits! It is a city of endless fascination and as the traditional seat of the Caliphate it gathered a multitude of different people—Turks and Arabs, Kurds and Circassians, Albanians and Bulgarians, Egyptians and Sudanese. It contains Muslims of every walk of life, of different fashions and tongues, yet nobody and nothing seem strange and you can find anything you want from any country.

(It is interesting to note that he omits to mention the non-Muslims, the Jews, Armenians and Greeks.) Abdullah and his brothers were effectively, *Istanbullus*. Their father married again while they were in the capital, his new wife being Adile, a granddaughter of Mustafa Reşit Paşa, the reforming grand vizier. By her his fourth son, Zaid, was born in 1900.

Faisal became King Faisal I of Iraq in 1921 and surrounded himself with a group of Arabs from Iraq and Syria, most of whom shared an Ottoman education.

King Faisal I, who died in 1933, never returned to Istanbul, but his nephew, Abdulillah, who was regent from 1939 to 1953, came to the city in 1945, accompanied by the perennial Iraqi prime minister, Nuri es-Said, a Baghdadi who had been at military college in Ottoman Istanbul, and others who had known the city thirty years earlier. The Iraqi party came by sea from Naples, and Nuri was seen gripping the rail of the ship with tears in his eyes as they passed by the sea walls. The regent's visit was the first visit of an Arab ruler since the end of the empire. The regent's maternal grandmother, one of the last harem-living women from the Caucasus, had been born in the city and was still living at Emirgân in a rather tumbledown house, fitted with fine Persian carpets, Bohemian glass chandeliers and alabaster Italian fountains. The Arab party all spoke Turkish. President İsmet İnönü arranged for the regent to stay at the Dolmabahçe Palace.

Faisal's family and household were thus integrated into the elite Ottoman world of the time and would have had the education of his class. He certainly had a knowledge of Persian and was able to use it when, in the 1920s, as King of Iraq, he went on a state visit to Iran. He also spoke French, again like any other man of his age and class.

So Faisal was not the desert *Bedu* of the film. He would have been as much at home in a western suit as in *Bedu* dress—as photographs of his family life indicate. As King of Iraq, he was happier wearing western dress.

Indeed, Turkish was an alternative language of the Hashemite family for most of the twentieth century. From 1968 to 1970 I was living in Amman, Jordan. My landlord, known as Monsieur Hans, was an Armenian barber who cut the hair of the Royal Family, including that of the great grandson of Sherif Hussein, the late King Hussein. I spoke with Monsieur Hans in a mixture of Turkish and French, as he spoke neither Arabic nor English. One day I asked him what language he spoke with the Royal Family. "Turkish," he told me. In 1970 President Cevdet Sunay of Turkey, a former general, paid a state visit to Amman. One evening was spent with Jordanian and Palestinian veterans of the First World War. The party ended with them all singing old Ottoman army songs.

The historiography of the independent Arab nations has emphasized the differences between Turks and Arabs. Secession was inevitable. But that is not how it seemed at the time. It was two years into the war before the Arab revolt took place. The nationalist demands before then were largely cultural. Arabs feared that their language was being marginalized by the expansion of education, where the principal language of instruction was Turkish. Decentralization was the principal demand. The elites of Damascus, Baghdad, Cairo and Jeddah were integrated into an Ottoman culture. A generation had studied in either a law school or a military college in Istanbul. Leading families had—and still have—property in the city. Many people of Arab origin were living there, and stayed on after Arab independence. Personal links continued to be extensive for fifty years after the fall of the empire and the political separation of Turks and Arabs.

In 1939 the Sancak of İskenderun (Alexandretta), part of the French mandate of Syria, became part of Turkey. The Turkish governor of the province of Hatay, as it became known in Republican Turkey, Ata Amin, was married to a sister of Faisal. And when King Abdullah of Jordan's son and successor, Talal, was deposed for mental instability, he retired to Istanbul and died at Emirgân in 1970.

## THE END OF THE BELLE EPOQUE

The First World War was a disaster for the Ottoman Empire. The casualties, the devastation and the humiliation are all painful memories. İsmet İnönü, who followed Atatürk as President of the Republic, was successful in his determination to keep Turkey out of the Second World War. The First World War saw an effective end to the glittering but fragile culture of Belle Epoque Istanbul

We have seen that many of the manifestations of "development"—the economy, investments, the transport system, the expansion of amenities and facilities—were largely to the benefit of the non-Muslims. During the First World War Armenians were perceived by the Ottoman government to be a fifth column of the Russians. In 1915 orders were issued for the evacuation of Armenians in eastern Anatolia for "security reasons." Hundreds of thousands of Turkey's Armenians died: some of them from starvation, some of them deliberately killed. In Istanbul, hundreds of Armenians—writers and intellectuals in particular—were rounded up. Turkish official sources have consistently denied that the Ottoman government had deliberately set out to eliminate the Armenians in what was a front line area in the war against Russia, but Armenians themselves and many others argue that what happened was genocide. The controversy still rages today, but like the events of 1948 in Palestine, emotion and rhetorical nationalist narratives are in danger of obscuring what happened, how and why. Hundreds of Turkish families took in Armenians. But by the end of the war Istanbul had unquestionably lost huge numbers of its Armenian population.

In November 1918 French, British and Italian troops entered the city of Istanbul, formally declaring an occupation in 1920. The occupation lasted until October 1923. The Bosphorus and the Dardanelles military installations were also in the hands of foreigners. Swathes of southern Anatolia were occupied by French and Italians. In May 1919 Greeks invaded Anatolia and occupied Izmir with the objective of annexing large parts of the Aegean coastlands. In Istanbul the occupation forces worked in cooperation with the last sultan and his ministers. But in May 1919 Mustafa Kemal raised the standard of national resistance against foreign occupation. Initially he and the nationalist forces claimed to be working in the interests of the sultan. It was not at first politic to repudiate a dynasty and a political system that could claim continuity for seven hundred years. But over the next four years the legitimacy of the old regime slowly but irreversibly crumbled as the nationalists, inspired and led by Mustafa Kemal Paşa, won success after success and cleared Anatolia of foreign occupation.

These political and military events discredited the foreigners. Russia before the war and Greece afterwards made little secret of their ambition to annex Istanbul. During the occupation local Greeks were perceived by many Turks to be favoured by the occupiers and to be potentially disloyal to a Turkey for the Turks. When the nationalists returned to Istanbul, the old sultan's regime with its economic, social and cultural associations was discredited. The sultan was sent into exile within weeks of the end of the foreign occupation of the city. The dual role of sultan and caliph—always dubious—was split. The sultan was deposed as ruler. His cousin, Abdülmecid, assumed the caliphate with purely religious responsibilities, but he too was removed and sent into exile in the autumn of 1924.

## THE LAST CALIPH: ABDÜLMECID EFENDI

There has, in recent years, been a revival of interest in and appreciation of the personality and work of the last caliph, known as Abdülmecid Efendi. He was an extraordinarily gifted man, whose life and work defy many of the received views and stereotypes of the Ottoman imperial family and the last years of the empire. Abdülmecid was a painter and musician, a creative intellectual who effortlessly bestrode the traditional Islamic legacy of the empire and nineteenth-century European culture.

Abdülmecid was the son of Sultan Abdülaziz, who was, as we have seen, himself interested in western music and culture. Abdülmecid was eight years old when his father was deposed and died shortly afterwards. His son insisted all his life that his father was murdered and had not committed suicide. He revered the memory of his father, who had arranged for him to have painting lessons from the Polish painter, Stanisław Chlebowski, attached to the imperial court.

Abdülmecid received the education of a male Ottoman aristocrat, studying Turkish, Arabic and Persian, as well as learning to speak fluent French. He also learned German and acquired a reading knowledge of English. During the latter part of the reign of his cousin, Sultan Abdülhamid II, his liberal views were eyed with suspicion and he was effectively under house arrest. From about the turn of the century he spent the summers at the building now known as his *köşk* in Bağlarbaşı, above Üsküdar on the Asian side of the Bosphorus. The winters were spent at the Feriye Sarayı, now part of the Kabataş High School and Galatasaray University. In 1916 his elder brother, Yusuf İzzeddin died, and he became second in line to the throne. From 1918, when he became crown prince, he moved to apartments in Dolmabahçe Palace, though he retained the Bağlarbaşı villa. When the sultanate was abolished in 1923, the caliphate was retained and Abdülmecid was elected to that office, but forced into exile the following year, when the caliphate was abolished. He went first to Switzerland, then Paris and finally ended up in Nice, dying there in 1944.

But for twenty-five years he was a major figure in the cultural scene of the city. Many of his paintings are in private hands, but some galleries in Istanbul, such as the National Painting and Sculpture Gallery in Beşiktas, the Dolmabahçe Palace, the Sabancı Museum in Emirgân and the Aşiyan Museum next to Boğaziçi University, have examples of his work.

He used to set aside one day a week—Wednesday—for his painting and would receive no callers. He was versatile in different genres. Devoted to his family, he frequently painted portraits of his son, Ömer Faruk, and of his daughter, Dürrüşehvar Sultan, who lived on to the twenty-first century, dying in London in 2006. Examples of these are on display in Dolmabahçe Palace. He was also proud of his Ottoman family background and produced portraits of those forbears who were reformers: Selim II, Selim III and Mahmud II. He painted landscapes and seascapes, still life, as well as domestic scenes—there is one of his daughter as an infant being bathed—and there are historical scenes; one is of the delegation calling on his cousin, Sultan Abdülhamid II, to announce that he had been deposed. Abdülmecid went to great lengths to make this picture authentic. He invited the five members of the delegation to Bağlarbaşı to be photographed. He also took a photograph of the room in the Yıldız Palace where the delegation met the sultan.

Perhaps the most interesting of his paintings, one that reveals an enormous amount about him and the world he lived in, is called "Beethoven in the Harem" and is now in the National Painting and Sculpture Gallery in Beşiktaş. In this oil on canvas painting we have a string trio playing in the ground-floor reception room in the villa at Bağlarbaşı. One woman is playing the violin, another the piano, while a man is bent over a cello. Four onlookers are in attendance in varying degrees of absorption. One is Abdülmecid, who has painted himself into the picture sitting in military uniform, one leg thrown over the other and gazing at a bust of Beethoven that is placed on a shelf below a seascape of Istanbul painted by Ivan Ayvazovsky, an Armenian from Crimea. A score of Beethoven's has been casually tossed on to the floor. The furnishings, with the potted palm, the screen, the flowers in an urn and the wall clock, could indicate the drawing room of any well-to-do household at the time in London, Paris, Berlin or Vienna. In a recess at the back is the darkened outline of an equestrian statue—perhaps not a normal European bourgeois fashion accessory.

Abdülmecid was a liberal and part of his liberalism was a passionate belief in the equality of the sexes, and the right for women to have an education and a full life. In the performance of chamber music, there is no clear leader, the contribution of each performer being judged on merit. Thus two performers are women, one a man; there is no hierarchy and nor is there a social hierarchy. The violinist is Abdülmecid's first wife, Şehsüvar Başkadın Efendi. The pianist is one of the Circassian harem officials, effectively a housekeeper, Ofelya Kalfa, otherwise Hatice Kadın, who had been the subject of a previous portrait painted by Abdülmecid. The cellist is Bihruze Kalfa, another court servant. Abdülmecid's second wife, Atiye Mehisti Kadınefendi, is one of the women looking on.

The casualness of the room with the Peters' edition of the Beethoven music on the floor and the rumpled up carpet indicates the idea that western music has been absorbed into the domestic culture. The scene was to some extent posed. Abdülmecid had arranged for things to be disorganized and was very annoyed when a servant tidied the room up. The Ayvazovsky painting of Seraglio Point was one that fascinated Abdülmecid, for one of his own landscapes was of a similar view.

But, apart from the presence of his two wives, there is another indication that this is no ordinary bourgeois family amusing themselves—the brooding equestrian statue. This statue can today be seen in the Beylerbeyi Palace. It is of Abdülmecid's father, Sultan Abdülaziz, and was cast in bronze in 1871 by the British sculptor, Charles Fuller. The statue had been in Topkapı Palace but Abdülmecid had it brought to his villa. It was an indication of the son's high regard for the musician father.

During the occupation of Istanbul, while Mustafa Kemal was mobilizing the nationalist forces, Abdülmecid and his family were sympathetic and there were proposals for Abdülmecid's son, Ömer Faruk, to cross over to Anatolia to join them. Mustafa Kemal declined the offer.

## MUSTAFA KEMAL ATATÜRK AND ISTANBUL

The maker of modern Turkey had a complex relationship with the city of Istanbul. In some ways Mustafa Kemal Paşa—known as Atatürk after the introduction of surnames in 1934—was a characteristic child of the Belle Epoque. He was indeed one of the last Ottoman *paşa*s. He appreciated European culture, loved western classical music, was competent in understanding German and fluent in reading, writing and speaking French; often French words—*déjà* was a favorite—would slip into his ordinary conversation. He enjoyed the bourgeois comforts of the city and, although he identified with the Anatolian Muslim soldier and peasant, was on easy terms with people of the Greek, Armenian and Jewish minorities.

Born in Salonica in 1881, he first came to the city at the age of seventeen when he entered the War College. The buildings are today the Military Museum in Harbiye, north of Taksim. They had been built in 1887 and were on the edge of the built up city, which was expanding to create the smart residential areas of Şişli and Teşvikiye. Conditions at the War

College were rough and food basic. (A regular dish was a bean stew that became a favorite with Atatürk for the rest of his life.) His contemporaries included men who were to be his colleagues and, in some cases, his rivals in the 1920s and 1930s. He graduated in 1902 as an infantry lieutenant, and went on to the Staff College. His contemporaries were all Muslims and came from different parts of the empire, although Turkish was the common language.

Mustafa Kemal was away from the capital during the revolution of 1908 and for most of the years before the outbreak of war in 1914, serving the empire in Syria, Libya and Macedonia. In 1910 he went on maneuvers in France and in 1913 he became military attaché in Sofia, Bulgaria. One consequence of the Balkan Wars was the transfer of his home town of Salonica to Greece. Muslim refugees, including Mustafa Kemal's mother and sister, moved into Istanbul, He set up a home for them in an apartment in Akaret in Beşiktaş, homes for public officials working in one of the nearby Dolmabahçe and Yıldız palaces. A near neighbor was the leading figure of the Young Turks, Enver Paşa, about whom Atatürk always had deep reservations.

Mustafa Kemal did not see much of the city during the war. He was busy humiliating the British and their allies in Gallipoli, and emerging as the empire's most successful soldier with further campaigns in eastern Anatolia and Syria. When he was in Istanbul he did not always stay with his mother. During a month's leave in 1917 he installed himself in the Pera Palas Hotel. By the latter days of the war, Mustafa Kemal was torn between disillusion at the turn of events, frustration at being unable to do much about it, and loyalty as an Ottoman public servant. As he recalled nine years later, "I had settled in a suite in the Pera Palace hotel in Istanbul. I was plunged in the sad thoughts that come to a man who believes that all is lost. But I also consoled myself like a man believing that all could also be regained."

At the end of 1917 he accompanied Mehmet Vahdettin, the younger brother and heir apparent of the ailing sultan, on an official visit to Berlin. Vahdettin was a prickly man but, appreciating his Gallipoli campaign, won Atatürk over by addressing him as "the commander who saved Istanbul."

At the end of the war, the leading Young Turks—Enver, Cemal and Talat—went into exile. Mustafa Kemal returned from Syria in the middle of November 1918, arriving at Haydarpaşa station to see the city under foreign occupation. He moved first to the Pera Palas, but found it uncomfortably full of Allied staff, and then moved to a house in Beyoğlu, owned by a Christian Arab, Salih Fansa, before renting a three-story town house in Şişli from an Armenian, which is today a museum. Here he met other discontented nationalist officers, disenchanted at the incapacity of the Ottoman authorities to prevent the foreign occupation of the Anatolian heartlands and the capital. For months Mustafa Kemal was unemployed, suspicious of the government and suspected by the regime. He wanted authority and tried to influence decision-making, with contacts at all levels from the palace—Vahdettin was now the Sultan Mehmet VI—to the press. As well as at the Şişli house there were meetings at the Cercle d'Orient in the Grande Rue de Pera and invitations to meetings at the ministry of war. Greeks complained of harassment by Turkish troops in eastern Anatolia where law and order had virtually broken down. At the end of April Mustafa Kemal was asked to be the Inspector of the Ninth Army, and to restore order in Anatolia east of Ankara. In early May 1919 the Allies occupying the city gave the green light to the Greek government for troops to invade Anatolia and occupy Izmir. The Greek prime minister, Eleftherios Venizelos, aspired to implement the Great Hellenic Idea of a Greek state taking over the whole of the Aegean coastlands of Anatolia. Mustafa Kemal selected his own staff, called on senior officials in the capital, and even had a private audience with the sultan.

"Paşa, you have already rendered many services to the state," Atatürk claimed the sultan told him. "They are now part of history. Forget about them, for the service you are about to render will be more important still. You can save the state."

On 16 May Mustafa Kemal boarded *Bandırma*, an old tramp steamer of questionable seaworthiness. On 19 May, as he says in the opening words of the great speech he gave in 1927, he landed at Samsun. In the next few years he established an alternative focus of authority in Ankara, led the military campaign to clear the invading Greeks from western Anatolia and embarked on the creation of modern Turkey.

It was eight years before Mustafa Kemal set foot in Istanbul again, eight momentous years in the history of the country. In October 1923 Ankara was designated the capital of the Turkish Republic. No longer was Istanbul, the home of the sultan, the capital of the empire. Many Istanbul families moved to the new capital, but returned to homes in Istanbul whenever they could. Most Greeks left, and the Armenian community had all but disappeared. Istanbul seemed to have been punished for being a cosmopolitan city, a not reluctant host to a foreign occupying power who had colluded with invaders. It was still a city of political activity—and not always sympathetic to the new Turkey. It was also the center for Turkish journalism.

In September 1924, when his authority over the country was not yet absolute, he boarded a boat at Mudanya and went on a Black Sea tour, passing through the Bosphorus. He did not leave the boat. Mustafa Kemal next trod the soil of Istanbul in 1927.

Yet in 1926 a statue of Atatürk was erected at Sarayburnu (Seraglio Point), the headland at the end of the old city that divides the Sea of Marmara from the Golden Horn. Statues were new to the country. The sculptor was an Austrian, Heinrich Krippel, who had already made a sculpture of the president for Ulus Square in Ankara, and was to produce others for Samsun and Konya.

By the summer of 1927 Mustafa Kemal had traveled extensively all over Anatolia, receiving adulation wherever he appeared. He decided it was time to come to terms with Istanbul. He arrived on the former imperial yacht *Ertuğrul* at the Dolmabahçe Palace as President of the Turkish Republic. City and president behaved graciously to each other. Streets were crowded with well-wishers and the president received delegations in the palace. The joyous visit was somewhat marred, however, by the discovery of a plot by Armenians allegedly to rob a casino in the Sultan Abdülhamid's former quarters at Yıldız Palace. The security forces were understandably nervous, for senior Ottoman figures from the war period—Talat Paşa, Cemal Paşa, Prince Said Halim—had all been assassinated by Armenians in revenge for the fate of their countrymen during the war.

Having exorcised his anxiety of embracing the city of Istanbul, Atatürk became a regular visitor after 1927. The city's identification with the Atatürk revolution was marked by the launch of one of the greatest reforms. In August 1928 in the Sarayburnu gardens, not far from his new statue, he announced the change of script from Arabic to Latin letters. Two days later he gave the first class in teaching the new script in the Dolmabahçe Palace.

On his visits to Istanbul, Atatürk enjoyed dancing and eating out at

Atatürk in conversation

hotels and restaurants, taking friends to night clubs in Pera (Beyoğlu). The Park Hotel on Taksim, destroyed by fire in the 1970s, was a favorite.

Atatürk was an intellectual and in the last ten years, after he had successfully driven through most of the reforms that have made Turkey what it is today, he encouraged scientific discussions of the language and history of the country. Few of his theories are accepted nowadays, but he was trying to define and present a distinctive Turkishness to the world. Much of his reported table talk revolved around the theory that the Turkish language was the source for other languages. The Hittites, he maintained, were really Turks, and so the Turks who invaded Anatolia from the tenth century onwards were simply claiming their own heritage. Dolmabahçe Palace was used for prestigious international conferences on such subjects.

Atatürk had a personal regime of heavy smoking, enjoying his *rakı* and drinking endless cups of Turkish coffee. He worked ferociously hard and usually did not get to bed before two or three in the morning. In his later years he followed the custom of many of his officials by coming to Istanbul for some of the summer months, away from the arid heat of Ankara.

From 1935 Atatürk had his own base in Greater Istanbul, in that year commissioning the construction of a summer residence at Florya, to the west of Yeşilköy, and separated from it by fields. The architect who gained the commission was Seyfi Arkan, responsible also for some apartment blocks in Istanbul. Atatürk was by now an ailing man, and the design had to take into consideration the president's health requirements, but more significantly his strong views about architecture. He kept in touch with experiments in contemporary design and disliked what many have seen as the appealing features of Ottoman towns—the narrow, winding, tightly packed streets—preferring the open wide streets of 1920s Ankara. Indeed, according to one designer close to him, he "detested every kind of architecture that was not modern, particularly eaves, pitched roofs and above all, domes."

Atatürk often came to Florya to swim and would check on the progress of his summer house which today is the Florya Atatürk Marine Mansion. Constructed of timber, the main building has only one story and is raised offshore on piles in the sea and connected by a pier to the mainland fifty meters away. From a distance the whole construction looked like a pier, and it did indeed fulfill the function of a pier, for Atatürk used to arrive here by boat. The modest buildings that make up an office and residential quarters with space for staff and bodyguards are brutally simple. There are no guest rooms—guests were accommodated on the shore. It combines elements of Expressionist and Art Deco architecture and is one of the iconic works of the Modernist Movement in Turkey. There are no eaves, pitched roofs or domes.

In early 1938 his health began to collapse. He was not good at following medical advice to cut down on smoking and drinking and to take more rest. In February he was at the Park Hotel for an all-night party. Fever followed and pneumonia was diagnosed. He went to Ankara but was back in Istanbul in May. He divided his time between the Dolmabahçe Palace and his home at Florya. But another distraction came his way: a luxury yacht, built for an American millionaire, the granddaughter of the builder of Brooklyn Bridge in New York. The government bought it as a gift for the president. The yacht, called *Savarona*, became another home for Atatürk in his last few months. It cruised around the Sea of Marmara and the Bosphorus, while the president received visitors on it—ministers and foreign visitors such as King Carol of Romania. But

Atatürk was terminally ill. In July he was carried in an armchair from the boat to a small downstairs room in the Dolmabahçe Palace. He declined and on 16 October went into a coma. He came to from time to time but relapsed into a final coma on 8 November and died at five past nine on the tenth.

In defiance of Islamic custom, his body was laid in state for seven days in the Throne Room at Dolmabahçe. Crowds of mourners came to pay their respects. On 12 November crowds got out of hand and eleven people were trampled to death. The body was taken to Ankara for a state funeral and a mausoleum was built on a hill in the capital to house his remains.

Clocks are often still stopped at five past nine.

*Savarona* lay in dock at Kanlıca during the Second World War and in 1951 became a naval training ship at Heybeli. It was gutted by fire in 1979, but the wreck was bought by the businessman Kahraman Sadıkoğlu, who spent $25 million on it. It can be rented—crew but not provisions included—for up to $400,000 a week. It can still be seen from time to time cruising the waters of Greater Istanbul.

*Chapter Seven*

# THE WATERS OF THE CITY

## THE BOSPHORUS

Like New York, Venice, Sydney and Stockholm, Istanbul is defined by water: the waterway linking the Black Sea and the Marmara Sea, the Bosphorus and its inlet, the Golden Horn. Few parts of the city are far from these stretches of water. Nearly every person nearly every day sees water. At the same time the Golden Horn has divided Stamboul from Pera in more than geographical ways. Although for two millennia the Asian suburbs have been intimately connected with the city—as places of retreat or of exile, and more recently as dormitory towns, there has at the same time been a real sense of taking a voyage from one shore to the other, literally to another continent. Muslim pilgrims bound for Mecca used to cross from Beşiktaş to Üsküdar to embark on the long overland journey. In the last forty years Üsküdar and its outer suburbs have been the first home for new immigrants to the city from Anatolia.

Bosphorus means "passage of the cow," derived from the legend of Io who was one of many lovers of Zeus. When Hera, Zeus' wife, suspected her husband of being involved in a love affair with Io, Zeus turned Io into a small cow and tried to send her away to avoid Hera's rage. She (the cow) swam across the strait, but Hera discovered her and sent a huge gadfly after the cow to bite and disturb her ceaselessly.

There is a story of a man from Üsküdar who used to row across to the city. He was outraged when a tax on boats crossing the Bosphorus was imposed. He swore a solemn vow never to pay any such tax. His son got a message to him that he was getting married in the old city, and the father, honoring his own vow, decided to walk to Istanbul, and did so, walking all round the Black Sea—to Trabzon (Trebizond), through parts of present-day Georgia, Russia and Ukraine, along through Romania and Bulgaria, eventually reaching the city through the land walls.

Philip Mansel may be unkind in describing the Bosphorus as a sewer flowing between housing estates. A century earlier, an American was quoted more poetically comparing the Bosphorus to Lake Como in the

185

Italian Alps as if drawn through a key-hole. But ribbon development has damaged the grace of its shores. The best way of seeing these shores is—as it always has been—by boat. (The second best way is from a low flying helicopter.) The roads on either side are choked with traffic. What could be a wonderful twelve-mile (twenty-kilometer) walk is a hazardous exercise, involving coping with badly designed pavements and dodging cars. Much of the distinctive character of each of the villages is lost. They used to be the residential areas of prosperous Greeks, Jews and Armenians. Today, newer settlers live around the churches, mosques and synagogues, although Rumeli Hisarı and Beylerbeyi have a longer established Turkish Muslim presence.

The level of the Black Sea is roughly fifteen inches (forty centimeters) above that of the Marmara. At surface level, water flows from north to south through the Bosphorus at an average speed of two to four knots. But because of the twists and turns of the channel and because of seasonal changes the currents are very unstable. The waters of the Black Sea have a low salt content, as it is mainly fuelled by fresh water from the three rivers, the Danube, Don and Dnieper. The heavier salt water is at the depth of the Bosphorus, and this drifts northwards but is blocked from entering the Black Sea by a ledge on the Bosphorus bed near the northern mouth. In short, the currents of the Bosphorus flow in opposite directions: the water nearer the surface flows from north to south, the lower waters from south to north. All this helps to explain the extraordinary turbulence of the waterway.

About 30,000 ships pass through each year—that is nearly a hundred a day: passenger ships, cruise liners, oil tankers, but mostly freight. Since the Montreux Convention of 1936 there is unrestricted transit by merchant shipping through these straits. Spills from the tankers and occasional collisions have put shoreline residents at risk, and there is an argument for greater control by the Turkish government.

Although temporary bridges of boats were built for military purposes in classical and medieval times, the first substantial bridge to span the Bosphorus was built in 1973 and opened to mark fifty years since the proclamation of the Republic. Spanning the Bosphorus was seen as sacrilege by some, but the lofty elegance of the structure has, with Nikogos Balyan's Ortaköy Mosque below, become an iconic image of modern Istanbul. Traffic pressure was relieved, but only temporarily, and a second bridge was thrown over the waterway fifteen years later, a few miles to the north. This latter bridge is officially called the Fatih Sultan Mehmet (or FSM) Bridge, after the conqueror of the city and builder of the Rumeli Hisarı which lies at its feet—another iconic contrast—but more generally it is known as the Second Bridge. The bridge was opened to commemorate 2,500 years after the building of a pontoon bridge by Darius the Great.

The villages along the shore were mostly fishing communities until the nineteenth century. The development of steamboat transport, especially from the 1850s when an Ottoman company, the Şirket-i Hayriye, was specifically set up to provide steamboat services for the Istanbul area, made the villages more accessible to the city. The nineteenth-century sultans built palaces to which preferred access was by boat, but from early Ottoman times, the court and senior officials liked to build houses on the waters' edge to retreat to. Such a house was called a *yalı*—the word is originally Greek. Certain villages became favoured by Ottoman, Hashemite and Egyptian ruling families. Others acquired a distinctively Armenian or Jewish character. Even today, Ortaköy on the European shore and Kuzguncuk on the Asian are multi-confessional with church, synagogue and mosque alongside one another. At Kuzguncuk one Jewish merchant built a house in 1923, with that date above the doorway, but also with the date of the Jewish calendar, 5683, and of the Muslim calendar, 1339.

The further reaches of the Bosphorus on the European side were where the summer retreats and offices of major embassies were situated. The German Ambassador's summer residence at Tarabya houses the German-Turkish Chamber of Commerce and Industry and provides a venue for German-Turkish events. The French Embassy is now used by the Marmara University School of Business and Political Science. The Spanish Summer Embassy at Büyükdere has been continuously occupied since 1783.

The British Summer Embassy at Tarabya was burned down in 1912. Some furniture and the carpet from the ballroom were salvaged. The ballroom was huge and the Foreign Office sent a message to all British missions in the world to see where there was a room big enough to find a home for the Tarabya carpet. Only the Consulate General in Cairo was able to meet the requirement and the carpet has found a home on the banks of the Nile. The Tarabya site is still owned by the British government and some consulate staff have homes there.

Forty years ago many of the *yalı*s were sinking into the Bosphorus and seemed to represent vestiges of a passing world. But one of the consequences of the prosperity of Turkey is that the *yalı* has become a coveted residence of the powerful and super-rich. The former prime minister, Mrs. Tansu Çiller, has a house overlooking the Bosphorus at Yeniköy. The Count Ostroróg or Red Yalı at Kandilli was recently bought by the leading Turkish entrepreneur Rahmi Koç for about US$10million. Money has been poured into their restoration and the last ten years have seen a revival of "yalı culture."

Other older buildings have been transformed for other purposes. These lie mostly on the European side. The restored *yalı*s on the Asian shore have mostly remained in private hands and are still residences. The Çırağan Palace, where Sultan Murat V lived for thirty years after his deposition in 1876, was devastated by fire in 1910 and for nearly a century stood as a ruined shell. In 1988 the Kempinski hotel chain bought it and restored it as a luxury hotel. The Esma Sultan Palace at Ortaköy is now a concert venue and restaurant. A palace built as a summer residence for the mother of the Hıdiv Abbas Hilmi in 1902 is now the Egyptian Consulate General. The residence of Mustafa Reşit Paşa, the great reforming vizier of Sultan Abdülmecid I and ally of the British Ambassador, Stratford Canning, is now the Baltalimanı Bone Diseases Hospital. Deli Fuat Paşa's *yalı* at İstinye now houses shipping-related administrative offices. The gorgeous Huber Mansion between Yeniköy and Tarabya, with outstanding work by D'Aronco, was built for an arms dealer. It served as a Catholic Girls' School during the Second World War and was then acquired by the Turkish government and is now the summer palace of the president. At Sarıyer the residence of Manuk Azaryan, an Armenian businessman who was in the Ottoman parliament before the First World War, today houses the Sadberk Hanım Museum of Art and Antiquities, set up by the Vehbi Koç Foundation in memory of the wife of Vehbi Koç, founder of the Koç Group, one of Turkey's major private sector operations.

The oldest wooden structure to have survived fire and decay is the former Köprülü family house. This is a few hundred yards south of the Second Bridge on the Asian shore. It dates back to 1699. The Köprülüs were a family of reforming grand viziers during the seventeenth century. The founder of the family's fortunes, Köprülü Mehmet, came from Albania. He was recruited as a youth into public service and in his seventies in 1656 was invited to be grand vizier. He re-established the authority of the sultan after years of virtual civil war. His son-in-law, Merzifonlu Kara Mustafa, was also grand vizier and was executed after the failed Ottoman siege of Vienna in 1683. Köprülü Mehmet's nephew, Amcazade Hüseyin Paşa, became grand vizier too, and built this *yalı*. Two and a half centuries later, another Köprülü, Fuat, was a distinguished historian and became foreign minister in the 1950s under Prime Minister Adnan Menderes. The *yalı* has suffered neglect, but there have been recent plans to restore it to something of its former glory.

The oldest *yalı* on the European side is the Şerifler Yalısı at Emirgân. Originally built in the 1780s, it was bought in 1894 by Hussein, the Sherif of Mecca, who raised the standard of revolt against the Ottoman Empire in 1916. This is where his sons, Abdullah and Faisal, future comrades-in-arms of T. E. Lawrence, were brought up.

## BÜYÜKADA, TROTSKY AND POPE JOHN XXIII

From the quay near Sirkeci railway station you can take a boat to *Adalar*, the islands. These islands, the Princes' Islands, lie off the Asian shore southeast of the southern end of the Bosphorus. Of the nine islands, five are inhabited. For centuries they were places of retreat. Until the introduction of steam-power in the middle of the nineteenth century, a journey from the city might take the best part of a day. In Byzantine times, monasteries attracted priests, scholars, and deposed patriarchs and emperors. The islands continued to be favored places of residence for Greeks, Armenians and Jews until the twentieth century. Churches and synagogues are still active on the islands, especially during the summer months.

In the twentieth century the islands and especially the largest of them, Büyükada, have attracted day trippers and summer residents. There are hotels and pensions. The biggest hotel on Büyükada is the Splendid Palas, which hosted King Edward VIII and Mrs. Simpson in 1936. The decor, the lifts and the spaciousness have not changed a great deal since then. "It is where Monsieur Hulot meets Monsieur Poirot," is how one visitor described it.

There has also been a roll-call of distinguished international residents. Leon Trotsky settled on Büyükada, between Moscow and Mexico. In 1928 he had been banished to Alma Aty (now Almaty) but in February 1929 Trotsky, with his wife and daughter, were suddenly and secretly escorted by train to Odessa and from there shipped across the Black Sea. The Turkish government was told by the Soviet government that he had come for his health. Trotsky was first housed at the Soviet Embassy, as a compulsory house guest. (It could be argued that he was also being protected from the large White Russian community that lived in Beyoğlu.) Nearly a year later, with the help of agents of the Soviet secret police, the OGPU, he found a place of seclusion on this island. His house was at 60 Çankaya Caddesi, today plaqueless and unoccupied and in poor shape, but with plans for restoration. The house used to belong to the Damascene Arap İzzet Paşa, had been requisitioned by the government and was already in a dilapidated and squalid state and full of cobwebs when Trotsky and his wife, Natalya Sedova, moved in. Trotsky's work room was on the first floor. The walls soon became lined with books and periodicals, arriving from Europe and America. Here he wrote *My Life* and *History of the Russian Revolution*. The house became filled with bodyguards, secretaries and guests. He was supported by money sent by American communists. The garden was left abandoned and was—then as now—full of weeds and hidden by trees.

Trotsky's house, Büyükada

As an escape from work, he used to go rowing and fishing with a local Greek resident, Haralambos. Occasionally he made trips to the city—on one occasion he went to see Charlie Chaplin's film, *City Lights*. He was also able to go to a conference in Denmark but was escorted in seclusion all the way. He traveled under the name of Leon Sedef—the name of another of the Princes' Islands. The residence on Büyükada was interrupted after the house was seriously damaged by fire, perhaps arson. Much of his library was destroyed, but Trotsky saved the manuscript of his *History*. He and his household then spent a year at a house in Kadıköy, surrounded by a high barbed wire fence. There too a fire broke out and more manuscripts and books had to be salvaged. Trotsky now wanted to leave Turkey, and his daughter committed suicide in the villa in 1932. He had few if any contacts in Turkey and in 1934 he was able to get a visa to go to France and settle at Barbizon, near the Fontainebleau Forest. Even so, he retained fond memories of the place. "I have been here for four and a half years," he wrote as he left. "My feet seem bound to the soil of Büyükada and I feel inside me a strong sensation at leaving."

Another resident of the island was the papal apostolic delegate to Turkey, Angelo Giuseppe Roncalli, from 1935 to 1944. A liberal, he was not in favor with the Vatican mainstream and his posting to Turkey was, like Trotsky's residence, a kind of exile. Roncalli had extensive European contacts and was instrumental in arranging for Jews to escape from Nazi-occupied Europe. The house of the apostolic delegate is near the center of the village, in Şehbal Sokak. Roncalli went on to be apostolic nuncio to France, Patriarch of Venice and finally, in 1958, pope. He is better known as Pope John XXIII.

## İSMET İNÖNÜ ON HEYBELIADA
The island of Heybeliada is forever associated with its most famous resident, İsmet İnönü, the second president of the Turkish Republic.

İsmet İnönü was Mustafa Kemal's closest ally. Born in 1884 in İzmir of a father who came from the east of Turkey and a mother from the Balkans, İsmet had a military education. He served in the Yemen in 1909 where—of all places—he developed a taste for western classical music. In the First World War he was an officer when the British army overwhelmed the Third Ottoman Army at Beersheba in Palestine in 1917. After the war he was working in the ministry of war in Istanbul and is believed to have secured the appointment of Mustafa Kemal as inspector of the army in Anatolia from where he led the revolt against the Ottoman authorities. He later slipped out of the city, joined the nationalist revolt and became Mustafa Kemal's chief of staff, and, to the end of Atatürk's life, his right hand man.

İsmet shared his leader's dreams, and was practical in implementing them, perhaps refining them. He was instrumental in defeating the Greeks in the War of Independence in western Anatolia, and, in the 1920s and 1930s served as Mustafa Kemal's prime minister. He was more pragmatic than his leader, a stickler for detail and a shrewd negotiator. The two men never always saw eye to eye and Atatürk was sometimes almost afraid of İnönü. A story dating from the late 1920s, soon after the introduction of the Latin script, illustrates this relationship. İnönü believed in the changes in the script and conscientiously never used the old Arabic script again. Atatürk and some companions were together making plans and scribbling some notes. Old habits are slow to die, and the notes were being written in the old script. İsmet İnönü was announced and the president and his companions, like naughty boys, hastened to hide the bits of paper. Nonetheless Atatürk had deep respect and affection for İsmet, who succeeded him as president after his death in 1938.

Twice Atatürk attempted to foster a multi-party system, paradoxically encouraging his own opposition. Both ventures failed but after skillfully succeeding in keeping Turkey out of the Second World War, İnönü, less charismatic, perhaps less sensitive to criticism, perhaps more of a gambler in this respect than Atatürk, did make possible the multi-party democracy that Turkey is today. Istanbul had been a city of detachment, and occasionally, opposition, to Atatürk. But, less than six months after Atatürk's death, İnönü gave a speech at the University of Istanbul, expressing his aim of creating a multi-party democracy. The Second World War stalled progress but the Democratic Party was launched when peace returned, fought in the elections of 1946 and actually triumphed in them in 1950. İnönü yielded his presidency to Celal Bayar. As a Turkish biographer put it, "İnönü considered this defeat to be his greatest victory."

Mindful of the disaster that the First World War had been to the country, he kept Turkey out of the Second World War until a month before the end. By declaring war in the final stages, he entitled Turkey to a seat at the newly formed United Nations. İsmet Paşa, as he was known long after such titles had been abolished, continued to be active in Turkish politics well into his eighties.

The Democratic Party, under Prime Minister Adnan Menderes, was in power until May 1960 when the army, fearing a dismantling of the Atatürk inheritance, took over the country. Menderes and colleagues were put on trial on the nearby island of Yassıada, and hanged. İnönü took no part in the coup although he was aware of the possibility and became the main beneficiary. He persuaded the army to give way to civilian rule and became the prime minister of a coalition government from 1961 to 1965.

He was prime minister in 1962 when I first went to Turkey. He never lost his love of western classical music and I saw him several times at concerts given by the Presidential Symphony Orchestra in Ankara. He was a small neat man with a tiny mustache, had a hearing aid and leaned forward slightly. There was sometimes a delay before the start of the concert, as the prime minister was late. He came in, took his place in the front row and the concert would then begin.

He continued to lead the Republican People's Party until he was in his late eighties. He resigned the leadership after he was challenged by one of the rising young men of the party, Bülent Ecevit, who took the party in a left-wing direction.

In the 1920s he rented a house—now 73 Refah Şehitler Caddesi—on Heybeliada for the summer. Ten years later he bought it (for 9,500 Turkish liras), and Mustafa Kemal furnished the house as a gift. As president, İnönü stayed at official residences at Florya and at Yalova, but his wife, Mevhibe, preferred to stay at this house with their children. During the 1950s, when he was the leader of the party and in opposition, he spent summers here. Again when he was prime minister between 1961 and 1965, and was based in the capital, Ankara, he stayed here whenever he could. He would withdraw only slightly from politics and came here for the summers, where the house would be used for political gatherings, including negotiations with the party as it edged to the left. He spent the winters in Ankara, where he died in December 1973 at the age of eighty-nine.

The house is now a museum belonging to the İnönü Foundation and has personal and official mementos of the man who did more than any person apart from Atatürk himself to transform Turkey in the twentieth century.

Many rooms of the house are as İsmet Paşa left it. There are some very domestic touches, such as the double bed he shared with his wife, Mevhibe, with pillows embroidered, one with the initial İ and the other, M. To the end, she always addressed him as "Paşa."

The *paşa* loved swimming and there are scores of photographs of him in old age, wearing a dressing gown on his way to the beach. He is followed by a crowd of young people and gracefully acknowledges their greetings. He had a curious way of diving from a pier into the sea, jumping in feet first. He never lost the wish to improve and when he was eighty-two he thought his swimming lacked style. He arranged for a swimming instructor from the island of Burgaz to teach him how to swim more gracefully.

Other photos have a more official appearance. The most interesting series is of his meeting, as president, and accompanied by Prime Minister Şükrü Saraçoglu, with Winston Churchill at Yenice near Adana in January 1943. The photos give a clear idea of the encounter. They met in train coaches at railway sidings. The carriages were very crowded and were likened by one of Churchill's staff to the Black Hole of Calcutta. Churchill, who had been the architect of the disastrous Gallipoli campaign, was very sensitive to Turkey's susceptibility to German approaches. He was on a frenetic and extended tour of the Mediterranean and came to woo İnönü, the man who had outmaneuvered another British political giant, Curzon, at Lausanne, twenty years earlier. İnönü greeted Churchill with an embrace. The confined railway compartment forced intimacy and probably reminiscences. The two statesmen chatted away in French, although İsmet İnönü knew English. When, in the year before assuming the presidency he was out of office, he worked hard at English, employing a regular tutor and reading books on British history and politics. İnönü's French was good, Churchill's was fluent if flawed. The neutrality of İnönü's government was reinforced, but little else resulted from the encounter.

Much is known of Atatürk's life and habits. İnönü, by contrast, was less flamboyant. He was a quiet man, with an unostentatious Islamic faith, and, as the villa and its contents disclose, had a life based on strong family ties. The grandfather of a friend of mine was a minister when İnönü was president. My friend has, in his possession, a sheaf of letters from İsmet Paşa and wondered how much they were worth. "Not an enormous amount," said a dealer. "But if you had some letters from Adnan Menderes they would be worth something."

## YEŞILKÖY

Most people, when they come to Istanbul, sweep down over the Marmara to arrive at the Atatürk International Airport. The airport used to be called Yeşilköy, meaning Green Village, after the village of that name. In the nineteenth century the village, which lived from fishing, was called by the Greeks and foreigners Agios Stephanos. In Byzantine times there was a monastery dedicated to St. Stephen. Agios Stephanos was, of course, the Greek name, but it has been better known to historians by the Italian form, San Stefano, famous for a treaty signed here in 1878.

San Stefano was transformed in the middle of the nineteenth century by two factors. The Armenian Dadian family owned several industrial plants between the city walls and Makriköy, today's Bakırköy, had their main residence at Beşiktaş, but also built a number of large weekend houses, *konaks*, here on the front. Secondly, access to the village became easier with the arrival of the railway.

In the 1840s Sultan Abdülmecid liked to vacation here and used to stay with the industrialist, Ohannes Bey Dadian. San Stefano became an attractive resort for prosperous Ottomans. By the time of his death in

San Stefano

1869, Ohannes Dadian owned almost the whole village and built places of worship for Greeks as well as Armenians. In 1842 he also built a fountain with a *namazgâh*, a praying area, for Muslims. The fountain still stands. Sultan Mehmet V built the mosque in San Stefano shortly before the First World War.

In 1877 war broke out between the Ottoman and the Russian empires. In the Crimean War the Ottomans had allies against the Russians, but none were forthcoming twenty years later. Russian troops swept through the Balkans and into Thrace and as far as San Stefano. The Ottoman government had no option but to make the best of matters and come to terms. The new young sultan, Abdülhamid II, asked the Dadians to make their San Stefano mansion available to the Russian commander, the Grand Duke Nicholas. Russians occupied the village in February 1877. The grand duke arrived by train where he was met by the Ottoman commander in chief and by Greek Orthodox clergymen, and moved into the *konak* owned by Arakel Dadian, brother of the late industrialist, Ohannes.

Peace negotiations were initiated in Arakel's house and continued and were concluded in another Dadian house, the Villa Neriman, which had been occupied by the Russian Ambassador in the city, General Ignatiev. The treaty was humiliating for the Ottomans and was to be revised, more in the interests of the empire, by Bismarck and Disraeli at Berlin later that year: but that is another story. In San Stefano during the negotiations, a party spirit seems to have prevailed. The Russians hosted a ball held in Arakel's house. The grand duke called on the sultan at Dolmabahçe palace, and a reception in honor of the grand duke was held at Beylerbeyi.

Seventeen years later, the Russians built a war memorial to their soldiers who died in the 1877–78 war. They erected it to the west of San Stefano, on land they had purchased for this purpose. The Grand Duke Nicholas returned to inaugurate the memorial in 1898. At the beginning of the First World War, the Ottoman authorities destroyed the war memorial by blowing it up with dynamite.

The Dadians, like the Muslim upper classes of Constantinople, married extensively into eastern Mediterranean Armenian and Christian aristocracy. One daughter married a Gulbenkian, another married into the family of Nubar Paşa, the Armenian prime minister of Egypt. A granddaughter of Ohannes married into the Coptic Butros Ghali family in Egypt, from which sprang the former secretary general of the United

Nations, Butros Butros-Ghali. The Dadians lost many of their assets during and after the First World War. One granddaughter in 1950 returned to Istanbul to claim back some of the Dadian lands. She got nowhere: some of her land formed part of the international airport.

There are few signs of San Stefano's brief moment of fame. The railway station has enabled the small town to become a genteel commuter suburb of the city, lacking the bustle of Bakırköy. An older quarter with narrow lanes to the west has some good restaurants around the churches. The Dadian mansions have gone, but the churches and the mosque remains. The hotel on the front has also disappeared, but in 2005 I stayed at a pension that had an echo of the past. It was managed by an elderly Jew called Isaac. The building is a freestanding wooden construction that had been the summer home of the French Levantine Crespin family and, during the First World War, was commandeered for senior German army officers. Isaac has run the hotel since the 1960s. His mother, he told me, was Spanish, his father Austrian. But as we talk further it turned out that his mother's family was indeed Spanish, but had emigrated from Spain to the city in the 1490s. His father was an Austrian Jew who, in the 1930s, came to Istanbul to buy carpets. Isaac's maternal grandfather had a shop in the Grand Bazaar and that is where his parents met. Agatha Christie and her husband Max Mallowan had been visitors to the shop and Isaac showed me a visitors' book with their signatures.

## Chapter Eight

# SAILING TO ISTANBUL

From the early nineteenth century Istanbul began to be added to the list of places to be visited on the Grand Tour. Every year accounts of outsiders' impressions of the city were being published. Numbers of visitors increased even more from the 1830s when steam power revolutionized travel in the Mediterranean. Some accounts—like those of A. W. Kinglake—have become part of English literature. Other people were profoundly affected by their time in Istanbul: in the case of Disraeli, it helped to define a political outlook. For others, like Byron and Thackeray and Thesiger, it was one port of call in a life much determined by travel and "abroad." Some, like Slade and Pears, settled in the city to work.

### LORD BYRON: AN ARISTOCRAT ABROAD

Lord Byron was in his early twenties when he came to Constantinople. He arrived in the middle of May 1810, with a friend, John Cam Hobhouse, and a valet, William Fletcher. They came after a long Mediterranean tour that had taken him to Lisbon, Gibraltar, Malta, Greece and Smyrna. They arrived on a frigate, *Salsette*, commanded by Captain Walter Bathurst, who was to be killed in the Battle of Navarino in 1827. They first stayed at a *han* in Pera, described by Hobhouse as "as bad as Wapping." The following day they called on the first secretary of the embassy, Stratford Canning, then aged twenty-three and on his first posting to the city. Canning and Byron had already met in 1805, when both played in their respective school teams in the cricket match between Eton (Canning) and Harrow (Byron), the first match between the two schools to be played at Lord's Old Ground in Dorset Square. Canning was a rather solemn young man—Hobhouse described him as "pleasing... with a vulgar voice"—but they got on well and went riding together. In later years Canning retained "a most agreeable recollection of [Byron's] good nature and varied conversation." The ambassador, Robert Adair, was ill but roused himself to greet Byron and Hobhouse and to express to them his personal dislike of the Turks.

Byron checked the city with Gibbon's description and found it accurate, and, with a *ferman* from the sultan, visited mosques. The mosque that was the Church of the Holy Wisdom, he found inferior to St. Paul's Cathedral: "I have been in both, surveyed them inside & out attentively." He appreciated its historical importance with its associations with emperors and sultans, but thought it "inferior in beauty & size" to the Süleymaniye Mosque. The walls of the Topkapı Palace reminded him of those of his Nottinghamshire home, Newstead Abbey, "only higher." He was more impressed by the city walls: "I never beheld a work of Nature or Art, which yielded an impression like the prospect on each side, from the Seven Towers to the End of the Golden Horn."

Byron also made a boat trip to the Black Sea, the Euxine, stopping at Yuşa Tepesi (Joshua's Hill), south of Anadolu Kavağı, then a favored spot for outings, "like Harrow and Highgate," as he helpfully explains. Ten years later, he versified his recollections of the trip in the fifth Canto of *Don Juan*:

> The wind swept down the Euxine, and the wave
> Broke foaming o'er the blue Symplegades;
> 'Tis a grand sight from off the Giant's Grave
> To watch the progress of those rolling seas
> Between the Bosphorus, as they lash and lave
> Europe and Asia, you being quite at ease;
> There's not a sea the passenger e'er pukes in,
> Turns up more dangerous breakers than the Euxine.

The British Ambassador recovered his health and was planning to return to London. He had to make farewell calls on the Sultan Mahmud II. The ambassador and his suite were on the point of setting off for the sultan's Topkapı Palace when Byron turned up in "scarlet regimentals topped by a profusely feathered cocked hat." As a peer of the (British) realm, he expected to be included in the ambassador's suite. The ambassador explained that British precedence and rank meant nothing to the Ottoman authorities: Byron had to follow, but not as a member of the ambassador's train, and was furious. The ambassador consulted the Austrian internuncio who confirmed his own opinion. Byron was told, and this time took it all in good part and wrote a dignified letter of apology.

Lord Byron, peer and poet

He followed the official train as a simple individual, impressing Canning with his cheerfulness and good-humored wit. The sultan was then under thirty and in the 1820s was to be the man against whom the Greek War of Independence was mainly targeted. Byron dressed in his red regimentals beneath fur robes and the sultan thought he was a woman.

After six weeks Byron and his companions left the city. As the *Salsette* sailed away, to Byron's presumed gratification, there was a salute in his honor. Byron and Hobhouse parted company at a port off the Greek coast, Hobhouse returning to England and taking with him letters from the poet, some of which expressed his moody boredom with Hobhouse's company. Byron stayed on in Greece for another eight months.

## ADOLPHUS SLADE: WITNESS TO CHANGE

Adolphus Slade (1804–77) was a younger son of a Peninsular War general who received a baronetcy. He committed himself as a boy to entering the Royal Naval College Portsmouth, where he received a good rounded education. He combined naval service with travel and was in South America for three years before he was twenty. In 1827 he was in the east Mediterranean, a witness to the Battle of Navarino, where, in the last major sea engagement between sailing ships, an Ottoman and Egyptian fleet was defeated by French, British and Russian forces, effectively sealing Greek independence.

After this first encounter with the Levant, Slade took three years on half pay to wander further in Ottoman lands and the Black Sea. He arrived again at Constantinople in May 1829 and was impressed by the glittering whiteness of the newly rebuilt Selimiye Barracks in Üsküdar opposite the Topkapı Palace—they had, as we have seen, been constructed between 1825 and 1827 by Krikor Balyan for Sultan Mahmud II to replace the previous wooden barracks built during the reign of Selim III.

Such was the casual nature of travel and nationality in the 1820s that Slade had no British passport, though he did receive a passport from the French authorities. When he landed at Tophane he was quizzed by an immigration official. Slade declared his nationality.

"Are you really an Englishman?"
"I am."
"Where is your English passport?"

"I have not got one."

"Why not?"

"Because it is not customary to have one."

"Why then have you got a French passport?"

"Because I travelled through France."

The officials were puzzled, paused for a smoke and resumed the interrogation: `

"Can you give us a reference?"

"Not I! I do not know a person in the *padishah*'s dominions."

"Wonderful! What then brings you to Turkey?"

"To see the great man, Mahmoud."

Slade was allowed to land and went to stay with a Dr. Musmezzi in Pera, described as a "Sclavonian," married to an Armenian. It was a comfortable establishment, his bed being sprinkled with rosewater.

The British Embassy was completely unstaffed, but Slade received hospitality from the Sardinian Consul General, and spent his time wandering around the city. Pera, he thought, induced idleness: "What with *chibouques* in one house, sherbet in another, a gaze on a beautiful scene here, a stroll in a cool shade there, the day slips away insensibly." Unlike many living in Pera he did cross the Golden Horn and see the sights. These included a baker who had been nailed to his door by his ears for demanding too high a price for his loaves. He also saw a prison which had in its grounds a mosque, a church and a synagogue.

Through his Sardinian contacts he dined out and met Giuseppe Donizetti Paşa, the brother of the more famous composer Gaetano Donizetti. Donizetti Paşa was also a musician and was employed by the sultan to train the army band. Slade was fascinated to hear the strains of Rossini's music coming from the quay.

A few days later, he met naval officers and the Capitan Paşa, the commander of the Ottoman navy. His ship had its own band, consisting of drums, cymbals, clarinets and fife, and played the Hunters' Chorus from Weber's opera, *Der Freischütz*, over and over again.

Slade moved in midsummer to Büyükdere with the diplomatic community. There was less etiquette by the Bosphorus. The Sardinian Ambassador, Slade recalled, made himself conspicuous by having mass performed in his house every morning, and by riding in an antiquated carriage every evening up and down the anchor-strewn quay. This nobleman had a knack of making himself disliked by persons of all ranks, nations, and sects. In character he was proud (with the low,) avaricious (though rich,) and a gourmand: in person he was tall, bloated, and corpulent. With the cunning of a Genoese citizen, he united the fawning of a Turinese courtier.

Slade took part in expeditions to the Belgrade Forest and on a plain opposite on the Asian shore, during the summer of 1829, sailors played cricket once or twice a week.

Slade wrote up an account of these early travels in two volumes that were published in 1832. He returned to the region later in the 1830s and clearly loved the country, apparently learning Turkish. In 1837 he served as liaison officer between the Mediterranean squadron of the Royal Navy and the Ottoman authorities in Istanbul. Then, in 1850, he was seconded to the Ottoman navy as a special adviser with the title of Müşavir Paşa. He spent seventeen years—until 1866—with the Ottoman Empire, becoming an admiral and seeing service in the Crimean War. After his retirement he wrote his Crimean war memoirs. He thus knew the country during the period of major reforms. His writings, with quotations from Dante and classical authors, have an arch, almost archaic, style, but display an understanding of the workings of the empire and a compassion for the men who worked under his command. His writings were known to Turks in Istanbul. He was not always sympathetic to the changes, which he felt were based on inappropriate foreign models. An elderly Turk, he reflected in 1867,

> looking back to the days of his youth, might draw conclusions from the survey not altogether unfavourable to the mixed government of Sultan, Beys, Ulema, and janissaries. Under it Turkey governed herself [badly he would admit], in her own way, and fought unaided her own battles: than which national pride has no greater aspiration. Under it Turkey was a lightly-taxed and a cheap country. With a reserved fund for war expenses, she never had recourse to usurers to defray current expenditure, and never gave people the trouble to call twice for payment of just claims. With a reasonable income, the old seraglio, one summer palace

of modest dimensions, and a few plain kiosks, sufficed for the accommodation and recreation of the imperial family. In those days Turkey clothed her population, and equipped her troops, ships, and fortresses, chiefly with native products. Her gentry then loved the chase, and the exciting game of *jereed*, which requires a strong arm, a sure eye, self-possession, and expert horsemanship; and her citizens, led by imperial example, relaxed themselves often with archery on the Okmeidan.

It may be that Slade paints a sentimental picture and by 1867 was out of step with most observers of the Istanbul scene. But there is nothing superficial about his observations, and he saw merits in the system that was being "modernized" to the applause of western commentators. Moreover, he empathized with the opinions and dilemmas of his Turkish colleagues—after all, he probably spent much of his time negotiating the implementation of reforms.

He returned to his home country. In spite of extensive overseas service he ended up as a British rear admiral with a KCB. He died in 1877, shortly after the outbreak of a virulently anti-Turkish campaign sparked by the repression of an uprising against Ottoman rule in the Balkan provinces, repression popularized in Britain by the Liberal leader, W, E. Gladstone, as the Bulgarian atrocities.

## DISRAELI; TURKISH PREJUDICES

Born in the same year as Slade, Benjamin Disraeli (1804–81) was in Constantinople one year after Slade first went there. But the future prime minister's visit was to have a profound impact on British relations with the Ottoman Empire in the 1870s. Disraeli spent eighteen months traveling around the Mediterranean in 1830 and 1831. He was twenty-six when he set off and had already published three novels. He was in poor health and constantly (and justifiably) worried about money. He traveled with a friend, the energetic and wealthy James Clay, by Malta, Corfu and Albania to the new Kingdom of Greece. From Piraeus he sailed to Constantinople, arriving there on 10 December 1830 and staying for six weeks. A new ambassador, Sir Robert Gordon, younger brother of the recent foreign secretary (and future prime minister) Lord Aberdeen, hospitably invited Disraeli and Clay to dine regularly at the embassy.

Disraeli was enchanted by the city. He wrote to his father,

A romantic engraving of the early nineteenth century

Cypress groves and mosquish domes, masses of habitations grouped on gentle acclivities rising out of the waters, millions of minarets, a sea, like a river, covered with innumerable long, thin, boats, as swift as gondolas, and far more gay, being carved and gilt... There are two things here which cannot be conceived without inspection—the Bosphorus and the Bazaar. Conceive the Ocean a stream not broader than the Thames at Gravesend, with shores with all the variety and beauty of the Rhine, covered with palaces, mosques, villages, groves of cypress and woods of Spanish chestnut. The view of the Euxine at the end is the most sublime thing I can remember.

He saw the Sultan Mahmud II from a distance. "He affects the affable activity of a European Prince, mixes with his subjects, interferes in all their pursuits and taxes them most unmercifully." He observed the European dress of the sultan—he had switched from traditionally Turkish dress three years earlier after the suppression of the Janissaries—and thought "the young Turks in uniforms which would not disgrace one of our cavalry regiments."

He visited some of the tourist sites. The Süleymaniye Mosque was "nearly as large and far more beautiful than Sophia." He played forfeits at parties given by the ambassador, who was assisted by two attachés. He confessed to his friend, Bulwer Lytton,

> that my Turkish prejudices are very much confirmed by my residence in Turkey. The life of this people greatly accords with my taste which is naturally somewhat indolent and melancholy... this is, I think, a far more sensible life than all the bustle of clubs, all the boring of drawing rooms and all the coarse vulgarity of our political controversies.

He became as familiar with the Ottoman Empire as an outsider could be, and felt an affinity with what he saw as a blend of oligarchy and meritocracy, based on an ideological solidarity.

Nearly half a century later, Disraeli, now the Earl of Beaconsfield, was prime minister. Reports of atrocities committed by Circassian auxiliaries in Ottoman uniform against Bulgarians stirred British public opinion and divided Britain. Disraeli believed that the alliance with the Ottoman Empire forged during the Crimean War was of paramount strategic importance. Turkey provided a check against Russia, which, during the middle of the century, was spreading its influence in Central Asia and, it was thought, threatening British possessions in India.

In 1876 Gladstone, who had formally if unconvincingly retired from frontline politics, embraced support for the Bulgarians and helped to stir up popular anti-Turk sentiment. An early Islamophobe, he railed against Disraeli who dismissed the stories of Bulgarian massacres as "coffee-house babble." But part of the opposition to Disraeli alluded to his Jewishness. The historian, Edward Freeman, thought he was "oriental in his sympathies and tastes." Judaism and Islam were blurred in some eyes. One member of parliament observed that "the Jews of every part of the world took the side of the Sultan against the Czar," going on to remark that "a common enemy is a great bond of friendship, and as the Christian was equally the enemy of the Mohammedan and the Jew, they were thereby brought into a certain alliance with one another." It was thought that Disraeli, "as a Jew, feels bound to make common cause with the Turk against the Christian." Freeman went further: "We cannot have England or Europe governed by a Hebrew policy... Throughout the East, the Turk and the Jew are leagued against the Christian."

The campaign against Disraeli mobilized the Nonconformist conscience of England and Wales, and to a lesser extent Scotland and Ireland. It led to a Liberal victory in 1880 and Gladstone's second government in 1880. Disraeli died the following year.

## A. W. KINGLAKE: TRAVEL CLASSIC

Alexander Kinglake (1809–91) was a retiring gentleman lawyer from Somerset. Educated at Eton and Trinity College Cambridge, he spent a year wandering around the Near East in 1834. It took him ten years to write and polish the account of his travels and published *Eothen, or Traces of Travel Brought Home from the East* in 1844. The book was an instant success and has remained a travel classic ever since. Kinglake wrote with a detached irony and created a persona for himself.

His traveling companion was John Savile. An Eton contemporary, Savile, also known then as Lord Pollington and heir to an earldom, had traveled extensively in Russia, the Caucasus and India. He had not traveled in the Ottoman Empire before, and he and Kinglake decided to travel to the Near East together. They went separately to Hamburg, and then together crossed Europe, with Pollington's Yorkshire servant, Steele. They arrived in the Ottoman capital at the onset of winter 1834. They had traveled overland from Belgrade with a polyglot interpreter by the name of Mysseri. The plague, presumably cholera, was raging in the city when they arrived. Savile, who in *Eothen* is called Methley, was already unwell. Mysseri took the travelers across the Golden Horn in a *caique*, and they "climbed up shelving steps, and threaded many windings, and at last came into the main street of Pera" to stay with a family, presumably Italian, by the name of Giuseppini.

Kinglake was impressed by the way that the sea and the city intermingled. The gondolas of Venice were one thing, but there "it is a hundred-and-twenty-gun ship that meets you in the street."

Methley/Savile/Pollington slowly recovered but Kinglake did not wish to abandon him. Nonetheless, he disregarded the cholera, explored the city, learned to smoke a Turkish hubble-bubble, took a horse and worked hard at the Turkish language, with the help of a phrase-book. The structure of the language, he observed, "especially in its more lengthy sentences, is very like to the Latin; the subject matters are slowly and patiently enumerated, without disclosing the purpose of the speaker until he reaches the end of his sentence, and then at last there comes the clenching word which gives a meaning and connection to all that has gone before." Kinglake wrote more about the way Turks negotiated in the bazaar than about any of the sights of the city.

Methley and Kinglake left Istanbul, and traveled by Troy to Smyrna, and on to Jerusalem, Cairo and back to Damascus.

Kinglake's first choice of profession had been soldiering, but poor eyesight blocked that path. His interest in military matters then brought him back to Constantinople twenty years after his first travels, on the outbreak of the Crimean War. In August 1854 he traveled with the editor of *The Times*, John Thaddeus Delane, and Henry Layard, traveler, archaeologist, member of parliament and future ambassador at Constantinople. They called on the ambassador, Stratford Canning—now Lord Stratford de Redcliffe. Kinglake was gratified to find that his old interpreter, Mysseri, had prospered on the fame of *Eothen* and was now running a hotel for western European travelers on the Grande Rue de Pera. (The spelling of his name varies in later travelers' accounts.) Kinglake went on to the Crimea where he was the guest of the British commander, Lord Raglan, and where he rode with Raglan's staff at the Battle of Alma. Raglan died in the Crimea in 1855, and the following year Raglan's widow asked Kinglake to write an account of the war. *The Invasion of the Crimea* appeared slowly in eight volumes, and is one of the great unread classics of military history. There are passages of eloquence, including an appreciation of Stratford Canning's Constantinople diplomacy, and of Florence Nightingale's work in the hospital at Scutari, Üsküdar.

## THACKERAY

William Makepeace Thackeray (1811–63) made a tour of the eastern Mediterranean between July and October 1844. He had had a success with his travel book, *Irish Sketchbook*, published under the pseudonym of Michael Angelo Titmarsh the previous year. He stopped off at Smyrna before arriving in the city. Fog obscured his first sighting, but when that lifted, his initial impressions reminded him of a Wencelas Hollar print of the Thames waterfront of London. "It is a scene not perhaps sublime, but charming, magnificent, and cheerful beyond anything I have ever seen— the most superb combination of city and gardens, domes and shipping, hills and water, with the healthiest breeze blowing over it, and above it the brightest and most cheerful sky."

Thackeray spent eight days at Constantinople, staying at the hotel run by Misseri (as he spells the name), made famous by the recently published *Eothen*. He arrived during the fasting month of Ramadan and found most of the tourist sites closed. But he did visit a hammam and saw the Sultan Abdülmecid I, then aged twenty-one, arrive by boat at Tophane to attend prayers. Thackeray thought he looked "like a French roué worn out by debauch." As he entered the mosque, "a shower of petitions was flung from the steps where the crowd was collected and over the heads of the gendarmes in brown."

He preferred the Mosque of Sultan Ahmet to the Church of the Holy Wisdom and strolled around Gülhane, which had the air of a homely English park, with macadamized roads and carpenters repairing some park palings. Topkapı, he thought, was not so much a palace as "a great town of pavilions, built without order, here and there, according to the fancy of succeeding lights of the universe, or their favourites. The only row of domes which looked particularly regular or stately, were the kitchens." An interesting observation, for these kitchens had been designed by the great Sinan.

He left on a vessel bound for Jaffa. The deck was "covered with Christian, Jew, and Heathen. In the cabin we were Poles and Russians, Frenchmen, Germans, Spaniards, and Greeks." Thackeray disembarked at Smyrna and went on to Lebanon, Palestine and Syria before returning home. The account of his travels was published as *Notes of a Journey from Cornhill to Grand Cairo* in 1846, under the authorship of Mr. M. A. Titmarsh.

## ADAM MICKIEWICZ: POET OF POLAND

Tarlabaşı is one of the grimmest quarters of Istanbul: tenement buildings of an undistinguished design, poverty-stricken people, squalor in the streets. The latest immigrants from abroad settle here. One older community of the quarter is made up of poor Kurds who make a delicacy, *midye dolması*, stuffed mussels, sold to late night revelers on İstiklâl Caddesi. But tucked away, a hundred yards from Dolapdere Caddesi, is a building that has seen better times, a villa that still has a faded glory about it. The villa houses a little-visited museum and commemorates the Polish connections with Istanbul. Here died Poland's national poet, Adam Mickiewicz, in 1855. After his death the house became a focal point for Polish exiles in the city.

From 1795 and throughout the nineteenth century Poland was subject to Russian rule. Many Polish artists and intellectuals, including Frederic Chopin, sought and found exile in France. Polish identity overlapped with Roman Catholicism, and it was Byzantine Orthodoxy that was the oppressor. On the principle that my enemy's enemy is my friend, a number of Polish intellectuals looked for inspiration in the Ottoman Empire and the visible world of Islam. Adam Mickiewicz, born in 1798, was exiled from Poland to southern Russia in 1824 and visited the Crimea which, like Poland, had been swallowed up by Russian expansionism. Crimea had been Ottoman until 1788 and was still a multicultural maritime province. Mickiewicz saw it as "the Orient in miniature." The Crimean peninsula inspired his *Crimean Sonnets.*

Mickiewicz spent the second half of his life in Paris, in a community of Polish exiles. For many years he was Professor of Slavonic Languages at the Collège de France. During the Crimean War, he set out for Constantinople, arriving in September 1855, initially staying at a convent in Galata.

Another Polish exile, Prince Adam Czartoryski, had been granted asylum in the Ottoman Empire after the failure of the Polish uprising against Russia in 1848. Czartoryski was an elderly nationalist who had known Mickiewicz for nearly forty years. The prince had been granted land by the sultan twelve miles to the east of Üsküdar, in a village now named Polonezköy.

A third man of Polish origin in Constantinople at the time was the colorful Michał Czajkowski, who had started as a dashing aristocrat back home. A successful novelist, he came to the Ottoman Empire, embraced Islam and became known as Sadık Paşa. The Poles aimed to raise troops to fight alongside the Ottomans in the Crimea. Sadık Paşa raised a division, made up of deserters from the tsar's army, Cossacks and press-ganged Jews. The Polish exiles in Constantinople formed another Polish army in the city, and Mickiewicz spent a fortnight with them at Burgas, now on the Bulgarian Black Sea coast. Mickiewicz took note of the Jews in the camp. He had sympathy with Jews as another oppressed people, and proposed to a less sympathetic Sadık Paşa the forming of a separate Jewish legion.

At Burgas he became ill. He left the front and came to Istanbul, to the house in Tarlabaşı. He settled in, worked at studying the Turkish language and busied himself with correspondence about a Jewish legion. But illness turned to cholera, violently and lethally. He collapsed in the presence of a Polish visitor to whom he started a sentence, "The regiment of Ottoman Cossacks..." He died two hours later, on 27 November 1855.

The villa housing the museum was rebuilt in 1870 and has panels celebrating Mickiewicz's patriotic poetry, in Polish and with translations into Turkish and English:

> Arise! United stand! With chains of harmony
> Let us encircle the vast world.
> Our spirits unified yet free.
> Then earth-bound human clod away!
> We point thee a more lofty goal,
> Till, freed from mouldy bark, thy soul
> Recall to long lost, verdant day.

Or more bathetically

> No frogs so sweet as Polish frogs e'er sang.

Adam Mickiewicz's body was taken to Paris, and in 1890 moved to Poland, still not yet an independent country, and he now lies in the cathedral of Kraków. Meanwhile Polonezköy, which is within the boundaries of Greater Istanbul, has become a favorite place for a day out or a weekend away. A few Central European-style houses survive, and secular *Istanbul-lus* are happy to eat at restaurants that provide a sort of Polish cuisine with illicit pork.

## MARK TWAIN

In the summer of 1867 Sultan Abdülaziz visited Europe as the guest of the French Emperor Napoleon III. He visited the Exposition Universelle in Paris, where the two monarchs progressed through cheering crowds. A bystander perched on a barrel to get a better look. He was a thirty-one-year old American from Missouri called Samuel Clemens who had achieved minor success as a travel writer, his travels till then not extending outside the North American continent. Clemens, who became better known as

Mark Twain, was on a five-month tour of the Old World and had been commissioned by a San Francisco newspaper to send letters regularly back for immediate publication.

Mark Twain had left the ship on which he had been traveling at Marseille and taken the train to Paris. He was not greatly impressed by the sultan, whom he saw as "a short, stout, dark man, black-bearded, black-eyed," wearing "dark green European clothes" and a fez, but "without ornament or insignia of rank." He had, for Mark Twain, the appearance of a butcher. "If he only had a cleaver in his hand and a white apron, one would not be at all surprised to hear him say, 'A mutton roast today, or will you have a nice porterhouse steak?'"

It was a chance encounter, and a little later in the early autumn of that year, Mark Twain and the cruise ship, *Quaker City*, a veteran of the American Civil War, reached the sultan's capital. He arrived at dawn and saw it as "by far the handsomest city we have seen."

Mark Twain did the usual tourist things, visiting the Church of the Holy Wisdom and the Grand Bazaar. He was not impressed by the former, dismissing it as "the rustiest old barn in heathendom." It was then a mosque and he had to remove his shoes and claims to have caught a cold as a result. He was more impressed by the mausoleum of Sultan Mahmud II, describing it as "the neatest piece of architecture."

His most vivid impressions were of the variety of crowded life in the narrow streets: beggars, cripples, physical freaks. The city was "an eternal circus. People were thicker than bees in those narrow streets, and the men were dressed in all the outrageous, outlandish, idolatrous, extravagant thunder-and-lightning costumes that ever a tailor with the delirium tremens and seven devils could conceive of." Veiled women looked like the shrouded dead who had risen from their graves. He wandered along the Grande Rue de Pera, noting dogs in the side streets. Three dogs were fast asleep and blocked one such road. A man led a herd of sheep past them. The sheep bounded over them, the dogs looking lazily up. "I thought I was lazy," reflected Twain, "but I am a steam-engine compared to a Constantinople dog." Elsewhere he was fascinated by a man driving a flock of a hundred geese through the street, controlling them with a ten-foot pole.

Twain went in for other experiences enjoyed by tourists. He was fascinated by reports of the slave trade, and seems disappointed that Georgian girls were no longer sold in public. He saw a *zikr*—the whirling of

Dervishes—and had a Turkish bath. He did not enjoy the latter. ("The place was vast, naked, dreary; its court a barn, its galleries for human horses. The cadaverous half nude varlets that served in the establishment had nothing of poetry in their appearance, nothing of romance, nothing of Oriental splendor. They shed no entrancing odors—just the contrary.") He smoked a hubble-bubble and choked, he thought, like an eruption of Vesuvius.

He left the city and cruised into the Black Sea and on to Odessa and the Crimea, and a week or so later returned, pausing for two days in the city, during which time he took boat trips on the Golden Horn. Then on to the Mediterranean and south to Palestine.

The letters were brought together and published in 1869 as *The Innocents Abroad*. Of all Mark Twain's books this sold best during the author's lifetime. It has been seen as the most successful of the "funny school" of travel writing. Abroad is dirty; foreigners are comical, and there is no place like home.

Mark Twain lived on for another forty years. The ship, *Quaker City*, sank four years later off Bermuda.

## THE PRINCE OF WALES, 1869

Official royal visits abroad were facilitated by the development of railways and steam boats in the middle of the nineteenth century. In 1867 Sultan Abdülaziz spent several days in Britain after his sojourn in Paris. To complement this courtesy visit, the British government arranged for Queen Victoria's son and heir to make an extended Near Eastern tour two years later.

The Prince of Wales, later King Edward VII, came to Istanbul, accompanied by his wife, later Queen Alexandra, his private staff and William Howard Russell. Russell had been *The Times* correspondent covering the Crimean War fifteen years earlier, and was familiar with the city. He later published his diary of the royal tour.

The party left London in November 1868, spent Christmas with the family of the Princess of Wales in Denmark and then traveled overland to Brindisi, from where they sailed to Egypt, visiting from there Jaffa and Jerusalem. They arrived at the Ottoman capital in a small flotilla. In sight of the city they trans-shipped to one of the Sultan Abdülaziz's steamers and were received by the reforming grand vizier, Ali Paşa, described by

PUNCH, OR THE LONDON CHARIVARI.—JULY 20, 1867.

THE ILLUSTRIOUS CONVALESCENT.

Mr. BULL. "YOU A SICK MAN! HA! HA!—I KNEW MY CRIMEAN DOCTORS WOULD SET YOU UP, AND THIS VISIT WILL DO YOU ALL THE GOOD IN THE WORLD."

*Punch* comments on Sultan Abdülaziz's visit to Britain

Russell as "a very small, slight, sallow-faced man, with two very penetrating honest-looking eyes. He has a delicate air, and looks timorous and nervous."

Russell found that there had been many improvements since he had last been in the city. "After the great fire of '64, orders were given that no houses of wood should be erected in future, and there are great open spaces yet to be filled in Stamboul. There is gas in all the main streets on both sides of the Golden Horn. The water supply is abundant. But the change in the aspect of the population is not so gratifying to the eye. The grand old turban is rarely seen. Moolahs and 'fanatics'—i.e. men who believe— are the only people who wear them; and the fez in all its ugliness, is the universal substitute."

The royal party stayed at a palace near Tophane. Dinner was accompanied by the sultan's band under his Italian bandmaster, Callisto Guatelli Paşa, who entertained the visitors with a medley of operatic music.

On the morning of their second day they received a delegation of

British subjects, led by Charles Hanson, one of the founders of the Ottoman Bank. "Like most delegations," observed Russell, "they were bald-headed, immensely respectable, and very tedious men, in evening clothes, and full of professions of loyalty." During the afternoon the prince and princess visited the Sweet Waters of Asia and spent the evening at the Naum Theatre on the Grande Rue de Pera where an Italian company played before a packed house. ("The spectators did not stare as much at the Sultan's box and its distinguished occupants as most European audiences would have done.")

The following day the royal visitors went to Topkapı, seeing the Baghdad Pavilion and "everything except the Holy Place where rests the Standard of the Prophet, never to be seen by Christian eye, unless it be unfurled against him in battle." After that the tourists went to the great mosque, formerly the Church of the Holy Wisdom, seeing the interior from "the Sultan's 'pew,' which is screened by lattice-work from the vulgar eyes below." Then on to the ministry of war, to be received by Hüseyin Paşa and Ömer Paşa; the latter had been the commander in chief of the Ottoman army in the Crimean War. After lunch and an exchange of toasts, they went to the Sultan Ahmet Mosque and down to the Golden Horn by way of the covered bazaar—the tourist route has not much changed in a century and a half.

The great event was a formal dinner at the Dolmabahçe Palace. The royal couple were there before seven and met all the sultan's ministers. The sultan received them and giving his arm to the Princess of Wales led the party into the dining room. The menu was of both French and Turkish food:

> Potage Sévigné
> Croquettes et Beurek
> Poisson (levrek) à l'Impériale
> Filets de Boeuf à la Jardiniere
> Midia-ile Yalandji Dolma
> Filets de Chevreuil
> Zeytoun-Yaghli Enghinar
> Turban de Volaille à la Princesse
> Kiata-Barbunia
> Foie Gras en Belle Vue

Asperges

Punch à la Romaine

Faisans et bécassines

Pilav

Ananas à la Victoria

Kaikmakly

Tel Cadaif

Timbales à la Sicilienne

Tauk Gueuk-su

Fromage glacé

Wines available were "Xeres, Sauterne, Bordeaux, Lafitte, Vin du Rhin (avec les plats froids), et Champagne frappé." After the meal the sultan gave his arm to the princess and escorted her to the Imperial Harem where she met the sultan's mother.

The following day, a Sunday, was spent with the British: church service at the British Embassy, lunch with the ambassador and then a trip to Scutari (Üsküdar) to see the cemetery of Crimean war dead.

The royal couple made a second trip to the bazaars, passing incognito as Mr. and Mrs. Williams. Then there was a return visit to Naum's theatre to see the opera, *Martha*, by the German Friedrich von Flotow. The story of the opera takes place in Richmond, Surrey, and the piece was, says Russell, "astonishingly well sung and played."

The royal party on one afternoon crossed the Bosphorus in fourteen-oared caiques and saw the sultan's new Beylerbeyi Palace. Open landaus were ready and took them up the hill to Çamlıca, the summer residence of Prince Mustafa Fazıl, brother of the Hıdiv İsmail of Egypt. The two princes were old acquaintances, and the Egyptian had the reputation of being a radical in politics. He had studied in Paris and had been a reforming minister of education, and then of justice, in the Ottoman capital. His radicalism manifested itself by his allowing his daughters to ride unveiled in his park. The Ottoman Egyptian prince was a gourmet and kept three chefs, a Turk, a Frenchman and an Egyptian, in three kitchens in each of his palaces. The choicest fruit—pineapples, melons, apples and pears—had been brought in from Paris.

On the same day, the prince and princess danced for England by attending a state ball at the British Embassy—the ballroom is still there. All ministers and all foreign ambassadors were present. Unusually, the sultan himself graced the occasion. He and his entourage arrived (late) and were met at the gate by the prince and the ambassador and received by the princess and the ambassador's wife at the top of the stairs. The sultan did not dance but looked on with benevolent serenity. The party went on till dawn.

The following afternoon His Royal Highness went to the arsenal at Tophane, where the master general of ordnance, another Ali Paşa, had studied at Woolwich, and was employing some British workmen. From there the prince visited the Crimean Memorial Church and then on again to Naum Theatre. This time they saw the opera *L'Africaine* by Giacomo Meyerbeer, first produced only four years earlier. The sultan attended the performance, his face "a study as he gave his attention to the march of events on the stage."

The prince spent one morning visiting Abdullah's photographic studios and the imperial stables, which included "a magnificent old charger, twenty-nine years of age, with a pedigree of 400 years" and a stuffed Russian bear, shot by a tsar and sent as a present to the sultan. Later he and the ambassador, "notwithstanding the bitter cold wind [rode] to an outlying cricket-ground in the suburbs, and saw the poor Ariadnes [the crew of the prince's boat] out-bowled and out-batted in one innings by the English inhabitants of Constantinople." (The outlying cricket-ground was probably at Okmeydanı, above Kasımpaşa, which was from time to time taken over by the British colony for polo and golf.) The royal couple went again to the British Embassy for a banquet.

On the last day the photographer, Abdullah, came to take portraits of the royal party, including some "cabinet photographs" of the princess. A final trip to Dolmabahçe by caique was followed by an afternoon "déjeuner," after which the sultan led the princess

> down the grand staircase to the Grand Hall, which is one of the—if, indeed, it be not the—noblest of rooms in the world. It is not possible to describe such a wonder of size and colour; but if you will fancy St Paul's, with the interior of its dome bright with metallic lustre, and decorated with the richest arabesques, you may come near it. A group, in which the Sultan stood prominent, was formed at one side of the vast circumference. In two lines, far apart, were eight officers of the Body

Guard in Arnaout uniforms. They stood, with heads downcast and arms folded across the breast, as if fixed to the earth, their eyes turned towards the ground. As the Sultan passed towards the great porch, these mutes turned slowly, like so many automatons, keeping their heads in the direction to which he moved; and when His Majesty strode back through the hall, and vanished through the pillared entrance, the satellites revolved on their heels slowly as he went.

Caiques took the royal party from the quay at Dolmabahçe Palace to the prince's boats, and, to the accompaniment of a band playing the Turkish national anthem, the Prince and Princess of Wales ended their visit to the city, heading up the Bosphorus to the Black Sea en route for the Crimea.

One week later they returned through the Bosphorus but did not land. They proceeded to Athens and then, after six months away from Britain, back to Brindisi and overland home.

## EDWIN PEARS: FORTY YEARS IN CONSTANTINOPLE

The man who drew the attention of the outside world to the Ottoman crisis of the 1870s was Edwin Pears (1835–1919) who arrived in the city in 1873 as a lawyer and who was to live there until the First World War. He was the worst type of British expatriate, arriving with a stock of mid-Victorian English liberal values through which he saw and judged Istanbul. He never traveled much outside Istanbul, and immediately saw the government machinery as "honeycombed with corruption." He deplored what he saw as the philo-Turk prejudices of the British community who had done well out of the "glamour" of the Crimean War. Soon after his arrival he became a correspondent for the London newspaper, the *Daily News*. In his self-revealing memoirs, *Forty Years in Constantinople*, he recalls that he "learned of the existence of the Bulgarian people" and then of the victims of "Turkish misrule" in the Bulgarian provinces. Atrocities had been committed in Bulgaria, but they were not exclusively committed by Turkish forces. But Pears' reporting was one-sided, and did not pause to reflect on the causes—endemic banditry in the mountains, rising expectations, an increasing sense of nationalism and a breakdown of administrative control.

During his years in the capital Pears continued to send negative reports on the politics of the country. He also wrote two volumes on the history of the city—on the Fourth Crusade and on the Turkish conquest in 1453. In the latter there is a constant motif that Turkish rule is bad—corrupt and cruel—and that the Turks are religious fanatics and hate non-Muslims. It is as if Turkish rule in Europe was illegitimate and that the sooner it ended the better. Pears did what he could, by his writings, to hasten that day. His active hostility to his hosts was well known and it is a tribute to Turkish hospitality and tolerance that he was allowed to stay. He used no Turkish sources in his historical writings. They are, however, written with a compelling narrative style, but show no empathy for Muslims and not much knowledge about Islam.

Pears became a senior member of the British community and briefed young diplomats about Ottoman law. He did know some of the emerging generation of Turkish public servants. Indeed, in 1909, when Mahmud Muhtar, a minister of war, was on the wrong side of a coup and was seeking refuge from the forces of the Young Turk Unionists, Pears gave him temporary refuge at his house in Moda—the suburb on the Asian shore that became the home of well-to-do British residents.

When war broke out between the British and the Ottoman empires, Pears, now Sir Edwin, a rather sad old man in his eighties, had to leave. But he continued to write articles, hostile and uncomprehending, about the country where for forty years he had lived and prospered.

He helped to fuel anti-Turkish prejudices and Islamophobia with the apparent authority of long residence in the country. Was it not Prime Minister Lord Salisbury who said, "If I wish to be misinformed about a place I consult an Englishman who has lived there for thirty years"?

## MARMADUKE PICKTHALL: CONSERVATIVE AND MUSLIM

Marmaduke Pickthall (1875–1936) was an English novelist and a Muslim convert. Although his translation of the Qur'an is one of the best known among Anglophone Muslims, he left little legacy. He was an oddball, a passionate and articulate supporter of unfashionable causes. An ardent supporter of the Ottoman cause during the First World War, his knowledge of the country was based on four months' residence in Istanbul during the Balkan Wars in 1913.

He had been a great supporter of the 1908 Revolution and wanted to see the capital for himself. At the age of thirty-seven he arrived in March

1913 and spent two weeks at the Pera Palas Hotel. He did not like the area. "Contrasted with the stricter morals and puritanical decorum of the Turks," he wrote in a dispatch to the journal, *The New Age*, "Pera, and its neighbour, Galata, are a huge plague-spot—a parasitic growth which threatens Turkey with corruption." He had letters of introduction from the Conservative member of parliament Aubrey Herbert and through a contact took rooms at a house in Erenköy, an elegant village far from the city center and on the Asian side. This belonged to a German lady, Fraulein Kate Eckerlein, who had spent many years in Turkey and whose name was turkified as Misket ("Miss Kate") Hanım. He studied Turkish with a Roman Catholic Arab from Diyarbakır who taught at the Galatasaray Lycée, and with the progressive imam of the local mosque at Göztepe. Pickthall was an accomplished linguist and within months he was able to discuss politics and read newspapers.

His two main contacts were Ali Haydar Bey, son of the reforming grand vizier of the 1870s, Midhat Pasha, and the foreign minister, Prince Said Halim. The latter was another member of the Egyptian Hıdival family who had settled in Istanbul. The prince, Pickthall wrote to his wife, Muriel, had "very blue eyes, very brown cheeks, very white collar, very black frock-coat, a very red fez which looks like a part of his head, and a cigarette in an amber holder stuck permanently in one cheek."

Pickthall himself bought and wore a fez. Each day he traveled by train and steamer to Galata Bridge. He traveled with a group of commuters from Erenköy, a group that "comprised ex-Ministers of State, doctors, khojas, and some journalists." He had his shoes cleaned, and called on Turkish friends and on *The Times* correspondent, Philip Graves. In contrast to most British visitors, Pickthall sought out and cultivated only Muslim Turks. He was contemptuous of the Christians of Pera, whose "population preys upon the empire with intent to kill."

He was in Istanbul in 1913 when the unionist grand vizier, Mahmud Şevket Paşa, was assassinated. Pickthall thought he was the only man "to have the will and capacity to save his country from the hundred enemies inside and out, who threatened its existence." Pickthall sympathized with the government's draconian punishment of the offenders:

> Twelve were hanged. To show you the value of a punishment which
> seemed to me excessive: a very peaceful, law-abiding Syrian merchant

whom I knew, being in Stamboul, went to see the bodies hanging on the gibbets, and touched one of them. He told the tale with placid satisfaction. "Then I felt more comfortable," he said, "for then I knew for certain that we had a government."

Pickthall was never fair to Ottoman Christians. While the Christian Balkan states were threatening what was left of European Turkey, he witnessed a funeral of an orthodox prelate, the procession escorted by Turkish troops. Would a Catholic bishop be allowed a public funeral in Belfast if that city was under siege by a Roman Catholic army, he wondered. "There was a glorious row," he wrote to his wife, "in the Greek Church at Pera on Good Friday; four different factions fighting about which was to carry the big Cross, and the Bishop hitting out right and left upon their craniums with his crozier; many people wounded, women in fits. The Turkish mounted police had to come in force to stop further bloodshed."

Pickthall left in July. The series of dispatches he had sent to *The New Age* were published the following year as *With the Turk in Wartime*. Pickthall was a founding member of the Anglo-Ottoman Society in January 1914. The other early members made up a rainbow coalition and included the MP Aubrey Herbert, the Persian scholar at the University of Cambridge, Professor E. G. Browne, the romantic Scottish aristocratic socialist, R. B. Cunninghame Graham, and one of the founders of the Labour Party, Keir Hardie. After war broke out between the British and the Ottoman empires, Pickthall wrote regularly and stridently for the press arguing the Ottoman case. In 1917 he came out as a Muslim and at the end of the war he was called up for military service, and agreed on condition that he did not have to be a combatant against Turkey.

Politically Pickthall was a conservative. But at the end of the war, he must have been regarded with grave suspicion by the British establishment as an infidel and a potential traitor. Indian Muslim friends in London came to his support and he went to Bombay to edit the *Bombay Chronicle* for two years. While he was in India he published his last novel, *The Early Hours*. This takes place in Turkey in the years before the First World War. There is a background of contemporary Turkish politics and a few scenes take place in Istanbul. The hero, like the author, stays in Erenköy, travels to the Galata Bridge with the same commuters and has his shoes cleaned on arrival.

After two years in Bombay Pickthall went on to Hyderabad and worked in various capacities for the Nizam. He was for ten years the first editor of *Islamic Culture*, a semi-academic quarterly. In it he wrote on the progressive Islamic philosophy of his old friend, Prince Said Halim, who had been gunned down by an Armenian nationalist in Rome in 1921. In 1931 his old links came in handy, when he negotiated the marriage of the Nizam's son and heir to Dürrüşehvar Sultan, the daughter of the last caliph of the Ottoman Empire, Abdülmecid II, who was living in exile in Nice. Pickthall died in Cornwall in 1936, Dürrüşehvar Sultan seventy years later, dying in London. Both are buried with yards of each other in the Muslim cemetery at Brookwood in Surrey.

## WILFRED THESIGER: "SHOWPIECES OF A DEAD PAST"

In the summer of 1930 Wilfred Thesiger (1910–2003) was twenty years old. He was born in Ethiopia, or, as he always called it, Abyssinia, where his father was the head of the British Mission. Wilfred had witnessed and relished the savagery of that kingdom. As a teenager he had been to India to stay with his uncle, who happened to be the viceroy.

In June of his first long vacation from Oxford he managed to secure a passage, working on a tramp steamer bound for the Black Sea. The steamer anchored off Istanbul and Wilfred received a message at the ship's office from the ambassador, Sir George Clerk, inviting him to call at the embassy—or the consulate general, for the embassy had been transferred to the capital, Ankara. Wilfred was embarrassed that he did not have clothes appropriate for calling on the ambassador, but went nonetheless. Clerk had known Wilfred's father (also called Wilfred) who had been an honorary consul at Van in the 1890s and received Wilfred who wore grey (albeit clean) flannel trousers.

Wilfred spent four days in the city, visiting Ayasofya, the Church of the Holy Wisdom, each day and seeing the mosques, the walls, the bazaar, the cisterns and the Topkapı Palace. He attended the Friday prayers in Ayasofya, along with a few hundred worshippers. But he was disappointed by the city, which he found "depressing, soulless, with drab crowds, deserted mosques, and palaces preserved as showpieces of a dead past." He returned in 1936. Ayasofya was now a museum and he was even more disappointed: "it was now debased into an ancient monument, open to the public for a fee."

## Chapter Nine

# CONTEMPORARY ISTANBUL

### THE CHANGING FACE OF THE CITY

The last century has witnessed an extraordinary demographic turnover in Istanbul. In 1914 the population of the Vilayet (governorate) of Istanbul was almost a million—as it had been at its most populous in the Middle Ages. Muslims in 1914 formed just over 60 percent of the population. Thirteen years later, the population had dropped to 700,000 of whom Christians numbered around 270,000.

The most significant emigration has been the departure of Greeks. Modern Turkish national identity has largely been based on the triumph of Mustafa Kemal over the Greeks and their expulsion after the First World War. By the 1920s Greek loyalty had become suspect for the majority Turkish population. Sixty years later, Greeks were not permitted to have dual nationality. By then the Greek community of Istanbul was down to 2,000. This was a transformation from the situation a century earlier, when Istanbul was the city with the largest Greek Orthodox community in the world. Indeed, in the middle of the nineteenth century there was actually immigration of Greeks, including numbers from the newly independent Greek kingdom: Istanbul offered more social and economic possibilities than Athens.

The main Armenian deportations and massacres took place in Anatolia. But the city also suffered. The Armenians of the capital had felt themselves safe, and some had had good relations with Young Turk leaders. But on the night of 23/24 April 1915, 235 leading Armenians were arrested and detained, and then exiled to central Anatolia. Most were never heard of again. One who did escape was a middle-aged composer, Soghomon Soghomonian, otherwise known as Komitas, who before the war had studied in Berlin and became a pioneering musicologist, attracting attention from Saint-Saëns and Debussy. Komitas returned to the city, but his mind was unhinged by his experiences. He immigrated to Paris and died there in an asylum in 1935. The date of the first arrests and deportations, 24 April, is held as the Armenian national day of mourning.

Many Armenians survived deportation and the massacres and continued to live in Istanbul. Districts such as Samatya have had a concentration of Armenians over the years. Today there are about 50,000 Armenians in Istanbul, including recent temporary migrants from the independent Republic of Armenia, formerly in the Soviet Union.

Jews and Armenians have had a comparable twentieth-century experience. Both have endured marginalization and economic persecution, but individuals have integrated themselves into Turkish mainstream culture, in the professions, sport and entertainment. This has not been the case to the same extent with the Greeks. Those still resident form an aging community. Congregations of Orthodox churches also include Arabic-speaking Christians from the region of Antakya (better known in English as Antioch) and İskenderun (Alexandretta) near the Syrian border, and visitors from Greece who visit in large numbers, particularly at Easter.

The non-Muslims have been replaced by millions of Muslims. During the nineteenth century, as the empire in Europe was replaced by independent Christian states, Muslims from those Balkan countries as well as from the Caucasus poured into the capital. The process continued after the First World War with Muslim migrants from the Soviet Union, and in particular from the Crimea. Then after the Second World War more migrants came from the Balkans when communist regimes were established. Unlike many of the Russians who migrated into Istanbul after the Bolshevik Revolution of 1917 and moved on to Paris or the United States, the people from the Balkans came to stay, many making a contribution to Turkish entrepreneurial culture.

But what characterizes Istanbul today, socially, economically and politically, has been the massive migration from rural Anatolia. There had always been a steady trickle of seasonal migration, and some groups—in particular the Laz from the eastern Black Sea coastal regions—built up their own networks in the construction industry, in hotels and catering services from the nineteenth century. The mass migration started from the 1950s, since when the population of the city has increased at least tenfold. In 1970 the population was three million, in 1975 four million, in 1985 six million, in 1995 nine million. Today the population of Greater Istanbul is in the region of fifteen million. The birth rates of the immigrants have been higher than those of the old *Istanbullus*. The immigration has followed patterns that can be replicated in many Third World cities: chain migration, with people following pioneer migrants from a family or a locality. Men of the first generation of immigrants from the country worked as laborers, and the women often obtained work as domestic servants.

Immigrants have shaped the physical appearance of Greater Istanbul. During the 1960s and 1970s many immigrants built houses without permission or regulation; the regulations were anyway unclear and ambiguous. Land that is not specifically owned belongs to the state and has been regarded as common land, for the use of Turkish citizens. The first immigrants settled in unused farmland or parkland. Property abandoned by non-Muslim emigrants was taken over. The law relating to *vakıf* property—endowments under Islamic law—was, after the Atatürk revolution, unclear. Houses were thrown up overnight, thereby claiming a legal status. Huge shanty towns—*gecekondu*—grew up around the city. Space between villas was filled in. Today you can travel through sixty miles (one hundred kilometers) of urban landscape from one end of Greater Istanbul to the other.

The writer, Latife Tekin, in her novel, translated as *Berji Kristen, Tales from the Garbage Hills*, first published in 1983, has written of the marginal life of the people of the *gecekondu*. When they first arrived they built houses from rubbish. Their ramshackle huts, constructed sometimes on toxic waste, were liable to demolition by bulldozers.

> In the huts the hammering and plastering never let up. No sooner was one wall repaired than another collapsed, and then a roof leaked, and one day bits of tin would be nailed to hut walls and on another bits of wood were put up to cover the gaps.

Latife Tekin writes how the people, immigrants to the city, were exploited and recruited into local factories on basic pay and with minimal health protection.

After 1980 shanty towns were slowly and partially replaced by new blocks of apartments. The first contracting entrepreneurs were often Turks from the Black Sea regions, who obtained a working capital by selling apartments before they had been constructed. Pressure from the immigrants obliged municipalities to facilitate permits and grant public land for housing development. As a result, around and within the perimeter of the city there are clusters of ten- to twenty-story towers, each with four or five apartments to a floor. The infrastructure may be dubious and the landscaping aesthetics appalling, but the tower blocks have facilitated social mobility.

Further collective control was provided by professional syndicates that had political and social leverage—doctors, military officers, journalists—creating cooperatives that owned apartment blocks. These either provided homes for their members or were rented out, providing an income for the syndicate.

Most people in modern Istanbul live in apartments. Prices suit all budgets. Even centrally it is possible to buy or rent an apartment at a fraction of the price of similarly located property in any Western European city. There are not many older villas. Some have been well restored at vast expense. In the Sultan Ahmet area, some older wooden houses, either survivors of the great nineteenth-century conflagrations or rebuilt in defiance or circumvention of regulations, were rescued from collapse or demolition in the last decade of the twentieth century to become boutique hotels. In less gentrified parts of the city older houses can still be seen, some rooms occupied by people—and rats and scorpions—while other parts of the building are visibly disintegrating.

The novelist, Elif Shafak, wrote about one old building in her novel, *The Flea Palace*. She described the contrasting variety of people who rent apartments and the rubbish surrounding the building, drawing out the tension between the dramas of the residents and the squalor of their environment. All live surrounded by the past and the dead: "In this city, the dead resided side by side with the living."

## ECONOMIC TAKE-OFF AND THE SKYSCRAPERS OF LEVENT

The 1980s saw also the economic take-off of Istanbul. Large contractors who had done well in the Gulf and Libya were well-placed to develop the physical environment for the new globalized middle-class areas such as Levent, Etiler and Maslak: new office tower blocks, shopping malls, residential units, exhibition grounds. For the upper end of the market of an international bourgeoisie there were gated compounds, swimming pools and proximity to golf courses. The problems of commuting—a journey of a few kilometers might take an hour by car at peak times—were partially offset by the construction of the Metro, the first section of which opened in 1989.

The city's booming economy since the 1990s has led to enormous disparities of wealth. According to the March 2008 issue of *Forbes Magazine*, Istanbul is the fourth city in the world for its number of billionaires—thirty-five—only exceeded by Moscow, New York and London. Successive "soft Islamist" governments have embraced global capitalism, and the areas north of Taksim, and particularly Şişli, Levent and the nearby Maslak compare architecturally with London's Dockland, Texas or the United Arab Emirates. During the 1980s and early 1990s, when Turgut Özal, Süleyman Demirel and Tansu Çiller were successively prime minister, the private sector was given every encouragement. In spite of banking crises—in 2000 private banks crashed—there has been no reverse of this trend, and Istanbul has continued to lead the country towards a Thatcherite free-market utopia. Many of the leading banks that had had their headquarters in Ankara moved to Istanbul. A Stock Market was founded in 1993.

For the first time, the architectural reference points are not Turkish nor Eastern Mediterranean nor Levantine, not even European, but global. The shopping malls are no longer—as in Beyoğlu—inspired by Paris, Brussels or Naples. They are vast spaces, shopping centers with drive-in facilities and giant department stores. Metrocity in Levent, with available valet parking, has become the twenty-first-century equivalent of the Grande Rue de Pera with its own classy international outlets: Swatch, Marks & Spencer, River Island, United Colors of Benetton, Sony, Mothercare and Starbucks. The clientele is prosperous.

Levent skyscrapers

The area of Levent was first settled in the 1950s. New social housing complexes were surrounded by squatter settlements. In the 1970s the older commercial and industrial complexes moved out from Eminönü and Beyoğlu and settled here. The changes were facilitated by the construction of the Bosphorus bridges and the new motorways that bypassed the older quarters of the city.

Banks set the pace, with the Yapı Kredi Plaza and the Oyak Bank in 1989. The first multipurpose skyscraper is the Akmerkez Commercial and Residential Center (the American spelling is indicative) in Etiler, built in 1993. It consists of three blocks, one of fourteen stories, another of seventeen. A third twenty-four story block contains luxury residential units. Three lower storeys serve as a shopping mall. In the following decade Turkish billionaires, international hotels and banks vied with each other to dazzle the spectator. The Sabancı Plaza, equipped with banking headquarters and conference halls and boasting a striking use of glass and steel, was designed by Haluk Tümay in 1993. The HSBC Bank, designed by the same architect, was built in 1998 and has a progressive elevation in a ziggurat form. This building was put out of action by terrorists in November 2003. At the turn of the century skyscrapers with competing altitudes were being put up. The Turkish Commercial Bank headquarters rose to 593 feet (181 meters) in 2000.

## THE SABANCI AND KOÇ FAMILIES AND CULTURE

In the way that the Armenian family, the Dadians, dominated manufacturing and commercial economy in the nineteenth century, so two Turkish families have had a major impact on the Turkish economy in the last fifty years. Both have made enormous contributions to culture and the arts: they are the Koç and the Sabancı families. Their styles and backgrounds have differed.

The Sabancı family come from Kayseri, a province with a reputation for producing people with talents for business. The founder of the dynasty was Hacı Ömer Sabancı, who was born in 1906 and moved to Adana in his twenties and became a partner in a cotton ginning factory. One of modern Turkey's first industrialists, he took over a number of abandoned assets—property and industrial plants—and made the Adana region a major industrial area of the country. Hacı Ömer founded Akbank in 1948 and died in 1966, leaving several sons to run the businesses. Subsequently the Sabancı empire shifted its base to Istanbul. Today Sabancı Holding owns 69 companies and has 53,400 employees. From its industrial base—textiles, tires, cars, cement, plastics and energy—it has expanded into hotels and financial services. The current chairman and chief executive officer is a granddaughter of Haci Ömer, Güler Sabancı, who took over from her uncle Sakıp Sabancı on his death in 2004. She used to be in charge of the tire production factory and has been known as the "rubber queen." Her office is in one of the twin towers belonging to Sabancı Holding at Levent.

The Sabancıs have founded a university, based at Orhanlı, near Tuzla, southeast of the city in the direction of İzmit on the Asian side, which has over 3,500 students. The Sabancı Foundation has also sponsored the arts, with a gallery and museum at Sakıp Sabancı's former mansion in Emirgân. All Sabancı ventures can be recognized from the highlighting of the two first letters in their name.

Akbank, owned by the family, has sponsored a chamber orchestra whose resident conductor is the dynamic young Cem Mansur, who has a passion for the democratic and therapeutic value of music. "Music is a miraculous path towards peace and democracy," he argues, eloquently elaborating—albeit unwittingly—the philosophy of the Caliph Abdülmecid II. "Playing in an orchestra alters your mindset, not to mention help you learn about history and geography. Making music together teaches people about living in a true democracy, while, at the same time, empowering people with the tools to accept the 'other' and forge links."

Koç Holdings also started from humble beginnings. Vehbi Koç, a slightly older contemporary of Hacı Ömer Sabancı, started with a family retail business in Ankara. He was well positioned for providing services to the new parliament and government in Ankara, and in the 1920s and 1930s concentrated on the importation of goods, especially cars. In the 1940s Vehbi Koç went into manufacturing, starting with the production of light bulbs and electrical goods. He soon expanded into tractors and agro-industry, textiles and household goods. In 1986 Koçbank was established, and in 2006 it merged with Yapı Kredi Bankası. There is also a Koç University, founded in 1993 and based near Sarıyer on the European shore of the Bosphorus. There are currently just under 3,000 students.

Koç Holdings is also a family concern. A grandson of Vehbi Koç, Mustafa, is chairman. The family has been remarkable for its cultural interests. The son of the late Vehbi, Rahmi, has been fascinated by machinery all his life. His private collection has grown into the Rahmi M Koç Industrial Museum at Hasköy, and is an extraordinary gathering of vehicles, computers and machines. Founded in 1994, it initially occupied a twelfth-century Byzantine building, which the Ottomans used as a foundry for making anchors for the navy in the eighteenth century. In the twentieth century it became a cigarette factory. A few years after acquiring this site, the dockyard opposite, alongside the Golden Horn, was up for sale. Rahmi Koç bought it to house the larger items of the museum. These include airplanes, submarines, buses and trams. In the open air museum you can see a crashed airplane, suitably damaged. It is a Liberator B-24, what was left of a plane used to bomb oil refineries in Romania in August 1943. After that action it headed back to its British air base in Cyprus but crash landed near Antalya. Parts of the plane were salvaged fifty years later and it was restored to its present dramatic appearance with the help of Roy Newton, one of the seven survivors of the crash.

Among the latest items is the 1966 Ford 105E that Harry Potter in the film, *Harry Potter and the Chamber of Secrets*, drove on the railway track ahead of the Hogwarts Express and then took off to the skies. Another recent addition is a discarded Routemaster bus from London. Traction engines, wheelchairs, prams, a field ambulance, mechanical toys, cameras, clumsy big computers dating from the 1970s, scooters, a penny farthing bicycle, antique printing presses, motorcycles traction engines and tractors reveal a manic passion for collecting. You can press a switch to listen to the sound of a Harley Davidson revving up, or a high speed train whizzing past. Rahmi Koç has an educational mission, a zeal for getting young people to understand how things work. Most visitors are schoolchildren and students. There is now a branch of the museum in a former *han* in the center of old Ankara, and an outreach program with a "müzebus" and education packs. You can even be educated in the toilets where there are framed posters of international industrial fairs and exhibitions.

Other large items include the reconstruction of a ship's bridge; the set of a film made in Turkey in 1996; an olive oil factory; one of the trams that ran from Kadıköy to Moda from 1934 to 1966 (the line was later replaced and is still working on the Asian side of the Bosphorus); a street of shops from the early twentieth century, with a pharmacy smelling of cloves; and the horse tram that once plied between Beşiktaş and Karaköy.

In the Rahmi M Koç Museum the visitor is greeted by the waxwork (made at Madame Tussauds) of a beaming Rahmi M Koç. He has every right to beam. He has an affection for each individual item. Asked whether there were any items he spent ages chasing after, he mentioned a London taxi cab built in about 1910. It was in a museum in New Zealand that was selling its stock by auction.

> We were outbid by a British antique dealer, who bought the vehicle. We bought some other items that we'd bid for, but when they were about to be shipped, the government revoked the auction, seized all the objects, and refunded our money. Some time later I was in London and stopped by the gallery of my friend Laurence Langford for a chat. What should I see but the very same taxi there. Cold sweat poured down my back. As it turned out, the dealer who'd bought the vehicle immediately paid up and took possession of it after the auction and left the country by plane, with the result that he was unaffected by the government's decision. He

subsequently sold the object. After a great deal of haggling and after three years had passed, we finally managed to buy this London taxi cab.

Much of the social history of modern Turkey is on display. One model is of a Bosphorus ferry-boat, *Kalender*, built in Newcastle-upon-Tyne in 1912: the actual steam engine can be seen alongside. A saw mill is still here, in working order. A tractor used on Atatürk's model farm near Ankara nestles in some straw. The winding engine for the first trains in the Tünel underground railway is here as well as the first carriages. There are some unique historical items, such as the railway coach used in 1867 by Sultan Abdülaziz on his visit to Europe.

Everything has been cleaned and polished and meticulously restored by a team of thirty. Not everything is on display simultaneously: this encourages the visitor to return. The museum is slightly off the beaten track and, although it receives 200,000 (mostly Turkish) visitors a year, its vastness makes it possible to wander round and enjoy it all without the distraction of crowds.

*Koç* is the Turkish for ram, and just as Sabancı enterprises can be recognized from the highlighting of S and A, so Koç enterprises are distinguished by the logo of a ram's head.

## ISLAMISM IN CONTEMPORARY ISTANBUL AND THE "CLASH OF CIVILIZATIONS"

Some areas of Istanbul have witnessed the arrival of a socially conservative Anatolian world. The area of Sultanbeyli, on the southeastern outskirts of the Asian side, hidden from many visitors by the more prosperous Bağdat Caddesi, has been one of the centers of Turkish radical Islam. In the early 1980s it was a village with a population of about 4,000, mostly Black Sea, immigrants. Over the next decade the immigrants increased the population to 80,000. An Islamist local mayor, Ali Nabi Koçak, originally from the central Anatolian city of Yozgat, led resistance to the metropolitan municipality's plans to demolish whole areas to make room for fast roads and luxury residential complexes. Under Mayor Koçak the local municipality offered new immigrants easy access to land and help with construction materials. The Islamic ideological character attracted rural and Kurdish immigrants. By the end of the century the population was over 200,000. For a few years there was an idea of Sultanbeyli being an ideal Islamic community, centered around the mosque, and with appropriately modest buildings, the tallest constructions in the neighborhood being minarets. The town became an alcohol-free and gender-segregated zone. Officials would pray in their offices, and visitors would leave their shoes at the door to keep the floor suitable for prayer, uncontaminated by the outside world.

In 1996, two years after the victory of the Islamist Welfare Party in the Greater Istanbul *municipal* elections, the *national* authorities erected a statue of Atatürk in the center of the main shopping area of Sultanbeyli. This represented an explicit assertion of the national ideology of revering the secular first President of the Republic. Mayor Koçak moved it to a park. This led to a confrontation, and Koçak was dismissed and the statue forcibly reinstalled. Within a few years alcohol was again available in Sultanbeyli and other manifestations of Islamic social engineering reversed. But Sultanbeyli is still one of the more deprived areas of the city, with unpaved roads and schools without access to running water.

Other poor, popular areas have been absorbed into the global character of modern Istanbul. Ümraniye behind Üsküdar is another former

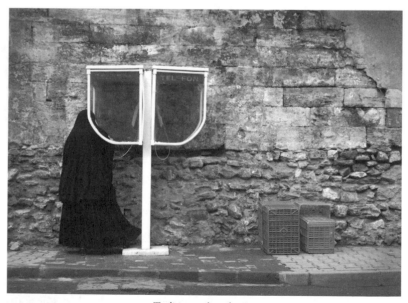

Tradition and modernity

squatter area. Chic restaurants, shopping malls and an IKEA store are neighbors to conservative Islamist quarters where middle-class apartments overlook small plots of grass where women wearing the *çarşaf* (the full, usually black, veil, equivalent to the Iranian *chador*) keep an eye on cows and wash their carpets.

The upheaval of millions of Anatolians from their rural roots meant the creation of new social networks, usually based on locality. The coffee house catered for people of particular areas. It became an effective social club, a venue for finding out about working possibilities and a base for political activity. It complemented the mosque as a focus of the new communities.

Meanwhile many older *Istanbullus* felt threatened by the wave of immigrants who had lost the "innocence" of their origins without acquiring the sophistication of the city. Their taste in clothes and music was scorned. The immigrant bought tapes of music that was a hybrid mix of cultures and was given the name *arabesk*, a word which has overtones of tackiness.

Yet the new immigrants were courted by the politicians. For Atatürk, the Anatolian peasant made up the foundation of the Turkish nation and was as far as possible from the urban, urbane sophisticates of Pera. The older *Istanbullus* were on the defensive, feeling swamped by the numbers of the immigrants. But Atatürk and the Kemalists had not taken into consideration the intense personal piety of the immigrants who did not share their secularist distaste for Islamic practices. It was therefore a shock when the Islamist Welfare Party displaced the Social Democrats in the municipal elections in 1994. They campaigned on a platform of public morality, social justice and hostility to corruption. Many feared the kind of Islamic social bullying that had taken place in Algeria or Iran. The new municipal regime did change some things. The red light district near Taksim was closed down. No longer was it possible to stroll down a street and gawp at prostitutes as they sat, stripped to the waist, smoking their cigarettes in the doorways. But the new Mayor of Beyoğlu stressed cultural plurality. "The first thing I ordered," he said, "was to clean up the garbage around the Armenian church." The municipality (now in the hands of the Justice and Development Party, also with an Islamist orientation: the mayor in the nineties is now prime minister) has introduced a benign Islamic practice. When the daily fast during the month of Ramadan ends at sunset, you can see marquees that have been set up in public places and near mosques.

Bowls of soup and bread are distributed to people, presumed poor, with which to break their fast. It is a revival of the Ottoman *imaret*s in twentieth-century form.

## SOCCER AND TRIBALISM

Soccer came to Istanbul at the end of the nineteenth century. The first to play were Greeks and visiting resident British men who established an Istanbul Football [Soccer] League. In 1903 a Turkish team, which in time became today's Beşiktaş, was founded: the first Turkish team to take part in the league. In the next few years the other two major Istanbul teams were founded: Galatasaray in 1905, and Fenerbahçe in 1907. These three teams dominate the scene. Partisanship is ferocious: both for one's own team and against their rivals.

Although Turkey competed internationally, it was only from the 1990s that Turkish soccer hit the international sporting headlines, due in large part to trainers and managers from overseas, and today—like western European clubs—Turkish teams feature many foreign players. Turkish players, conversely, play for clubs in Britain and other countries. One outstanding example is the Turkish international player, Tuncay Şanlı, who played for Fenerbahce before coming to Britain to play first for Middlesbrough before being transferred in August 2009 for a fee of £5 million ($7.8 million) to Stoke City.

Almost everyone in the city will claim allegiance to one of the three teams, but in Istanbul support is seen to break down in class terms. Galatasaray was founded by pupils of the French-medium secondary school in Pera (Beyoğlu), whose alumni have formed an educational élite in the country. Supporters of the soccer team are traditionally made up of older official classes, but another group of supporters come from an entirely different class. In 1988 the hard-line Kurdish leader of the PKK, Abdullah Öcalan, gave an interview to the newspaper *Milliyet*, and declared his enthusiastic support for Galatasaray Football [Soccer] Club. As a result and paradoxically, it is the team that enjoys the support of Kurds, even though Kurdish spectators do not always join in the singing of the national anthem at matches.

Fenerbahçe, based on the Asian side, is regarded as the team of the "newer classes," the smart meritocrats, while Beşiktaş is the team of the working class.

Beşiktaş supporters

The main teams receive sponsorship, currently from mobile phone companies. All three teams have shops and make plenty of money from the sale of shirts, flags and badges. These can be seen all over the country. And for all three teams, soccer is just one of the club activities. All have sections devoted to other sports.

A soccer match is an intensely emotional occasion and tickets are no longer cheap. Passions run high and security is tight. Spectators are frisked as they enter the terraces, and supporters of the visiting teams are penned in behind a tall wire fence with up to three lines of police protecting them. Police also guard the visiting players as they emerge from the tunnel and go on to the pitch, turning to face the crowd. After a match there can be riots on the streets, and even in provincial cities the supporters of an Istanbul team might pour on to streets to celebrate a victory or bemoan a defeat.

Beşiktaş includes the national flag with its own club colors, black and white, which were chosen as the colors of mourning after the loss of

Ottoman lands after the Balkan Wars of 1912–13. After Beşiktaş lost 8–0 to Liverpool in 2007, supporters of rival teams chanted derisively "Sekiztaş," *sekiz* being the Turkish for eight. Their stadium between Taksim and the Bosphorus was built in 1947 and named after the then president, İsmet İnönü. It is on the site of the former stables attached to the Dolmabahçe Palace. The legendary Brazilian soccer player Pele claimed that the stadium commands better views—of the Bosphorus and Dolmabahçe Palace—than any other soccer venue in the world. Their supporters include the present president, Abdullah Gül.

Galatasaray was founded by Ali Sami Yen, then a student at the secondary school. It has been the most successful of the three teams and also has the best international record. Malcolm Allison, the flamboyant former manager of Manchester City and Crystal Palace, spent a season managing Galatasaray in the 1970s. He was not the first Englishman to be involved with the club: in its early years before the First World War, the team was managed by one of their English players, Horace Armitage. Their supporters have a formidable record of intense and intimidating chants and behaviour on the terraces: their scarf wave before a match involves them holding up the red and yellow scarves, standing on the seats, chanting and jumping up and down in unison. When one of their players scores they sing the song, *I Will Survive* (the words are in English but they sing "La La La" to the tune). Less charmingly, their stadium in Şişli is known by their rivals as Hell.

Fenerbahçe, founded in 1907, has in recent years had two Brazilians players, who have taken Turkish nationality (one has played for the Turkish national team). Their stadium has been on the same site in Kadıköy for most of their history but in recent years it has been completely renovated. Orhan Pamuk, Turkey's leading contemporary writer, is a Fenerbahçe supporter. The team's great rivals are Galatasaray, and when Chelsea beat Fenerbahçe in April 2008, one of the chants of the Galatasaray supporters was—in English—"Thank You Chel Sea." The colors of the players are yellow (symbolizing the supposed admiration and the envy of others) and navy blue (symbolizing nobility). Opponents, however, see the supporters of Fenerbahçe as too wedded to western values and to the idea of America; according to this interpretation, yellow and navy blue represent the skin and the blue eyes of westerners.

## ETHNIC AND CULTURAL IDENTITY

It is impossible to generalize about the mixed political mood in Istanbul today. In the last ten years there have been shifts in different layers of opinion, but each layer has a heritage that goes back a century, and is interwoven with Turkey's history.

The constitution upholds an official ideology that, to some outsiders seems to have the authority of religious dogma, and much of modern Turkey goes directly back to the major reforms of Mustafa Kemal Atatürk in the 1920s. In the last eight years of his life the ideology of "Kemalism" became the orthodoxy. *Ne mutlu Türküm diyene!* "Happy is he who can say, 'I am a Turk'!" is the most widely quoted of Atatürk's sayings, and can be seen everywhere on statues and below busts of the great man. In the 1920s Turks were emerging, defeated and humiliated, from a war that had been devastating in its social impact. One of the paradoxes of the Atatürk revolution was that laicism—or secularism—was a defining tenet of Kemalism. Being Turkish was implicitly defined by what one was not; if a *Turk* was not Greek, Armenian or Jewish, it implied being Muslim, with Turkish as the first language. For many years Armenians, Greeks and Jews—though each community had contributed hugely to the reality of what is contemporary Turkey—could not share in that Kemalist Turkishness. There have been crises that made these minorities vulnerable, encouraging them to take whatever opportunities they could to emigrate. From the 1920s to the 1990s the proportion of non-Turkish Muslims in Istanbul has slumped. At the same time, Muslims of a non-Turkish background—Albanians, Arabs, people from the Balkans and Crimea, but not Kurds—have found it easy to be absorbed into a Turkish identity.

In the Second World War Atatürk's successor, İsmet İnönü, upheld the country's neutrality. But in November 1942 the government introduced a property tax, *varlık vergisi*. There was a campaign against "war profiteers" and a need to raise revenue. Property owners, big farmers and businessmen would have their assets taxed according to an arbitrary assessment by civil servants. The lists divided the tax payers according to religion: Muslim, non-Muslim, foreigner and *Dönme*, those people who had followed the teachings of Sabbatai Zevi, the messianic Jewish mystic who had converted to Islam in the seventeenth century. The non-Muslims (who also provided a disproportionate number of businessmen) were taxed most. No appeal was allowed and those who resisted or were unable to pay were sent to work in mines in eastern Anatolia, where many died. In 1944 the measures were dropped, outstanding debts were canceled and defaults forgiven. The lasting psychological impact it had on the Jewish community is illustrated in the novel *Young Turk* by Moris Farhi, who was brought up in that community.

In 1955 Cyprus was a British colony. Most of the Greek community, who formed 80 percent of the population, wanted union with Greece, and the Greek government supported this demand. The British, meanwhile, wanted to retain control of the island for strategic military reasons—it played a major role the following year in the invasion of Egypt—and the minority Turkish community was loyal to the British. Talks between the British, Turkish and Greek governments broke down in September 1955. There were then reports of Atatürk's birthplace in Salonica in Greece being damaged in an explosion. On the night of 6 September riots broke out in İzmir and especially Istanbul, targeting Greeks and their properties. The riots turned into wholesale looting and damage to thousands of Greek shops and houses. The army was brought in to quell the trouble.

Although the *varlık vergisi* and the September 1955 riots were exceptional events, they figure largely in the collective memory of the minorities. After 1955 most of the remaining Greeks chose to leave Istanbul. The Turkish authorities put no obstacle in their way.

In the 1990s and the first years of the twenty-first century the possibility of Turkey joining the European Union sharpened the nation's sense of its own identity. The ruling Islamist party has been keen for membership, and the successor to the ideologically pro-western Kemalist Republican People's Party less enthusiastic. But the prospect of membership has liberalized and opened up the country. The death penalty has been abolished. There is a greater readiness to discuss in public the Armenian massacres of the First World War and to acknowledge Kurdish cultural (if not political) claims. Such openness has led to clashes and rearguard action. The nationalist argument is that Turkey's integrity is at stake. "If we give in to the Kurds," a leading Istanbul journalist, Mehmet Ali Birand, put it in the 1990s, "then the Laz or the Alevis or ethnic Georgians will start asking for things. Turkey is an ethnic mosaic, and the example of what happened in Yugoslavia has really frightened us. When it comes to defending the country, then everything else—democracy, human rights—disappears from the agenda." Hence reactions that are sometimes ugly, like the prosecution of Orhan Pamuk in 2006 for the crime of "insulting Turkishness," or the murder of the Armenian journalist, Hrant Dink, in January 2007. But ugly reactions are often accompanied by more reassuring demonstrations. On the day of Dink's funeral, 100,000 people marched through Istanbul, chanting *Hepimiz Ermeniyiz*, "We are all Armenians."

The hundred thousand who followed Dink's coffin were not likely to be supporters of the Islamists, nor were they the hard-line nationalists. But they did represent an international liberal outlook that has been encouraged by increasing political openness to discuss the darker episodes in the nation's past.

## ORHAN PAMUK AND NÂZIM HIKMET

Orhan Pamuk is Turkey's best-known writer. Seven of his novels have been translated into English. His work has been translated into over forty languages and in 2006 he was awarded the Nobel Prize for Literature. In Turkey attitudes to him have varied. While most people are proud of his international reputation, he has been the target of strong criticism by nationalists who resent his position on Kurds and Armenians. The award of the Nobel Prize was even seen as a gesture against Turkey. But Pamuk first received critical acclaim within Turkey for his early novel, *Karanlık ve Işık* (Darkness and Light), written when he was in his twenties.

Orhan Pamuk is from a middle-class family, originally from outside Istanbul, but was born there and brought up in Nişantaşı. His brother, Şevket, is a leading historian of Ottoman banking. Orhan, after schooling at the English-medium Robert College, studied first to be an architect, but gave that up and trained to be a journalist. He opted to be a full-time writer in his early twenties. His international fame spread in the 1990s with two novels, translated as *The Black Book* and *The White Castle*. Both have an Istanbul background, the former in the twentieth century, the latter in the seventeenth.

Pamuk has written a semi-autobiographical work, *Istanbul*, published in 2005. He describes his family background, and themes that come into the novels can be traced to this work: a shifting sense of identity and an indefinable melancholy. "As a child," he wrote, "I had no sense of living in a great world capital but rather in a poor provincial city." These qualities, in Pamuk's view, are characteristics of modern Istanbul. Pamuk writes of wandering around the city at all hours, and *Istanbul* is illustrated by old pictures and modern photographs that draw out this melancholy or *hüzün*, as he calls it. His last (2009) novel, translated as *The Museum of Innocence*, is located in the Istanbul of the 1970s and explores issues of sexual identity in a changing moral environment.

Orhan Pamuk's reputation stands in contrast to another Turkish writer who has received—and continues to receive—international critical recognition. Nâzim Hikmet (1902-63) spent most of his adult life either in prison or in exile. In contrast to Pamuk, he was born into Ottoman aristocracy. Both grandfathers were *paşas* and senior government officials. Like Mustafa Kemal Atatürk, he was born in Salonica where his father was in public service. Nâzim went to the elite Galatasaray school in Istanbul and then—in the First World War—straight into the navy. He joined Mustafa Kemal in Ankara in the early years of the national struggle, but the 1917 Russian Revolution had inspired the young poet and he went to the fledgling Soviet Union to study in Moscow. On his return to Turkey he was a prolific writer of revolutionary verse and was first imprisoned in 1928. Released in 1933 but unrepentant, five years later he was before a military tribunal and sentenced to twenty-five years' imprisonment on charges of sedition and subversive activity among military students. In or out of prison, he was writing poems all the time and acquiring an international reputation. He was freed from prison in 1950 and immediately went to the Soviet Union where he spent the rest of his life.

Nâzim Hikmet commemorated on a Soviet postage stamp

Nâzim Hikmet's poems were innovative. He experimented with free verse, and wrote love poems to his wife and one long poem about Sheikh Bedreddin, a fifteenth-century Sufi revolutionary whom Nâzim saw as an early socialist. In contrast to Orhan Pamuk, he saw Istanbul in a very different and idealized light, albeit from behind bars or two thousand miles away in Moscow:

> My God, how lovely you are!
> Istanbul's air and water are in your laugh,
> Istanbul's delights in your look.

Turks have been ambivalent about the international reputation of Nâzim Hikmet, as his communism and chosen exile in Moscow ran counter to nationalist orthodoxy. But there has been a slow rehabilitation, and it may be that appreciation of the love poetry led the way. In any case, his Turkish patriotism was undeniable. Fittingly, his Turkish nationality of which he was stripped in 1959 was restored in 2009. His work is easily available in Turkish and in many foreign translations.

## EARTHQUAKE FEARS

In August 1999 a major earthquake struck Istanbul. Although the center of the earthquake was at İzmit, fifty miles (eighty kilometers ) to the east, the city and its extensive suburbs were severely damaged, physically and psychologically. The quake measured 7.6 on the Richter scale. The official estimates were that 17–20,000 people were killed, but unofficial estimates were double that. Tower blocks collapsed. Tens of thousands of people were made homeless, and essential services were shattered. Many died because of the effects of the quake during the following winter. Although there had for centuries been earthquakes in the Istanbul area, this was the first major quake since the city had become a megalopolis and had attained its new global status.

Istanbul was traumatized. The hastily built tower blocks were seen as death traps. Were they thrown up with inadequate safety checks? Had contractors bribed officials to approve unsafe housing? Could the quake happen again? Reliable international experts stated that there was a "65% probability that Istanbul will be hit by a major earthquake by 2030." People checked where they were living. There was a rise in the purchase of "steel-girded flats." The World Bank poured in millions for quake readiness. Most *Istanbullus* prefer not to think about potential disaster but it is always at the back of people's minds.

There was one positive consequence to the earthquake. Istanbul received immediate international support, but the first to respond were the Greeks, who sent in teams and equipment within hours. It inaugurated a new happier relationship between Turkey and Greece.

## ENVOI

The next twenty years are likely to see as many changes as the last twenty. Public transport in the city has been racing (with moderate success) to keep pace with urban growth. Innovations over the last generation have been quickly absorbed—even taken for granted. The Bosphorus bridges were perhaps the greatest changes, while the Metro has linked the main airport to the center of the walled city with efficiency, and the construction of the funicular between Kabataş and Taksim has built up a new radial line of communication. Kabataş has become a major port for boats to the Asian suburbs.

Within a few years a new rail link will be opened under the Bosphorus. That too will be absorbed into the system.

But the main physical and logistic features of Istanbul today will continue to be recognizable to any of the citizens and visitors over the last millennium.

Constantine's decision to build a capital city was brilliant. Certain features of the city have since his time been unchanged. International trade, a cultural center for the world, a social and cultural meeting point, a mixed population, a hub of entertainment and amusement. It has been able to integrate outsiders with ease. It is not difficult to be an *Istanbullu*.

Today only one in ten—or even fewer—of inhabitants have been *Istanbullus* for more than a generation. It is always instructive to ask friends where their parents and grandparents were born and brought up: an Anatolian town or village, the Balkans, Crimea or the Caucasus, Thrace. Many of those who have been originally Kurdish, Albanian, Laz or Alevi are now citizens of the city and officially and often indistinguishably Turkish. Hundreds of thousands of *Istanbullus* also have experience of living in Western Europe. They have returned home, fluent in one or more West European language, having returned from Kreuzberg or Stoke Newington.

Tensions in such a melting pot are inevitable. A Kemalist nationalist ideology aspires, not always successfully, to provide a comprehensive rallying point. But it has to adapt to a changing liberal, globalized world. The fault lines in Istanbul are religious, ethnic and political. Beyoğlu could be Milan, London's West End or New York; Sultanbeyli or Fatih could be a small town in Iran. All I*stanbullus* are mindful of the fact that in the last half century, the tensions have been so overwhelming that on three separate occasions the army, who see themselves as the guardians of Atatürk's revolution, have intervened, overthrowing secular governments, and have brought the country back to the prescribed path.

But it was ever so. We have seen how the first Roman capital, as well as early Ottoman Istanbul, encouraged immigrants. The outbursts of ethnic or political violence, and of terrorism, have been atypical of the general pattern of mutual acceptance, toleration and even celebration.

Above all, Istanbul has been a city of creative excitement. It has outstanding examples of the architectural innovation from almost each of the last fifteen or sixteen centuries. In the twenty-first century it has also become a global cultural city. Architecture, painting, music, sport, dance: all are vibrant, and operate in an international context. This globalism has benefitted the national economy. Turkey is one of the top ten destinations in the world for international tourism. About thirty million tourists came to Turkey in 2008, about the same number as came to the United Kingdom. Most visit the well-developed resorts of the Mediterranean and Aegean coasts, but a quarter come to Istanbul. Germany provides the largest number of visitors. About a million and a half come from United Kingdom. About 70 percent of tourists arrive by air, but 7 percent arrive by boat as Istanbul is becoming a major port for visiting cruise ships. This is not always beneficial to the national economy for the cruisers will dine and sleep on board. Even so, a thousand passengers pour into coaches each day, adding to the traffic congestion of the city, to head for the major sites—the Church of the Holy Wisdom, Topkapı, Galata Tower and Kariye Camii—where the visitors contribute to $19 billion that Turkey earns each year from the tourist industry.

The continuities of the city are, for those with sensitivity, mingled with the contemporary. A new block of apartments may be built round a fountain or tomb. Older buildings are used and reused, a palimpsest of centuries of human activity. You are never far from the waters of the

Marmara, Bosphorus or Golden Horn. Recovered after marginalization during the first fifty years or so of the Republican period, and no longer a dusty and neglected urban museum, Istanbul resumes its place as one of the most fascinating and culturally rich cities of the world.

# Further Reading

Abdullah, King of Transjordan, *Memoirs*. Translated by G. Khuri, edited by Philip P. Graves. London: Jonathan Cape, 1950.

Ágoston, Gábor, *Guns for the Sultan, Military Power and the Weapons Industry in the Ottoman Empire*. Cambridge: University Press, 2005.

Akaş, Ceyda, ed, *Industrial Archaeology by the Golden Horn*. Istanbul: Rahmi M Koç Müzesi, 2006.

Akmeşe, Handan Nezir, *The Birth of Modern Turkey, The Ottoman Military and the March to World War I*. London: I B Tauris, 2005.

Andiç Fuat and Andıç, Süphan, *The Last of the Ottoman Grandees, The Life and the Political Testament of Ali Paşa*. Istanbul: The Isis Press, 1996.

Ascherson, Neal, *Black Sea*. London: Vintage, 2007.

Asbridge, Thomas, *The First Crusade, A New History*. London: Simon and Schuster, 2005.

Atatürk, Mustafa Kemal, *A Speech*. Istanbul: Ministry of Education, 1963.

Baker, B. Granville, *The Walls of Constantinople*. London: John Milne, 1910.

Bali, Rıfat N., *The Jews and Prostitution in Constantinople 1854-1922*. Istanbul: The Isis Press, 2008.

Barillari, Diana, ed, *"Osmanlı Mimarı D'Aronco, 1893-1909 İstanbul Projeleri*, Exhibition Catalogue. Istanbul: İstanbul Araştırmaları Enstitüsü, 2006.

Barsley, Michael, *Orient Express*. London: Macdonald, 1966.

Batur, Afife, ed, *Architectural Guide to Istanbul*. Istanbul: Chamber of Architects of Turkey, 2005, 4 vols.

Baynes, Norman H, *The Byzantine Empire*. London: Williams and Norgate, 1925.

Baytar, İlona, ed, *Florya Atatürk Deniz Köşkü*. Ankara: Milli Saraylar Daire Başkanlığı, 2008.

Beckwith, John, *The Art of Constantinople*. London: Phaidon, 1961.

Berktay, Halil, *Renaissance Italy and the Ottomans, History's Overlaps and Faultlines*, Exhibition Catalogue. Istanbul: Sakıp Sabancı Müzesi, 2004.

Berridge, G. R., *Gerald Fitzmaurice (1865-1939), Chief Dragoman of the British Embassy in Turkey*. Leiden and Boston: Martinus Nijhoff Publishers, 2007.

Berridge, G. R., ed, *Tilkidom and the Ottoman Empire, The Letters of Gerald Fitzmaurice to George Lloyd, 1906-1915*. Istanbul: The Isis Press, 2008.

Bilgin, Mustafa, *Britain and Turkey in the Middle East*. London and New York: Tauris, 2008.

Blake, Robert, *Disraeli's Grand Tour*. London: Weidenfeld and Nicolson, 1982.

Byron, Robert, *The Byzantine Achievement*. London: George Routledge, 1929.

de Busbecq, Ogier, *Turkish Letters* (1927). Translated by E. S. Forster. London: Eland, 2005.

Buturović, Amila and Irvin Cemil Schick, eds, *Women in the Ottoman Balkans*. London and New York: I B Tauris, 2007.

Campbell, Caroline and Chong, Alan, eds, *Bellini and the East*, Exhibition Catalogue. London: National Gallery, 2005.

Çelik, Zeynep, *The Remaking of Istanbul, Portrait of an Ottoman City in the Nineteenth Century*. Berkeley: University of California Press, 1993.

Clark, Peter, *Marmaduke Pickthall, British Muslim*. London: Quartet, 1986.

Colonas, Vassilis, *Greek Architects in the Ottoman Empire (19$^{th}$-20$^{th}$ Centuries)*. Athens: Olkos, 2005.

Coles, Paul, *The Ottoman Impact on Europe*. London: Thames and Hudson, 1968.

Criss, Nur Bilge, *Istanbul under Occupation 1918-1923*. Leiden: Brill, 1999.

Cuddon, J. A., *The Owl's Watchsong*. London: Barrie and Rockliff, 1960.

Crawford, F. Marion, *Constantinople*. New York: Charles Scribner, 1895.

Crowley, Roger, *Constantinople: The Last Great Siege 1453*. London: Faber and Faber, 2005.

De Gaury, Gerald, *Three Kings in Baghdad* (1961). London: I B Tauris, 2008.

De Gaury, Gerald, *Travelling Gent, The Life of Alexander Kinglake (1809-1891)*. London and Boston: Routledge and Kegan Paul, 1972.

Deleon, Jak, *Ancient Districts on the Golden Horn*. Istanbul: Gözlem Gazetecilik Basın ve Yayın, 1991.

Deleon, Jak, *A Taste of Old Istanbul*. Istanbul: Istanbul Library, 1989.

Deleon, Jak, *The Pera Palas, A Historical Hotel Overlooking the Golden Hor,*. 2nd edition. Istanbul: Gözlem Gazetecilik Basın ve Yayın, 1998.

Deringil, Selim, *The Well-Protected Domains, Ideology and the Legitimization of Power in the Ottoman Empire, 1876-1909*. London and New York: I B Tauris, 2004.

Der Nersessian, Sirapie, *Armenia and the Byzantine Empire*. Cambridge, Mass: Harvard University Press, 1947.

Deutscher, Isaac, *The Prophet Outcast, Trotsky 1929-1940*. Oxford: University Press, 1970.

Devrim, Shirin, *A Turkish Tapestry, The Shakirs of Istanbul*. London: Quartet, 1996.

Djemaleddin, Bey, *Sultan Murad V, The Turkish Dynastic Mystery 1876-1895*. London: Kegan Paul, Trench, Trubner, 1895.

Dufferin and Ava, The Dowager Marchioness of, *My Russian and Turkish Journals*. London: John Murray, 1916.

Eldem, Edhem, *Bankalar Caddesi, Voyvoda Street from Ottoman Times to Today*, Exhibition Catalogue. Istanbul: Ottoman Bank Historical Research Center, 2000.

Eldem, Edhem, *A History of the Ottoman Bank*. Istanbul: Ottoman Bank

Historical Research Center, 1999.

Eminoğlu, Münevver, ed, *Bir Beyoğlu Fotoromanı, A Beyoğlu Photoromance*, Exhibition Catalogue. Istanbul: Yapı Kredi Kültür Sanat Yayıncılık, 2000.

Farah, Caesar E., *Arabs and Ottomans: A Checkered Relationship*. Istanbul: The Isis Press, 2002.

Farhi, Moris, *Young Turk*. London: Saqi, 2004.

Faroqhi, Suraiya, *The Ottoman Empire, A Short History*. Translated by Shelley Frisch. Princeton: Markus Wiener Publishers, 2009.

Faroqhi, Suraiya, *Subjects of the Sultan, Culture and Daily Life in the Ottoman Empire*. Translated by Martin Bott, London: I B Tauris, 2007.

Finkel, Caroline, *Osman's Dream: The Story of the Ottoman Empire 1300-1923*. London: John Murray, 2005.

Freely, John, *The Bosphorus*. Istanbul: Redhouse Press, 1993.

Freely, John, *Galata, A Guide to Istanbul's Old Genoese Quarter*. Istanbul: Archaeology and Art Publications, 2000.

Freely, John, *Istanbul and Around the Marmara*. Woodbridge: Companion Guides, 2000.

Freely, John, *John Freely's Istanbul*. London: Scala, 2005.

Freely, John, *The Princes' Isles*. Istanbul: Adalı, 2005.

Freely, John and Freely, Brendan, *A Guide to Beyoğlu*. Istanbul: Archaeology and Art Publications, 2006.

Gibbon, Edward, *Decline and Fall of the Roman Empire* (1776-88). London: J M Dent, 1957-62, 6 vols.

Gilbert, Martin, *Road to Victory, Winston S Churchill 1941-1945*. London: HeinemannMinerva, 1989.

Giraud, Ernest, ed, *La France à Constantinople*. Istanbul: Isis Editions, 2002.

Godfrey, John, *1204, The Unholy Crusade*. Oxford: University Press, 1980.

Goodrich-Freer, A., *Things Seen in Constantinople*. London: Seeley Service, 1926.

Goodwin, Godfrey, *A History of Ottoman Architecture*. London: Thames and Hudson, 1971.

Goodwin, Godfrey, *Life's Episodes, Discovering Ottoman Architecture*. Istanbul: Boğazici University Press, 2002.

Goodwin, Godfrey, *Topkapı Palace*. London: Saqi Books, 1999.

Goodwin, Jason, *Lords of the Horizons*. London: Vintage, 1999.

Graves, Philip P., *Briton and Turk*. London: Hutchinson, c 1941.

Greene, Graham, *Stamboul Train*. London: William Heinemann, 1932.

Grosskurth Phyllis, *Byron, The Flawed Angel*. London: Hodder and Stoughton, 1997.

Güçlü, Yücel, *Eminence Grise of the Turkish Foreign Service: Numan Menemencioğlu*. Ankara: Ministry of Foreign Affairs, 2002.

Gulbenkian, Nubar, *Pantaraxia*. London, Hutchinson, 1965.

Gülersoy, Çelik, *The Çerağan Palaces*. Istanbul: İstanbul Kitaplığı, 1992.

Gűlersoy, Çelik, *Dolmabahçe Palace and Its Environs*. Istanbul: İstanbul Kitaplığı, 1990.

Gűrsan-Salzmann, Ayşe, Anyos Munchos i Buenos, *"Good Years and More", Turkey's Sephardim: 1492-1992*. Istanbul: Gözlem, 2003.

Haidar, Princess Musbah, *Arabesque*. London: Hutchinson, c 1945.

Haldon, J. F., *Byzantium in the Seventh Century*. Cambridge: University Press, 1990.

Haldon, John, *Byzantium at War AD 600-1453*. Oxford: Osprey, 2002.

Hamilton, J. Arnott, *Byzantine Architecture and Decoration*. London: Batsford, 1933.

Hanioğlu, M. Şükrü, *A Brief History of the late Ottoman Empire*. Princeton and Oxford: Princeton University Press, 2008.

Harris, Jonathan, *Byzantium and the Crusades*. London: Hambledon Continuum, 2007.

Harris, Jonathan, ed, *Byzantine History*. Basingstoke: Palgrave Macmillan, 2005.

Heper, Metin, *İsmet İnönü, The Making of a Turkish Statesman*. Leiden: Brill, 1998.

Herbert, Aubrey, *Ben Kendim*. London: Hutchinson, c1925.

Herrin, Judith, *Byzantium, the Surprising Life of a Medieval Empire*. London: Penguin, 2008.

Hinkle, Richard and Vander Sluis, Rhonda, *From the Bosphorus*. Istanbul: Çitlembik, 2005.

Howard, Douglas A., *The History of Turkey*. Westport, Conn. and London: Greenwood Press, 2001.

Hutton, William Holden, *Constantinople, the Story of the Old Capital of the Empire*. London: J. M. Dent, 1900.

Ibn Battuta, *Voyages, Texte Arabe accompagné d'une traduction* (1854). Translated by C. Defremery and B. R. Sanguinetti. Paris: Editions Anthropos, 1968, 4 vols.

Inalcik, Halil, *The Ottoman Empire, The Classical Age 1300-1600*. Translated by Norman Itzkowitz and Colin Imber. Phoenix, London, 2000.

Jones, A. H. M., *Constantine and the Conversion of Europe* (1949). Harmondsworth: Penguin, 1972.

Kalinowska, Izabela, *Between East and West, Polish and Russian Nineteenth Century Travel to the Orient*. Rochester: University Press, 2004.

Kara Pilehvarian, Nuran, Urfalıoğlu, Nur and Yazıcıoğlu, Lütfi, *Fountains in Ottoman Istanbul*. Istanbul: Yapı-Endüstri Merkezi Yayınları, 2004.

Karmı, Ilan, *The Jewish Community of Istanbul in the Nineteenth Century*. Istanbul: The Isis Press, 1996.

Karmı, Ilan, *Jewish Sites of Istanbul, A Guide Book*. Istanbul: The Isis Press, 1992.

Khairallah, Shereen, *Railways in the Middle East 1856-1948*. Beirut: Libraire du Liban, 1991.

Kibris, R. Barış, ed, *Istanbul: The City of Dreams*, Exhibition Catalogue. Istanbul: Pera Museum, 2008.

Kinglake, A W, *Eothen*. London: Harrison, 1864.

Kirimtayif, Süleyman, *Converted Byzantine Churches in Istanbul, Their Transformation into Mosques and Masjids*. Istanbul: Ege Yayınları, 2001.

Koç, Vehbi, *My Life Story*. Istanbul: Vehbi Koç Foundation, 1977.

Landau, Jacob M., *Exploring Ottoman and Turkish History*. London: Hurst, 2004.

Lane-Poole, Stanley, *The Life of Stratford Canning*. London: Longmans Green, 1888, 2 vols.

Levey, Michael, *The World of Ottoman Art*. London: Thames and Hudson, 1975.

Lewis, Bernard, *The Emergence of Modern Turkey*. Oxford: University Press, 1961.

Lewis, Bernard, *Islam in History*. Chicago and La Salle, Ill.: Open Court, 2003.

Lewis, Geoffrey, *Turkey*. London: Ernest Benn, 1965.

Lindsay, Jack, *Byzantium into Europe*. London: The Bodley Head, 1952.

Loti, Pierre, *Constantinople in 1890*. Translated by David Ball. Istanbul: Ünlem Yayınları, 2005.

Luke, Harry, *The Old Turkey and the New*. London: Geoffrey Bles, 1955.

Mackintosh-Smith, Tim, *Travels with a Tangerine*. London: John Murray, 2001.

Maclagan, Michael, *The City of Constantinople*. London: Thames and Hudson, 1968.

Mamboury, Ernest, *The Tourists' Istanbul*. Translated by Malcolm Burr. Istanbul: Çituri Biraderler Basımevi, 1953.

Mango, Andrew, *Atatürk*. London: John Murray, 1999.

Mango, Andrew, *Turkey and the War on Terror*. London and New York: Routledge, 2005.

Mansel, Philip, *Constantinople, City of the World's Desire, 1453-1924*. London: John Murray, 2006.

Marchand, Leslie A., ed, *'In my Hot Youth', Byron's Letters and Journals,* Vol. 1. London: John Murray, 1973.

Melville Jones, J. R., *The Siege of Constantinople 1453: Seven Contemporary Accounts*. Amsterdam: Adolf M Hakkert, 1972.

Neale, John Mason, *The Fall of Constantinople* (1857). London: J M Dent, c1913.

Necıpoğlu, Gülru, *The Age of Sinan, Architectural Culture in the Ottoman Empire*. London: Reaktion Books, 2005.

Nelson, Robert S., *Hagia Sophia, 1850-1950*. Chicago: University Press, 2004.

Nestor-Iskander, *The Tale of Constantinople.* Translated and edited by Walter K. Hanah and Marios Philippides. New Rochelle, NY: Aristide D Caratzas, 1998.

Nicolson, Harold, *Sweet Waters, An Istanbul Thriller* (1921). London: Sickle Moon Books, 2000.

Oman, C. W. C., *The Byzantine Empire*. London: T Fisher Unwin, 1892.

Orga, Ateş, ed, *Istanbul, A Collection of the Poetry of Place*. London: Eland, 2007.

Orga, İrfan, *Portrait of a Turkish Family* (1950). London: Eland, 2004.

Ostrogorsky, George, *History of the Byzantine State*. Translated by Joan Hussey. New Brunswick, NJ: Rutgers University Press, 1957.

Öztuncay, Bahattin, *Kırım Savaşı'nın 150nci Yılı*, Exhibition Catalogue. Istanbul: Vehbi Koç Vakfı, 2006.

Pallis, Alexander, *In the Days of the Janissaries, Old Turkish Life as Depicted in the "Travel Book" of Evliya Chelebi*. London: Hutchinson, 1951.

Pamuk, Orhan, *Istanbul, Memories of a City*. Translated by Maureen Freely. London: Faber and Faber, 2005.

Pamuk, Orhan, *Other Colours, Essays and A Story*. Translated by Maureen Freely. London: Faber and Faber, 2007.

Pears, Edwin, *Forty Years in Constantinople*. London: Herbert Jenkins, 1916.

Pears, Edwin, *The Destruction of the Greek Empire and the Story of the Capture of Constantinople by the Turks*. London: Longmans Green, 1903.

Phillips, Jonathan, *The Fourth Crusade and the Sack of Constantinople*. London: Pimlico, 2005.

Pickthall, Marmaduke, *The Early Hours*. London: Collins, 1921.

Pickthall, Marmaduke, *With the Turk in Wartime*. London: J M Dent, 1914.

Procopius, *The Secret History*. Translated by G. A. Williamson and Peter Sarris. London, 2007.

Pruszyński K., *Adam Mickiewicz*. London: Fore Publications, 1959.

Psellos, Michael, *Fourteen Byzantine Rulers*. Translated and edited by E. R. A. Sewter. London: Penguin, 1966.

Quataert, Donald, *Manufacturing and Technology Transfer in the Ottoman Empire 1800-1914*. Istanbul and Strasbourg: Isis Press, 1992.

Quataert, Donald, *The Ottoman Empire, 1700-1922*, 2nd edition. Cambridge: University Press, 2005.

Quataert, Donald and Zürcher, Erik Jan, eds, *Workers and the Working Class in the Ottoman Empire and the Turkish Republic*. London and New York: I B Tauris, 1995.

Rıfat Samih, Kıbrıs, Barış and İnankur, Zeynep, eds, *Portraits from the Empire*, Exhibition Catalogue. Istanbul: Pera Museum, 2005.

Rodley, Lyn, *Byzantine Art and Architecture, An Introduction*. Cambridge: University Press, 1994.

Rugman, Jonathan, *Atatürk's Children, Turkey and the Kurds*. London: Cassell, 1996.

Runciman, Steven, *The Eastern Schism*. Oxford: Clarendon Press, 1955.

Runciman, Steven, *The Fall of Constantinople 1453*. Cambridge: University Press, 1969.

Runciman, Steven, *The Great Church in Captivity*. Cambridge: University Press,

1968.

Runciman, Steven, *The Medieval Manichee*. Cambridge: University Press, 1960.

Russell, William Howard, *A Diary in the East during the Tour of the Prince and Princess of Wales*. London: George Routledge, 1869.

Ryan, Andrew, *The Last of the Dragomans*. London: Geoffrey Bles, 1951.

Schatkowski-Schilcher, Linda, *Families in Politics: Damascene Factions and Estates of the 18th and 19th Centuries*. Stuttgart: Franz Steiner Verlag Wiesbaden GMBH, 1985.

Schlumberger, Gustave, *Les Iles des Princes*. Paris: De Boccard, 1925.

Şerıfoğlu, Ömer Faruk, ed, *Abdülmecid Efendi, Ottoman Prince and Painter*, Exhibition Catalogue. Istanbul: Yapı Kredi Yayınları, 2004.

Şeyhun, Ahmet, *Said Halim Pasha, Ottoman Statesman and Islamist Thinker (1865-1921)*. Istanbul: The Isis Press, 2003.

Shissler, A. Holly, *Between Two Empires, Ahmet Ağaoğlu and the New Turkey*. London: I. B. Tauris, 2003.

Slade, Adolphus, *Records of Travels in Turkey, Greece, &c*. London: Saunders and Otley, 1832, 2 vols.

Slade, Adolphus, *Turkey and the Crimean War*. London: Smith Elder, 1867.

Smith, Elaine D., *Turkey: Origins of the Kemalist Movement (1919-1923)*. Washington, D.C.: Judd and Detweiler, 1959.

Stephens, W. R. W., *The Life and Letters of Edward A. Freeman*. London: Macmillan, 1895, 2 vols.

Sumner-Boyd, Hilary and Freely, John, *Strolling Through Istanbul* (1972). Istanbul: Sev (Redhouse), 2001.

Talbot Rice, David, *Byzantine Art* (1935). Harmondsworth: Penguin, 1962.

Talbot Rice, David, *Art of the Byzantine Era*. London: Thames and Hudson, 1963.

Thesiger, Wilfred, *The Life of My Choice*. London: Collins, 1987.

Titmarsh, M. A. (William Makepeace Thackeray), *Notes of a Journey from Cornhill to Grand Cairo*. London: Chapman and Hall, 1846.

Tromans, Nicholas, ed, *The Lure of the East, British Orientalist Painting*. London: Tate, 2008.

Tuckwell, W, *A W Kinglake, A Biographical and Literary Study*. London: George Bell and Sons, 1902.

Tuğal, Cihan, "The Greening of Istanbul", *New Left Review*, 51. May June 2008, 65-80.

Tugay, Emine Foat, *Three Centuries: Family Chronicles of Turkey and Egypt*. Oxford: University Press, 1963.

Tuğlaci, Pars, *The Role of the Balian Family in Ottoman Architecture*. Yeni Çığır Kitabevi, Istanbul, 1990.

Tuğlaci, Pars, *The Role of the Dadian Family in Ottoman Social, Economic and Political Life*. Istanbul: Pars Yayın ve Ticaret, 1993.

Turnbull, Stephen, *The Walls of Constantinople 324-1453*. Oxford: Osprey,

2004.

Ünsal, Behçet, *Turkish Islamic Architecture*. London: Alec Tiranti, 1959.

Vambery, Arminius, *The Story of My Struggles*. London: Thomas Nelson, c 1915.

Vambery, Arminius, *Arminius Vambéry, His Life and Adventures*. London: T Fisher Unwin, 1885.

Varol, Marie-Christine, *Balat, Faubourg Juif d'Istanbul*. Istanbul: Isis Editions, 1989.

Vasiliev, A. A., *History of the Byzantine Empire 324-1453* (1928). Madison: University of Wisconsin Press, 1961.

Vryonis, Speros Jr., *Byzantium and Europe*. London: Thames and Hudson, 1967.

Walker, Christopher J., *Armenia, The Survival of a Nation*. London: Croom Helm, 1980

Warr Michael, *A Biography of Stratford Canning, Mainly His Career in Turkey*. Oxford: Alden Press, 1989.

Waterfield, Gordon, *Layard of Nineveh*. London: John Murray, 1961.

Waugh, Evelyn, *Helena*. Harmondsworth: Penguin, 1963.

Webb, Nigel and Webb, Caroline, *The Earl and His Butler in Constantinople*. Oakham: Legini, 2006.

Wheatcroft, Andrew, *The Ottomans, Dissolving Images*. London: Penguin, 1995.

Wilson, Mary C., *King Abdulla, Britain and the Making of Jordan*. Cambridge: University Press, 1990.

Woolf, Leonard S., *The Future of Constantinople*. London: George Allen and Unwin, 1917.

Wortley Montagu, Mary, *The Turkish Embassy Letters*. Edited by Malcolm Jack. London: Virago, 2004.

Wright, Thomas, ed, *Early Travels in Palestine*. London: Henry Bohn, 1848.

Young, George, *Constantinople*. London, Methuen, 1926.

Young, George, *Corps de Droit Ottoman*. Oxford: Clarendon Press, 1905-06, 7 vols.

Zürcher, Erik J, *Turkey A Modern History*, 3rd edition. London: I B Tauris, 2005.

# Index of Historical & Literary Names

# Index of Places & Landmarks